The Paris Commune

Acknowledgements
I would like to thank the many people who have helped with this book, including Dick Barbor-Might, Pete Cannel, Neil Davidson, Nick Howard and Chanie Rosenberg. Special thanks for invaluable advice are due to Ian Birchall, John Charlton and Chris Harman, and for help in its preparation to Penny Gower, Mary Philips and Peter Robinson.

All quotes at the start of chapters and sections are from "The Internationale" by Eugene Pottier—see Appendix 3.

The Paris Commune

A Revolution in Democracy

Donny Gluckstein

Haymarket Books
Chicago, Illinois

First published in July 2006 by Bookmarks Publications Ltd in London

This edition published in 2011 by
Haymarket Books
P.O. Box 180165
Chicago, IL 60618
773-583-7884
info@haymarketbooks.org
www.haymarketbooks.org

Trade distribution:
In the US, Consortium Book Sales and Distribution, www.cbsd.com
In Canada, Publishers Group Canada, www.pgcbooks.ca
In the UK, Turnaround Publisher Services, www.turnaround-uk.com
All other countries, Ingram Publisher Services International, IPS_Intlsales@ingramcontent.com

ISBN 978-1-60846-118-9

Cover design by Josh On. Cover image of the Place Vendôme, ©BHVP / Roger-Viollet / The Image Works.

Special discounts are available for bulk purchases by organizations and institutions. Please contact Haymarket Books for more information at 773-583-7884 or info@haymarketbooks.org.

This book was published with the generous support of Lannan Foundation and the Wallace Global Fund.

Entered into digital printing February 2018.

Library of Congress CIP data is available.

To my parents; always an inspiration

Contents

Introduction

The system we live under concentrates obscene wealth at the summit of society while condemning millions to poverty, oppression, war and disease. A movement of resistance to this has arisen and mobilized millions of people across the world. Slogans such as "Another world is possible" and "Think globally, act locally" echo through discussions and debates from Porto Alegre in Brazil to Mumbai in India, and protest marches from Seattle to Sydney. These demands raise many questions: what sort of new world is possible, which social forces can bring it about, and what sort of local action is needed to achieve global transformation?

The Paris Commune of 1871 provides answers, despite its distance in time. It involved the working class taking control of their city and driving out the French government. Free at last to pursue their dreams, socialists, communists, anarchists and radical Jacobins threw their energies into a social experiment on a huge scale. The ambitions of the communards were boundless, and their belief in the possibility of social justice, equality and international solidarity was intense. A new form of government based on mass active democracy was generated—the first workers' state. Alas, the Commune lasted barely 72 days. In hand to hand fighting at the barricades during May 1871, the forces of the government, cheered on by the ruling classes of the world, reoccupied the French capital using the utmost brutality.

When the blood had finally dried little seemed to remain of the Commune's aspirations. However, and in spite of the rulers' efforts to erase the event from memory, Eugene Pottier's famous song, "The Internationale," written during the Commune's final agony, keeps alive a link to its history and still recalls its message of struggle and liberation. "The Internationale" was sung in Petrograd in 1917; in Madrid as they fought fascism in the 1930s; in Tiananmen Square, Beijing, in the 1980s; and continues to be heard across the world today. Its verses evoke the first, but certainly not the last, time a new and just society was within reach.

So the Paris Commune deserves to be more than an obscure, if inspiring, reference point. Studying its life and death reveals a fascinating story of political and social daring, as well as great heroism. This is all the more remarkable in that the insurgents had no prior experience of a successful anticapitalist movement to draw upon. They were truly pioneering and cut a new path for others to follow.

In this book the participants speak for themselves wherever possible. Though huge changes have occurred in the century and a half since the Commune, it is remarkable how fresh and contemporary they sound. The chapter structure used does not deal with events chronologically. The achievements of the movement are covered first, followed by the background events that made it possible. Then follows a discussion of the problems the Commune faced in its civil war with the French government. The book continues with an account of how the Commune was crushed, and rounds off by considering the different ways this unique movement has been interpreted.

Cannons of Montmartre, March 18, 1871 (top);
the Buttes Montmartre, March 18 (below)

Crowd swarms around toppled Vendôme Column (above);
A group on the debris of the column, May 16 (below)

One

The Commune's Achievements

The Revolution of March 18, 1871

The soldiers too will take strike action

The Paris Commune was born in the early hours of March 18, 1871, when the French army attempted to disarm the Parisian militia—the National Guard. In protest at this action a popular uprising expelled the government from the city and put it in the hands of the working class. Even in the long history of French insurrections this outcome was unprecedented. The authorities had been challenged before, but this was the first time the working class had not just fought but also won on its own account. Typically, the establishment had such contempt for ordinary people that it could not conceive of revolts truly happening from below. Mass actions had to be the result of outside agitators manipulating gullible followers. So the "Red Professor," Karl Marx, was accused of orchestrating the Commune from his London office of the International Working Men's Association (later known as the First International).

The evidence of that dramatic day refutes this conspiracy theory. The uprising was initiated by the most exploited and oppressed people in Paris. Indeed, there were no well-known radical leaders present on March 18, because the most prominent were either under arrest or elsewhere.[1] Benoit Malon, socialist and future member of the Communal Council, confessed "never had a revolution more surprised the revolutionaries."[2] The Central Committee of the National Guard (a democratically organized militia composed of hundreds of thousands of mainly working-class Parisian men) expected nothing. Its meeting was arranged for 11 o'clock in the evening.[3] The First International did indeed have thousands of supporters in Paris. Yet so disoriented was it by events that it failed to make any statement on the revolution until March 23.[4]

Therefore the revolution was not sparked by left-wing agitators but by government provocation. If there was a dark conspiracy, it came from above, from the enemies of Paris. The French ruling class and the government saw the city and its increasingly radical working population as a threat to their position. They must be comprehensively crushed, and to do so their National Guard units had to be disarmed. Their cannons were stored on the heights of Montmartre and so this became the focus of the French army's operation.

General Vinoy was in charge of capturing the cannons. To him Paris was not a city of compatriots but hostile enemy territory. His language was one of military assault, nothing else: "The attack must be pursued at several different points at the same time… Two columns of the Susbielle division had to attack Montmartre."[5] Repression was planned to be severe and far-reaching: "It was not simply a matter of limiting ourselves to lifting the cannons, but…to take all the steps necessary to immediately arrest all the leaders of the insurrection."[6] To accomplish this, police gendarmes followed each column bearing lists of left activists, with special attention paid to the International's HQ.[7] The army propaganda claimed that March 18 was "the day the government chose to repress the uprising."[8] Yet it was the government's action that created a full-blown revolt where none had been before.

Due to a disastrous war with Count Bismarck's Prussia the previous year, the authorities had only 25,000 soldiers and 3,000 gendarmes available. By seizing the artillery in the dead of night they hoped to keep these meager forces free from "contamination" by the "mob."[9] The soldiers left their barracks at 3 o'clock in the morning[10] and swiftly climbed to Montmartre. The cannons were weakly defended and only one National Guardsman—Turpin—was cut down in capturing them. Vinoy excitedly telegraphed news of success to the capitalist government at Versailles.[11] However, a gross miscalculation had been made. The horses needed to haul this heavy equipment away did not arrive.[12]

When morning came the troops were still on the Montmartre heights. When their presence was discovered the local population realized what was afoot. Government propaganda could not turn back the tide of anger. In vain did an official poster promote the preposterous idea that the National Guards "have already caused you so much harm [and] have seized cannons which, if they are fired, would only thunder down upon your homes, your children and you yourselves."[13] The workers of Paris knew the opposite to be true. It was the Versailles forces who were trying to remove the people's means of self-protection and who were prepared to shell Paris.

Louise Michel, the tireless local activist based in that area, takes up the story of the events on March 18:

> Montmartre was waking up; the drum was beating. I went with others to launch what amounted to an assault on the hilltop. The sun was rising and we heard the alarm bell. Our ascent was at the speed of a charge, and we knew that at the top was an army poised for battle. We expected to die for liberty.
>
> It was as if we were risen from the dead. Yes, Paris was rising from the dead. Crowds like this are sometimes the vanguard of the ocean of humanity. The hilltop was enveloped in a white glow, a splendid dawn of deliverance… But it was not death that awaited us on the hilltop where the army was already hitching up the cannons to take them off, and combine them with those already lifted from Batignolles during the night. No, it was the surprise of a popular victory.
>
> Between us and the army were women who threw themselves on the cannons and on the machine guns while the soldiers stood immobile. When General Lecomte ordered the soldiers to fire on the crowd, a subaltern came out from the ranks and standing in front of the company called out in a voice louder than Lecomte's, "Turn your guns around and put your rifle butts up in the air!" The soldiers obeyed. It was Verdaguerre who, for this action, was shot by Versailles some months later. But the revolution had been achieved.[14]

Even hostile witnesses acknowledged the central role played by women, and also by children, in encouraging the mutiny. An officer in the Versailles army wrote of how the army's action was: "stopped by a crowd of several hundred local inhabitants, principally children and women. The infantry detachment which was there to escort the cannon completely forgot their duty and dispersed into the crowd, succumbing to its perfidious seductions, and ended by turning up their rifle butts."[15]

So it was the most downtrodden elements of society who took the lead at Montmartre. This was their moment. Elsewhere in Paris similar mutinies and revolts were occurring.[16] On the Rue Lepic an eyewitness stumbled across 50 or 60 cavalry—Vinoy and his general staff: "A yell rose from the ranks of the swelling crowd. Vinoy stopped for a moment, then left, head down, while some intrepid kids pursued him and slapped the horses of his escort with sticks. It was a really pitiful retreat."[17] The "attack" by this mighty military commander was defeated by children with sticks!

By midday the entire government was in full-scale flight.[18] Adolphe Thiers, its leader, realized that any further contact with ordinary people would destroy what little remained of military discipline. He therefore decided to withdraw his troops and government officials to nearby Versailles.[19] In one day victory was complete. The writ of the government no longer ran in the capital. It was not just a few ministers and all their officials who had fled: one Commune sympathizer recorded this ironic comment in his diary:

> Legally we had no more government; no police force or policemen; no magistrates or trials; no top officials or prefects; the landlords had run away in a panic abandoning their buildings to the tenants; no soldiers or generals; no letters or telegrams; no customs officials, tax collectors or teachers. No more Academy or Institute; the great professors, doctors and surgeons had left… Paris; immense Paris was abandoned to the "orgies of the vile multitude."[20]

A New Power

No saviour from on high delivers
No faith have we in prince or peer
Our own right hand the chains must sever

The revolution did not simply destroy the old structure. It was much more than a successful defense of bits of iron, or a mass protest, or a mutiny. For this was a moment when popular discontent was transformed into popular power, and in the process the participants were themselves changed. On March 19 *La Commune* newspaper described what had occurred the previous day as:

> a revolution without example in history. Your revolution has a special character that distinguishes it from others. Its fundamental greatness is that it is made entirely by the people as a collective communal revolutionary undertaking, anonymous, unanimous, and for the first time without leaders.
>
> Nothing of the personal, of the individualistic! There was no surprise attack, no coup de main, but...a massive achievement strong in its authority of the workers! This is a natural power, spontaneous, not false; born from the public conscience of the "vile multitude" which has been provoked and attacked and now legitimately defends itself. Such power owes nothing to the influence of the great names, to celebrity status, to the prestige of leaders, to the artifice of parties...[21]

What was particularly galling for the former rulers was precisely that this movement from below had created its own organs of authority. The *Journal Officiel* published at Versailles was infuriated that the names of members of the National Guard's Central Committee were "unknown to almost all who read them. They had suddenly emerged from obscurity."[22] How dare they!

Some modern accounts of the Commune minimize the radical dimension of this first successful workers' revolution, and thus imply that ordinary people cannot really bring change. But listen to the voices of that time. Here is a letter from Désiré Lapie, semi-literate carpenter and rank-and-file communard: "Yes my sister we are now in charge and before us are these people who bow down before monarchy and tremble at the thought of our revolution, these men who betrayed us we have them, even Bismarck is forced to recognize us, you see how we are strong..."[23]

A leading member of the Communal Council, Vermorel, agreed. The March 18 revolution:

> marks the achievement of political power by the proletariat... The [National Guard] Central Committee, which took power after March 18, was composed solely of workers, of proletarians. And by far the majority of the Commune is composed of workers, of proletarians even though it also contains some bourgeois devoted to the people's cause...[24]

Arnould, another council member, watched an aged National Guard on duty:

> This fighter had dreamed, for perhaps 50 years, of the triumph of the people and here, one fine day, all of a sudden, he was living his dream! He saw workers there like him, his workshop companions, his favorite club orators commanding, being obeyed! He saw the bourgeois, the big businessmen, the great industrialists, the bosses, begging for an audience, humble, submissive and polite, coming to ask for permits for their merchandise or for their families to pass! "At last!" said his look...[25]

Such assessments of the Commune were not confined to its supporters. They were held by opponents too. Take for example, Edmond Goncourt, a well-known diarist living in Paris but bitterly opposed to the Commune. He wrote:

> What is happening is quite simply the conquest of France by the working population and the subjugation, under its despotic rule, of the nobility, the bourgeoisie and the peasants. The government is falling from the hands of those who have into those who have not, from those who have a material interest in the conservation of society into those who are completely uninterested in its order, stability or preservation.[26]

Barral de Montaud, who stayed behind in Paris to spy for Versailles, reached the conclusion that "the third class in society...the people, made March 18... But Paris was only a means. Its express aim was the dominance of the working class..."[27]

Between left-wing and right-wing eyewitness accounts we have this from an unaligned middle-class woman of Paris who wrote:

> [To the people of Paris] the Versailles government represented and meant privilege, the possessors of blankets facing the poor without sheets. Perhaps the people did not understand the idea of the Commune at all, nor even tried to understand it. To them all this was irrelevant. They were obsessively aware of one single idea: that the rich existed alongside the poor, the man wearing gloves alongside the man with soiled hands; the salaried official functionary alongside the needy worker...[28]

Around the world messages of sympathy began to be sent. From a Brussels mass meeting came these words: "There has been no more momentous hour. The working people have shown a stamina that is the mark of classes that can be subjugated no longer..."[29] A First International meeting in Geneva "hailed the advent of the working class to political power in the Communal Revolution of March 18..."[30]

One of the many crimes of Stalinism in the twentieth century was to take over phrases such as "a workers' government" and pervert them. The March 18 revolution showed the meaning of workers' power. It had nothing in common with Stalinist Eastern Europe, or Western capitalist democracy for that matter. In both these latter examples the political system is designed to keep the population entirely passive. After March 18, by contrast, there was an explosion of mass popular involvement. A recent commentator has explained:

> There was, first of all, an immense, a grandiose festival, a festival that the people of Paris, the essence and the symbol of the French people and of humanity in general, created for itself and created for the world. Spring festival in the city, festival of the disinherited and of the proletarians, revolutionary festival and festival of the revolution, total festival, the greatest of modern times, it grew above all from the magnificence of joy. The historic day of March 18, 1871, broke the passivity and resignation that had ruled... The people of Paris broke the dykes and flooded onto the streets. In a warm and fraternal mass they enveloped those who would have fought them, the soldiers of the established powers, and disarmed them. A collective hero, the popular genius rose up in all its natural youth and vigour. It had triumphed simply by appearing on the scene... What force did this? A fundamental will to change the world, to change life as it is, the highest thought being the project of total revolution. This was an "all or nothing" gamble.[31]

How was this "will to change the world" expressed? We are encouraged to think of politics in terms of distant hierarchical bodies ruling over us. However, power can take other forms. It does not need to be above or apart from the population, residing solely in some boardroom or grand chamber. The Paris Commune was a classic example of an alternative politics. Its very name escaped these strictures. The dictionary definition for commune is "parish, township" as a noun, and "common, general, universal, most people, common people, the mob" as an adjective.[32] The newness of the emerging power meant the National Guard Central Committee had difficulty in finding a straightforward term to describe what they were promoting: "Its name is indistinct—municipal assembly, Communal Council or Commune."[33]

Following the revolution a council was elected on March 26, 1871. It sat at the town hall (Hôtel de Ville) and was like no previous parliamentary institution. Membership of this body was not a license to betray the electors in the interests of the rich and powerful, as this article from *Le Proletaire*, an 11th arrondissement newspaper, explained:

> It is up to the people alone to judge men and their acts. The mission of those we mandate is limited... Do not reach judgement or make decisions in the name of the people or in their place. Remain in your role as simple messengers and be content to furnish the people with the information that they have charged you to communicate.
>
> Servants of the people, do not assume the false airs of sovereigns. That is no more appropriate for you than for the helots you have replaced... Your persons are of little weight in the scales of the Commune. The people are tired of 'saviors.'[34]

As this statement shows, although the council at the Hôtel de Ville was frequently labelled "the Commune" it was not the only place that it was to be found. It existed on the streets, in meeting halls, homes and barracks. Lissagaray, a journalist and participant in the Commune who wrote a famous history of it, makes this point clearly:

> Seek it before you, and not at the faltering Hôtel de Ville. These smoking ramparts, these explosions of heroism, these women, these men of all professions united, all the workmen of the earth applauding our combat, all monarchs, all the bourgeois coalesced against us, do they not speak loudly enough our common thought, and that all of us are fighting for equality, the enfranchisement of labor, the advent of a social society?[35]

Running the Great City

Arise ye starvelings from your slumbers

When the national government decamped to Versailles this brought new opportunities for the people of Paris, but also risks, because it amounted to a deliberate act of sabotage. After Thiers ordered public officials out of the capital, fewer than a third remained.[36] The situation was critical as Andrieu, the person put in charge of public services, explained:

> Of all the weapons of war that the government of Versailles deployed against the Commune, that which appeared likely to be most effective was the sudden interruption of public services. A few more days and the

removal of the cemetery accounts would have made it impossible to bury the dead in Paris; the gas would have been cut off; the water in public fountains would no longer have been flowing, rubbish would not have been collected from the streets; financial resources for street sweeping and cleaning would have dried up... Paris would have seen its rubbish dumps and its sewers fill and overflow.[37]

However, very soon services were running normally as "the respiratory and digestive apparatus of the great organism functioned without disturbance."[38] Shops were open, theaters were playing and "elegant people promenaded as usual on the boulevards."[39] The working class proved that it did not need an elite of highly paid bureaucrats to run a major city. Key government departments were restarted "under the superintendence of workmen or former subordinate employees." Lissagaray tells us of the postal system under Albert Theisz, a manual worker and prominent member of the International. He "found the service quite disorganized, the divisional offices, closed, the stamps hidden away or carried off, the material, seals, the carts, etc. taken away, and the coffers empty... Theisz acted with promptitude and energy... And in 48 hours the collection and distribution of letters for Paris was reorganized..."[40] At the Mint the director was another figure from the International, "Camélinat, a bronze-mounter,"[41] and so it went on.

The energy and enthusiasm for building a new world swept people along. Many hardly slept in the 72 days the Commune lasted. Michel wrote, "During the entire time of the Commune, I only spent one night [at home]. I never really went to bed during that time. I just napped a little whenever there was nothing better to do, and many other people lived the same way. Everybody who wanted deliverance gave himself totally to the cause."[42] Was the artist Gustave Courbet a little carried away by overwork at the Arts Commission when he declared:

I get up, have breakfast and preside over meetings for 12 hours each day. My head has begun to spin, but despite this mental torment which I am not used to, I am enchanted. Paris is a true paradise! No police, no nonsense, no exaction of any kind, no arguments! Everything in Paris rolls along like clockwork. All the government bodies are organized federally and run themselves... The Paris Commune is more successful than any form of government has ever been.[43]

The effectiveness of the Commune's efforts was testified to by many eyewitnesses. English clergymen were enthused by a subject dear to their hearts—the streets were cleaner than ever before. And on these boulevards now closer to godliness no tobacco was sold; there was no begging, busking or prostitution. Even line fishing on the Seine ceased.[44] These actions were not enforced by any overbearing police force for most had run away, and those who remained only dared to patrol in threes, having to call in the National Guard if any action was needed.[45] With the exception of the handful of right-wing "battalions of order" that remained in Paris, this National Guard was the (male) working class itself: "Every citizen was armed, and all looked after their own salvation and that of everyone else."[46]

A sign of the new order was the lack of deference to "superiors." Entrance to the Hôtel de Ville was by password and nothing else would do, not even the very identifiable red sash fringed with gold of a Communal Council member: "The sentinels would reply, 'Having the sash makes no difference, nor does showing a pass. Anyone could get hold of a sash or steal a card.'"[47] In other fields the people's law and order was a striking success. A number of sources noted that there were very few robberies or crimes in general, and not a single murder in the two months of the Commune.[48]

Throughout the short life of the Commune Paris was under siege. A year previously, when a pro-business government was running the city and the Prussians were besieging it, there had been terrible hunger and deprivation. Even though mass unemployment persisted, that did not happen this time.[49] Public assistance schemes, which the left had previously advocated in the teeth of government opposition, were now given free rein.[50] Canteens were set up to feed the people, while wood, coal and other necessities like bread, salt, sugar and coffee were distributed free to those in poverty, or at low prices to others.[51] A town hall official describes how the system functioned: "During the day there was an uninterrupted procession of poor women, lacking bread and work, or whose husbands had been killed at the forward positions. We distributed money tokens or basic goods and took note of their home addresses to check out their claims... I requisitioned without hesitation all that was asked for (except for wine, of course)..."[52]

So, according to Arnould:

> During [the Commune's] short reign not a single man, woman, child or old person was hungry, or cold, or homeless... It was amazing to see how with only tiny resources this government not only fought a horrible war for two months but chased famine from the hearths of the huge popula-

tion which had had no work for a year. That was one of the miracles of a true democracy.[53]

While the Commune was much more than the council elected to the Hôtel de Ville, that body was of central importance as the movement's leadership. They swiftly marked themselves out from previous administrations by deciding "in conformity with democratic principles" to set a maximum salary of 15 francs a day, or 6,000 francs per year for itself and all public servants.[54] This salary was a fraction of the swollen salaries paid under the previous regime and this disturbed the Commune's opponents. Barral de Montaud, the Versailles spy, warned his masters that "the low pay given to the members of the Commune is a characteristic fact..."[55] This meant that even though François Jourde was a member not only of the Communal Council's highest body, the Executive Commission, and head of finance, his wife had to continue to take in washing to live.[56] The Commune's stance showed that, unlike the state under capitalism, it was not standing as separate from and above the people. The salaries of MPs reflect not only personal greed but an identification with the capitalist class (whom they usually serve). Inflated incomes for "important people" reinforce this idea that great accumulations of wealth are justified.[57] The Commune turned this idea on its head.

The council's structure reflected its subversive character in another way too. Under capitalism the state claims to be a neutral instrument available to be used by any democratically elected government. This helps disguise the preponderant influence of big business. The Commune made no such false pretense of neutrality. It had an Executive Commission with nine other subordinate commissions, ranging from finance to education, justice, security and military affairs. The duties of the Commission for Labor, Industry and Exchange included "the propagation of socialist doctrines. It must find means of creating equality in work and income." The External Relations Commission was to "contribute to the emancipation of the country,"[58] and so on.

Other features marked out its real democratic nature. Conventional states reduce accountability by separating legislative (parliamentary) and executive (governmental) functions. Consequently elected representatives, MPs, can talk but do not really control executive decisions. Furthermore, they cannot be mandated or sacked, and so once elected are free to act as they wish until the next ballot. Aneurin Bevan, a minister in British Labour's 1945 administration, described the operation of "the Mother of Parliaments" in these terms: "The House of Commons is the most unrepresentative of representative assemblies. It is an elaborate conspiracy to prevent the real clash of opinion which exists outside from finding an appropriate echo within its walls. It is a social shock absorber put between privilege and the pressure of popular discontent."[59]

By contrast the Commune "was to be a working, not a parliamentary body [but] executive and legislative at the same time."[60]

This meant that Communal Council members debated, voted and then carried out the decisions they took in the districts (or arrondissements) where local commissions were set up to assist.[61] In the 4th arrondissement, for example, the latter consisted of "simple workers, or small businessmen [who] met once a week with the members of the Commune."[62] This close link between the central power and localities created a punishing workload for representatives who shared the burden of total commitment. While Courbet worked 12 hours a day,[63] Arnould "could not recall being undressed and lying down more than ten times in two months. All we had was an armchair, chair or bench for a few moments. Even then we were often interrupted."[64]

A state built from below needs to be grounded in direct democracy with representatives made accountable. This aspect was stressed by the National Guard Central Committee, which played the central role in Paris until the election of the Communal Council on March 26. In preparation for that election the Central Committee issued this statement:

> The members of the municipal council will be constantly watched and kept under surveillance. Their actions will be publicly debated, making them revocable, accountable and responsible. It is such an assembly, for a free city in a free country, that you are establishing. Citizens, it is your honor to contribute by your vote to founding this system. You will want to win for Paris the glory of having placed the first stone of the new social edifice, of being the first to elect the republican commune.[65]

A safeguard of such accountability was the principle of instant recall that was carried into the Communal Council from the National Guard: "The Commune can be strengthened or renewed at any time because the voters always have the right to meet together at the request of the majority and through the organs of permanent electoral committees."[66]

The Commune in Action

We've enough of languishing in slavery

Grand schemes for radical change, we are always being told, can never succeed because they are "unrealistic." "Realism" in this sense means continuing to tolerate the inequity and injustice of the current economic system. The Commune did not dream of radical change—it made it a reality.

Having restored basic services, it addressed the pressing issues raised by the recent actions of Thiers's government. The city had just passed through a lengthy siege by Prussia. Prolonged mass unemployment resulted in a complete inability to pay rents and other debts (especially bills of exchange). So desperate was the situation that a moratorium on payment of rents and bills of exchange had been granted in the months before the Commune was established. In addition 900,000 people had come to depend on the tiny salary of 1.50 francs per day paid to each man serving in the National Guard.[67]

After the armistice with the Prussians Thiers's government decided that, even though the economy had not yet recovered, back rents and bills of exchange would have to be paid. The National Guard was also to be disbanded. This threatened disaster for the mass of the population. The Commune swiftly intervened to reverse these decisions. So from the first day, from the first action, the two assemblies—at Versailles and Paris—were set on a collision course. An insurgent explained what was at stake: "Paris is revolutionary, Versailles is royalist and bourgeois... To the inevitable question of who will pay the 5 billion francs Prussian reparations and the 10 billion francs damages? Versailles replies without hesitation: 'Labor!' Paris replies with confidence: 'It will be Capital.'"[68]

On its first day the Communal Council at the Hôtel de Ville confirmed an earlier Central Committee decision not only to retain the National Guard, the democratic workers' militia, but to abolish the permanent army, which only served the cause of imperialism or internal repression: "Conscription is abolished. No military force other than the National Guard can be created or enter Paris. All valid citizens are part of the National Guard."[69]

In a city where 19 out of 20 were tenants who paid rents on a quarterly basis[70] Thiers's decision to end the moratorium on payments provoked widespread anger. One person addressed the landlords in this way: "What

I object to is your coming back and saying [to me]: 'During seven or eight months you have done no work, you have been obliged to pawn your furniture to buy bread for your wife and children; I pity you from the bottom of my heart—be so kind as to hand me over my three quarters' rent.' No, a thousand times no..."[71]

The Paris Commune cut through the rent problem after three quarters of an hour of discussion in a decree of three lines. A Central Committee decision already forbade landowners from evicting lodgers[72] and the Communal Council, again on its first day, resolved to annul back rent payments on the grounds that "work, industry, and commerce have borne the full burden of the war. It is fair that property also makes a sacrifice."

What a refreshing approach! Whenever capitalists run into any difficulties such as falling profits or increased costs it is always the workers or the poor who have to bear the burden through cuts, unemployment or rising prices and this is portrayed as inevitable and not even worth questioning. But why should those who have the most not sacrifice something for those who have the least? The phrasing of the decree showed how the Commune gave power to ordinary people at the expense of the landlords: "All leases can be cancelled, *if the tenant so wishes*, during the next six months. All rent holidays that have been given can, if the tenant so wishes, be prolonged for three months."[73]

The decree on rents opened the way to further encroachment on "the rights of property." As German bombardment of Paris and its suburbs had created a mass of homeless refugees it was decided to requisition housing,[74] including all vacant apartments.[75] A motion requiring landlords who had collected rent since the outbreak of the war to "disburse this amount into the municipal coffers" ran out of time[76]; but hotels were taken over to house refugees.[77]

Ordinary people now knew that in Paris the state was not there to oppress or exploit them and the sense of empowerment was palpable. Take the case of Nicholas Dugène, former petty criminal but now a National Guard corporal. His landlady tried to evict a neighbor and seize her belongings because she had burned the furniture for firewood and not paid rent. He turned up with a squad of guards to show the landlady "that the boot was now on the other foot."[78]

The debate on bills of exchange was mostly a middle-class concern. Nevertheless, given the small size of most Parisian enterprises, it affected a large number of people. The decision was to phase in repayment of debts over three years, in contrast to the Versailles period of three months. At a First International meeting in London Marx declared that "the decrees about rent and commercial bills were two master strokes: without them three quarters of the tradespeople would have become bankrupt."[79]

The apparently obscure question of pawnshops raised the important issue of the relative roles of direct political action and campaigns by non-governmental bodies. To stave off starvation during the siege many Parisians were compelled to hand over vital possessions in return for cash worth a fraction of the value. By the spring of 1871 there were one million items in hock.[80] The Commune banned the sale of such articles by pawnshops. As a charitable act under the previous government, the Archbishop of Paris and Lord Mayor of London had funded the return of items for free if they were worth up to 20 francs.[81] The Commune also paid for free redemption up to the same value. One recent writer is scathing about what he sees as a stingy attitude on the part of Charles Longuet (Karl Marx's future son-in-law and council member). He was "no more generous than the Lord Mayor of London and the Archbishop."[82]

This misunderstands the context. Unlike charities, the Commune based its entire policy on the need for social transformation. The pawn system preyed upon the poorest in the community. For the items they pawned—articles of primary necessity such as mattresses, clothing and blankets—they were given only about a fifth of the market value, because their resale value was so low. So buying them back from the pawnshop was all the more difficult. By contrast luxury items such as jewelry commanded two thirds of their market value.[83] It may not have been more financially generous than the archbishop, but the Commune did not want to affront people's dignity and targeted its measures at returning "tools, clothing, blankets and bed linen" through monthly payments over five years. It said: "This measure is all the more socialist because men are proud and will not easily bring themselves to ask for charity, even if disguised."[84] However, this could only be a temporary arrangement until the start of socialism (a goal definitely not shared by the archbishop):

> It is fully understood that the liquidation of the pawnshops must be the consequence of a social organization which gives the worker real guarantees of assistance and support in the case of unemployment and ill health... We are convinced that the establishment of the Commune will

> create new institutions that will help put workers out of the reach of exploitation and the need to loan money from usurers...[85]

A New Foundation for Social and Economic Relations

The actions of the Commune over rents, debts, the Guards' salary and pawnshops were against a backdrop of a universally dominant laissez-faire Victorian ideology. This, like neoliberal ideas today, stressed that the state should concentrate on assisting capital at home and abroad. If the Commune had stopped at relieving economic distress, it would still have been a pioneer in founding a welfare system. But it went much, much further because, as its statement on the "liquidation of the pawnshops" showed, it did not just intend to apply a bandage to the ills of society, but to found another world entirely.

Although the members of the Communal Council came from very different political traditions, on one principle they were agreed. As Lissagaray put it, "All socialist decrees passed unanimously; for though they differed they were all socialists."[86] There was, at a deep level, a remarkable unanimity around the idea of the Commune as bringing social equality, justice and workers' emancipation through breaking the capitalist state. Different individuals emphasized particular aspects, but like the rays of the sun, each could trace the origins back to a single source of energy—the revolution of March 18.

In this context the work of the Commission for Labor and Exchange acquires an exceptional importance. However, unlike the political revolution of March 18, which could be accomplished in a day, the two and a half months of the Commune were certainly not enough time to produce a social and economic revolution, which requires a whole epoch. Nevertheless, a new kind of society can be fleetingly glimpsed in its actions.

The central figures in the Labor Commission were Leo Frankel[87] and his chief assistant, Bertin. The latter noted that some people criticized the Commune as a mindless act of violence or wished to reduce its scope to reforming some elements of the system:

> The movement that has just occurred was so unexpected, so decisive that the professional politicians understood nothing of it and did not see in this great movement anything but a revolt without logic and without aim. Others have chosen to circumscribe the very idea of this revolution

by reducing it to a simple demand for what they call municipal rights, a sort of municipal autonomy.

But he rejected such views entirely:

> The 18 March revolution…is a great victory of popular rights in the implacable struggle that it maintains against all tyrannies. The slave, followed by the serf, began the struggle and the proletariat will have the glory of closing the cycle by its revolution and consequent social equality.
>
> The people (who are not blinded by governmental fictions)… created its political organism as a means of realizing the very aim of the revolution, that is the emancipation of labor, the abolition of monopolies, privileges, bureaucracy, speculative, capitalist and industrial feudalism…[88]

This final aim is one thing, reaching it quite another. The commission would have little time to achieve "the emancipation of labor" and Frankel himself was disappointed by the slow progress that was made. By April 28 he complained to the Communal Council that the abolition of night work at bakeries was "the only truly socialist decree that has been made by the Commune…"[89] However, hidden in this apparently modest measure were some important signs for the future. Bakery workers had been campaigning against their antisocial hours for at least two years. The bakeries were tiny and it would have been very difficult for them to have a successful strike. The Commune could provide a solution, and 3,000 of them marched to the Hôtel de Ville to make their case.[90]

Night work was abolished but only after prolonged argument. It was not that there was disagreement with the bakers' case as both sides of the debate regarded night shifts as unacceptable. Avrial declared: "Their working conditions are unfair; you cannot create two classes in society like this. You can't make workers, who are men like us, only work at night and never see the day." Vermorel agreed: "It would be against all justice and all human rights to allow a particular class of workers to be separated from society in the interests of the aristocracy of the stomach."[91] In striving to create a different society, brand new issues arose that had never been aired in a representative chamber before.

The row was about how to solve the problem in this new world turned upside down. Some believed that use of centralized state power would weaken the independent action of the people. They opposed a decree banning night work because they rejected state action on principle. Workers' self-activity would be better: "I am opposed to all these constant regulations that you seem to want to make... Let the workers themselves safeguard their interests in relation to the owners; today they are powerful enough to act as they wish" (Billioray).[92] Many of the most radical members of the Communal Council adopted this approach[93] so this stance was not an expression of neoliberal or laissez-faire attitudes, quite the opposite:

> Let's call the owners and the workers together and say to the former: "Here are the demands that the workers have formulated, discuss them, and if you owners don't want to accede to them, if you threaten to shut your establishments, on that very day we will requisition them. We will let the workers run your production (after paying fair compensation)." That is what should be done. We should not take decisions ourselves on this.[94]

However, the majority was for a decree and Malon expressed their views: "It is said that we cannot concern ourselves with social questions; I must say that until now the state has intervened enough *against* the interests of the workers. It is at least fair that today the state intervenes *for* the workers."[95]

On May 15 a 1,500-strong march of bakery workers went to the Hôtel de Ville carrying red flags and shouting, "Long live the Commune."

Another problem confronting the Labor Commission was the way orders for Commune military supplies were fulfilled. When the Versailles government attacked Paris this was an urgent issue. Initially the Commune bought equipment at the lowest price, but this meant bosses given Commune contracts actually cut their workers' pay by a third. The Communal Council was shocked because this struck "a blow against the very principles of the social revolution that we must defend at all costs."[96] Proposals were made to amend the contracts, but Jourde, commissioner for finance, resisted because rewriting contracts in the middle of a vicious civil war could lead to dangerous delays in the production process: "The change that is proposed would be an obstacle to our supplies... We must not forget that there are urgently needed supplies that have to be paid for within 24 hours. The contracts for these operations cannot be revised... If you revise the contracts already made it will make it impossible to agree to new ones."[97]

The workers involved took a very different view, as this reaction from one female garment worker shows: "Is it true what I have just learned? Are we under the Empire or under the Commune?... You are playing the game of Versailles... if you do not know what to do, at least bring in the male and female workers to advise you on what should be done."[98]

The issue involved here is fascinating. How can the general interests of the working class (in defending itself) be squared with the particular interests of a section of workers? Frankel realized that effective defense of the workers' revolution depended as much on their belief in the cause as the military supplies that might be produced. He agreed with the garment worker that the situation was a "shameful...affront to the dignity of the Commune [because] exploiters are profiting from public misery to lower salaries, and the Commune is blind enough to collaborate in this type of maneuver." He warned the Communal Council not to "forget that the March 18 revolution was made exclusively by the working class. I don't see what the point of the Commune is if we who believe in social equality do nothing for that class."

Frankel was successful. Revised contracts were introduced specifying a minimum wage agreed jointly by the workers' representatives, the Military Supplies Agency and the Labor Commission. Employers were not consulted. Furthermore, in an important additional clause it stated that where possible they should be entirely bypassed and contracts should awarded "directly to the workers' own corporations."[99]

Workers' corporations—the key labor organization in Paris—had an enormous significance that is perhaps obscure for us now. There is no contemporary equivalent for the Parisian "workers' corporation" because of large-scale production replacing handicrafts. The term "workers' corporations" can been translated as "associations," or "cooperatives," or even "trade unions." The Labor Commission chose to promote this body as its main socialist vehicle.

On April 16 the Communal Council decreed that workshops whose owners fled to Versailles would be passed to "the cooperative association of workers who were employed there." A jury would decide the level of compensation to be paid to the owner.[100] Later on a more ambitious proposal was developed: to investigate "all the large workshops, the monopolies and their tools" with a view to handing them over to any workers' association that requested them. (However, no decision was taken on this.)[101] At the same time the Commune put its own workshops under workers' control.

The International in Paris welcomed the Commune's decree as: "An important day in the life of the working class. The revolution has made a real step... The Paris Commune (our creation) is taking the lead by putting the workers' societies in a large bureau in the Office of Public Works to proclaim to all the world that the past is dead..."[102]

Lefrançais, a prominent communard, said this decree constituted "the social revolution."[103]

In practice there was little time to do very much. The decree inviting unions to meet and discuss implementing the decree went out on April 24. Ten corporations responded and their first meeting was on May 15.[104] Versailles forces were within the walls just a week later. Even so, as a recent history states:

> Despite the short time at its disposal the operation did not have as derisory results as has been supposed. There were a dozen confiscated workshops, above all those linked to military defense, repair of arms, fabrications of shells and bullets. Five corporations had begun searching out the available workshops, ready for their confiscation. Let us add that the Commune also had at its disposal the industrial establishments belonging to the state—the mint, national printshop, army bakery, cigarette manufacture and some munitions enterprises dating from the siege. It began to entrust the management of these to their workers.[105]

How did workers' control function? The Louvre armament works was an example. Its regulations stated: "The managing delegate will be nominated by the workers and is revocable as soon as it is considered he has failed in his duty... Workers' meetings also nominate the workshop leader and the section leaders. Like the delegate they will be revocable... The delegates are renewed every 15 days."[106] Others were encouraged by this example. Even the café workers began to set up a trade union.[107]

The "Petroleuses": The Commune and Women's Liberation

Working-class women played a central role in the Commune from the revolution of March 18 till the final battle against invading Versailles forces. For this last struggle they were accused of being arsonists or *petroleuses*. A correspondent in *Le Vengeur* newspaper understood the fear they evoked: "I have seen three revolutions and never have women been involved with such determination... It seems that they see this revolution as precisely their own, and in defending it they defend their own future."[108]

To see just how big a break from the past this was, consider the previous role of women in France. The Catholic church allotted women a subordinate and inferior role and prominent politicians like Thiers agreed.

He wrote that "Christianity, which has done so much for society, compels the man to respect the weakness of the woman, which is like that of a slave." He located women's role within a "divine hierarchy—family, fatherland, humanity, god."[109] This divine role meant that the female workers earned just half the average male wage.[110]

The Commune began to dismantle this mountain of prejudice and discrimination and it did so in the most practical of ways. An early measure was to eradicate differences between "legitimate" and "illegitimate" relationships. The council decided to pay pensions to the families of fallen guardsmen. Such war pensions had not existed previously.[111] But who should be entitled to them? On April 10 the Hôtel de Ville agreed that pensions would be paid to dependents irrespective of marital status.[112]

Until this time, in a typically hypocritical fashion, men who committed adultery and kept mistresses were accepted while unmarried women who had relationships with men were pilloried. At the same time the subordinate position of women was anchored in the "legal" family. The Commune's short decree on war pensions was a double blow struck at this edifice—giving unmarried women equality with married, and so undermining the traditional family. Arnould realized its significance:

> The Commune did more for the emancipation of women, for their dignity, than any of the moralists and legislators of the past... This was perhaps one of the most audacious acts of the Commune, for it radically cut through a moral question and set a landmark for a profound modification of the current constitution of the family.
>
> This decree...puts a woman legally and morally on an absolutely equal footing with a man, placing things in a real moral position and striking a mortal blow against the religio-monarchic institution of marriage... The union of man and woman must be an act that is essentially free, accomplished by two responsible persons. In this union, the rights like the duties must be reciprocal and equal.[113]

Other steps were directed against the oppressive role of the family. The Commune considered a proposal that all children regardless of legitimacy should enjoy equal rights. In place of religious vows, civil marriage was to be instituted, the only requirement being a declaration at the town hall that they were not married to someone else.[114] For those already married, the Commune:

> reestablished divorce, abolished since 1816. For the Commune marriage

> ceased to be a solemn contract and became a written engagement between two people of the opposite sex to live together. This simplified ceremony implied a just-as-easy dissolution, by mutual consent. A simple declaration written by hand by both partners was enough. It was only necessary to take it to the delegate of the arrondissement.[115]

Along with this came the granting of alimony "to women demanding separation."[116]

These measures outraged priests who thought divorce to be one of "the most scandalous subjects [and] audacious blasphemies" and an example of "the most revolting impiety uttered against god and religion." What was particularly galling was "that both male and female citizens had unanimously pronounced in its favor."[117]

The argument is sometimes made that addressing the grand issues of the state and public power leaves domestic and social relationships untouched and unreformed. The Commune's measures regarding women and the family show that the two spheres cannot be separated. Lefrançais from the Communal Council understood this. The family institution was a key method of controlling and passing on property from one generation to the next. Property could not be challenged if the family was untouched, and equality could not be achieved if property rights came first. The Commune's actions represented "a challenge thrown down to the pretended principles of conventional morality. Until now society denied all equality, and had the unique aim of safeguarding property."[118]

While gender issues were bound to be prominent in building the new society that the Commune wanted, it never forgot that it had itself been created by the working class, and working-class women in particular. Mere sexual equality, ordinary people sharing the same poverty and exploitation, was not the aim. The revolutionary women were clear on this. Speakers at the Women's Deliverance Club based at Trinity Church declared: "The social wound that must be closed first of all is the existence of bosses, who exploit the workers and enrich themselves through their sweat. No more bosses who consider the workers to be mere production machines. Let the workers unite together, join their labors in common and they will be happy."[119]

This plea for unity of men and women in the fight for a new world was most powerfully articulated by the Women's Union. It was founded in April by a Russian—Elisabeth Dmitrieff, who had just been sent to Paris by the International's General Council. The Women's Union contrasted with an earlier Women's Association that, along with International members, included women regardless of class.[120]

The occupations of 60 of the union's core members have been ascertained and they give a good idea of how representative it was. There were:

> fifteen seamstresses, nine waistcoat-makers, six sewing-machine operators, five dressmakers, five linen drapers, three makers of men's clothing, two bootstitchers, two hat-makers, two laundresses, two cardboard makers, one embroiderer of military decorations, one braid-maker, one schoolteacher, one perfume-maker, one jeweller, one gold-polisher, one book-stitcher and one bookbinder.[121]

At its height three to four thousand attended the union's meetings.[122] The manifesto the Women's Union put to the Labor Commission was a magnificent combination of political strategy, women's emancipation, immediate practical steps and the overcoming of the alienation under capitalism:

> In the old social order women's work was the most exploited… In the current situation of terrible and rising poverty due to the collapse of employment opportunities it is to be feared that the women of Paris, who have been revolutionized for a time, will return to the passive or more or less reactionary state that the old order created for them, due to continual privation.
>
> The "immediate and essential reforms"[123] were therefore:
>
> (a) A variety of work in each trade—a continually repeated manual movement damages both mind and body.
> (b) A reduction in working hours—physical exhaustion inevitably destroys man's spiritual qualities.
> (c) An end to all competition between male and female workers—their interests are identical and their solidarity is essential to the success of the final worldwide strike of labor against capital.
>
> The association therefore wants:
>
> (1) Equal pay for equal hours of work.
> (2) A local and international federation of the various trade sections in order to ease the movement and exchange of goods by centralizing the interests of the producers.
>
> The general development of these producer associations requires:
>
> (1) Informing and organizing the working masses… The consequence of

> this will be that every association member will be expected to belong to the International Working Men's Association.
> State assistance in advancing the necessary credit for setting up these associations: loans repayable in yearly installments at a rate of 5 percent.[124]

During the Commune changes that today we can only dream of—an end to monotonous labor, long hours and sex discrimination, the introduction of real equal pay, international workers' control, all backed by the state—were posed as "immediate" reforms!

Under capitalism such demands might, at very best, be politely listened to by politicians and then conveniently forgotten. But the Commune was no conventional state working from top down. The Women's Union was not patronized and sent away after lobbying. It was quickly incorporated into the fabric of the Commune. Frankel secured 8 to 10 million francs to back its proposals and the union set up committees in every arrondissement.[125] Funds were disbursed at a rate of 100,000 francs every week.[126] With Labor Commission backing, it began setting up an entire structure of syndical chambers out of which would emerge production units under workers' control and a Federal Women's Chamber.[127]

Although there was practically no time for these grand plans to reach fruition, Lissagaray gives us a glimpse of what was achieved as he strolled toward the former parliamentary chamber:

> Let us enter the Corps Legislatif (parliament building), transformed into a workshop. Fifteen hundred women are there, sewing the sand sacks that are to stop up the breaches. A tall and handsome girl, Marthe, round her waist the red sash with silver fringe given her by her comrades, distributes the work. The hours of labor are shortened by joyous songs. Every evening the wages are paid, and the women receive the whole sum, eight centimes a sack, while the former contractors hardly gave them two.[128]

The achievements of the Commune in the field of women's liberation are all the more extraordinary when we remember that the context was the mid-nineteenth century in a devoutly Catholic country. The current disintegration of the conventional family and the spread of alternative family structures, the independent attitude of women gained through large-scale employment, the retreat of religious dogma from the domestic sphere were all in the future. The idea of liberation, however, could be expressed far more straightforwardly, as this woman speaking at a club showed:

> They tell us that the Commune is going to try and do something so that the people no longer die of starvation even though they are working. It's about time. I am a washerwoman. For 40 years I have worked hard all week without any holidays. Why should certain people have the right to rest and others not? Is this just?[129]

The Triumph of Reason

For reason in revolt now thunders

It is sometimes thought that a workers' revolution will have narrow economistic aims barely more ambitious than a glorified trade union. But as the Commune unfolded it became clear that every aspect of the old society was to be put under the microscope and that great emphasis would be placed on the social and cultural development of the individual of the future. A new society needs new people and so education, as one council member put it, was "the mother of all issues."[130]

Transforming education meant confronting the influence of the Catholic church, which wished to maintain its monopoly on the shaping of young minds. Ever since the days of the Enlightenment in the eighteenth century, education had been an ideological battleground. The Enlightenment philosophers believed that human progress would come through knowledge and the rejection of superstition. Diderot, for example, developed the *Encyclopédie* because he saw rational thought and science as weapons that would defeat blind faith in the established order. During the Great French Revolution (1789–1794) a law was passed that set forth the principle of free secular education. (That stance should not be confused with the recent French ban on Muslim women wearing headscarves. In the post–September 11 climate this smacks of racism masquerading as anti-clericalism, even though many on the left have been seduced by the secularist arguments put forward.)

Later governments wanted to bring change to a halt and foster respect for the establishment. Thus Napoleon Bonaparte brought the church apparatus back into primary schools in 1808, and the return of the monarchy in 1815 saw it spread into secondary schools. Now it was argued, "The priests and still less the feudal lords should not have been dispossessed. Bishops have the divine right to determine, control and manage education."[131] By 1870 five out of six girls in education were taught in religious institutions[132] while there was a tripling of church schools for boys between 1850 and 1863.[133]

Religion played the role of today's mass media in bolstering conservatism and reaction. Thiers, that inveterate and articulate ruling-class warrior, conveyed this superbly. Ordinary people must not learn too much of the world:

> I say that we must be careful before extending primary education too far, either in terms of availability or in terms of content... Reading, writing, arithmetic, that is what we need—the rest is superfluous.
>
> I formally demand something other than these detestable little secular teachers. I want the religious brothers back, even though in the past I have been against them. Also I want to make the influence of the clergy all-powerful. I want the action of the priest to be stronger, much stronger than before, because they need to propagate that good philosophy which teaches that *man is here to suffer*, and not that philosophy which says the contrary—*be happy*... If you think that here below you are entitled to *a little bit of happiness*, and if you do not find it in your actual situation, you will strike at rich people fearlessly for having kept you away from your happiness. By taking the surplus from the rich person you will guarantee your well-being and that of all those who are in the same situation as you...[134]

Happy human beings? Never!

The Commune abolished the use of religious oaths because "it is irrational and immoral to take as witness to an oath a divinity whose existence, and consequently whose authority over humanity is officially denied by science."[135] This led to the following exchange between Rigault, the insurgent in charge of the "ex-Prefecture of Police," and an arrested Jesuit:

> Rigault: What is your profession?
> Jesuit: Servant of god.
> Rigault: Where does your master reside?
> Jesuit: Everywhere.
> Rigault: Scribe, write! This is someone who says they are a servant of someone named god who lives as a vagabond.[136]

The Commune did not take a purely repressive approach to religion. Catholic priests were themselves victims of the system and the right of priests to marry was introduced.[137] However, on April 2 the Hôtel de Ville decreed the separation of church and state and took over all ecclesiastical property.[138] Reclus, the communard diarist, "shook with joy" on learning of this. It was "one of the most decisive acts that had been taken...because it separates the world of the past from the world of the future. The old world would never pardon us for this."[139] He was right. Although the true motivation for the brutal massacre of Bloody Week was the defense of property, the Commune's challenge to religion was a major excuse. In today's Paris the one symbol recalling the Commune is the highly visible church of the Sacré-Coeur at Montmartre built in "expiation" for the "terrible crimes" of 1871.

The way was now open to reforming education, a process eased by the departure of the majority of teachers to join Versailles.[140] Education was one of the nine commissions though the Commune was able to provide few resources. Edouard Vaillant, and André Leo, a leading female writer, were also members. The commission planned to offer compulsory free education for both sexes up to the age of 12.[141] This was not because the economic system required a productive workforce, trained into dumb obedience and unthinking consumption. The motive was exactly the reverse: "Any official direction which is imposed on the judgement of the pupil is fatal and must be condemned...it tends to destroy individuality... We declare that, due to the principle of equality, the Commune owes to every one of its members free education at all levels."[142]

Secular education was a prominent feature throughout: "Schools are open to all the community whatever their beliefs... Religious instruction is left to the initiative of families but is banned for both sexes in all schools."[143] The newspaper *Père Duchêne* stressed girls' education, a revolutionary idea for the time:

> If only you realized, citizens, how much the Revolution depends on women, you would have your eyes opened on girls' education. You would not leave them, as has been done until now, in ignorance! *Foutre*! In a good Republic, perhaps more attention should be paid to the education of girls than to that of boys. After all it is mothers who give us our first ideas and so it is important that these should be those of good *citoyennes*. Thus, citizen members of the commune, if you want to have men, the morals of the Nation must be reformed. And in order to transform morals women must be given a good solid education.[144]

People like Thiers wanted to produce factory fodder on the one hand, while imparting culture to ruling-class children on the other. The

Commune aimed at "professional education" to encourage a rounded creative personality:

> We need a situation where the younger generations, those born or yet to be, are intelligently guided as their capacities develop... The people of 1880 need to be able to produce, but also to speak and to write. From a young age the child must be able to move alternately from the school to the workshop, so that from early on he or she can earn a living at the same time as developing their mind by study and thought. The person who wields a tool must be able to also write a book with feeling and talent... The artisan must be able to relax from daily work through enjoying culture—the arts, letters or sciences—without ceasing to be productive...[145]

In place of dominating and regimenting young people, the 17th arrondissement brought in a system operating on principles of "justice, freedom from oppression, respect for all human beings without distinction of race, nationality, belief, social position, sex, or age... Violating freedom of conscience demoralizes, perverts and coarsens character." Teaching would be based on "scientific and experimental methods that are always based on observation of facts, whether in nature, physics, morality or intellect..."[146]

The Commune combined great vision with poignant tragedy. Under capitalism it is hard to imagine ever hearing a speech like this one, uttered at the opening of a boys' school on the Rue Rollin:

> The Commune, my little friends, wants all children to be healthy in mind and body, generous, lovers of the truth and of justice, and to ardently desire equality in duties as well as rights.
>
> Above all don't forget, that at this moment when I am talking to you about these high ideals, thousands of citizens confront death so that your well-being can be improved, that education is given to all, that there is no more injustice or privilege, and that the strong and powerful do not crush the weak...
>
> So whatever happens, please remember that the people of the Commune love you deeply and when you in turn grow up, defend their memory against those who will insult them.[147]

Despite its brief existence the Commune's reorganization of schooling laid the basis for professional education thereafter. It was far ahead of its time. The Third Republic that followed would only bring in compulsory free education after ten years, a fully secular schools system 33 years later, and equal pay among teachers after 44 years![148]

The Commune's Internationalism

"The Internationale" unites the human race

Before the Commune rabid nationalism and racism had been typical tools of the government. France was a major imperialist power that sought to dominate the European continent as well as snatch colonies further afield. The insurgents could not have been a greater contrast to this. They stood for a completely different world founded on human solidarity. Their vision lives on in the song, "The Internationale." In place of capitalist competition leading to bloody war, the Commune wanted peace and antimilitarism.[149]

This principle was more than a vague sentiment. It was rooted deep in the hearts and minds of the communards because of the bitter lessons of the past. Previous governments had sacrificed hundreds of thousands to the banner of nationalism, but in the recent war showed more interest in defending French capitalism against French workers than resisting foreign occupation. Such experiences convinced Parisians that, as the International's paper put it:

> "Fatherland" is no more than a word, a fallacy! Humanity is a fact, a truth. Priests invented the Fatherland and kings, like the myth of god. It has always served to herd human beings into pens like animals. Here, in the name of a debased illusion and in the grip of the bosses, they are sheared and bled for maximum profit... Enough blood! Enough stupidity! People! The Fatherland is nothing but a word. France is dead. Humanity lives![150]

Rather than admit that ordinary people oppose their system, the establishment always tries to blame sinister external forces for manipulating them into protest action. In 1871 the target was foreigners. *Le Figaro* published a list of 44 non-Frenchmen who were leading insurgents. This was supposed to shame the Commune, but of course it did it honor. The Commune was accused of having recruited:

> The tramps and brigands from all over Europe. Polish forgers, Garibaldian adventurers, Slavic pimps, Prussian agents, Yankee filibusters all frolic at the head of its battalions. Paris has become the main sewer for the scum and dregs of two continents.[151]

Worse still, an officer in the Versailles army saw evidence that the "legislators of the International have applied their program, which means...no more property, no more country!"[152] "Instead they want to efface nationalities and mix everyone together in the name of a common higher interest."[153] A multicultural society—what a horrible fate.

The way the Commune welcomed non-French people into its most prominent positions was without precedent. The trend was set early in a debate about whether "foreigners can be part of the Commune." In particular, what attitude should be taken to Frankel, a Jew and leader of the International's German-speaking section in France (when Germany had been at war with France just a few weeks previously)? The answer—"We consider that the flag of the Commune is that of the universal republic...citizen Frankel is admitted [to the Communal Council]."[154]

As head of the Labor Commission, Frankel had the most important domestic post in the Commune. The highest military position—Delegate for War—went to Cluseret, a naturalized US citizen. Dombrowski, a Pole, became the Commune's chief general, and he was ably assisted by other foreign officers such as Wroblewski (also Polish) and La Cécilia (Italian). The hero of Italian unification, Garibaldi was actually made head of the National Guard.[155] *Père Duchêne*, a newspaper bearing the name of the famous populist journal of the Great Revolution, put the general view well, even if it was a little confused on the details:

> Isn't Garibaldi, an Italian, a bloody good bloke?
> And isn't citizen Cluseret, an American, a bloody good bloke?
> And citizen Dombrowski, a Russian. Isn't he a bloody good bloke?
> And isn't citizen Frankel, a Swiss, a bloody good bloke?
> Of course they are!
> And they're all better than...Thiers, aren't they?[156]

The Commune's internationalism found its symbolic expression in the demolition of the Vendôme Column. Topped by Napoleon Bonaparte's statue, forged out of captured cannons, and erected in memory of his army's victories, Thiers saw it as an emblem of "national glory and military virtues."[157] On April 12 this decree appeared:

> The Commune of Paris considers that the imperial column in the Place Vendôme is a monument to barbarism, a symbol of brutal force and false glory, an affirmation of militarism, a negation of international rights, a permanent insult to both victors and vanquished and a menace to one of the three great principles of the French republic—fraternity... The column in the Place Vendôme will be demolished.[158]

On May 16, in front of huge crowds, the column was brought down. Place Vendôme was then renamed Place Internationale.[159] Imagine Nelson's column receiving the same treatment.

The Commune's Legal System

Equality needs different laws

The Commune's brief existence was overshadowed by constant civil war, but it still fought to create a new type of state founding a new society. One of its first actions (March 28) was abolition of the death penalty, "to prove to the whole of France and the entire world that its representatives are humane, not the bloodthirsty hangmen they are accused of being."[160] As a symbol of this new approach a guillotine was placed before a statue of the Enlightenment philosopher Voltaire and ceremonially burned.[161]

Alas, the communards discovered that military pressures made such magnanimous arrangements impossible to sustain. Courts-martial with the power to inflict capital punishment were reinstituted. However, unlike previously, these were democratically organized and consisted of officers and rank-and-file National Guards, the former, of course, being elected and subject to instant recall.[162] Each battalion also had an elected and recallable disciplinary committee. As the noose tightened around Paris, an atmosphere of suspicion developed and by popular demand the methods of the Great Terror of the 1789 Revolution were revived. In fact, apart from the hostages killed in the final hours in a vain attempt to deter Versailles troops from indiscriminately massacring the Parisian population, only three people were executed by courts-martial for military offenses under the Commune.[163]

At a less dramatic level, Eugène Protot, as head of the Justice Commission, took steps that have recently been described as "a century in advance of what we have today."[164] Under the old legal system run by a "judicial aristocracy"[165] of lawyers, administrative costs had been so exorbitant that justice was only available to the very rich. Protot pegged legal salaries to the council's level of 6,000 francs per year.[166] Magistrates were elected for the first time and functions that formerly carried charges (such as witnessing documents, registering children and marriage contracts) were to be provided free.[167]

"The Inauguration of Luxury"

And give to all a happier lot

Although the March 18 revolution was in direct response to immediate issues, the Commune and its working-class supporters had their sights on winning more than a crust of bread. There was a higher goal of human liberation—to think, feel and create as never before. Culture, in the broadest sense of the term, was to be revolutionized alongside politics and economics. It was in this sense that the Commune was described at the time as "a celebration" or a "festival"[168] taking place "in face of the enemy cannons in the most splendid place on earth."[169]

Festivals need festivities and artists came forward to provide them. Four hundred people met over a three-day period to set up an Artists' Federation.[170] Stretching from those in the fine arts to manual workers who earned their living from state commissions for public buildings, it was presided over by the painter Gustave Courbet and a 47-strong commission including 16 painters, ten sculptors and medal engravers, five architects, and so on.

The Artists' Federation wanted "to create socialist establishments everywhere." Vaillant, under whose commission culture fell, argued that:

> Exploitation in the arts is perhaps even more terrible than in the workshops, with all those working in theaters exploited from top to bottom. The female dancer is forced to sell herself to live. In a word it is robbery from start to finish. We must apply to the theaters a regime of equality, the regime of association [cooperatives]... Theater managements are charged with replacing the existing regime of proprietors and privilege with a system of association to be run entirely by the artists themselves.[171]

So the federation wanted self-government in place of exploitation by the capitalists, government censorship, and dependence on commissions from the rich.[172]

In a move a century ahead of its time, the federation overthrew the elitist division between fine arts and applied arts and promised that both would enjoy equal status in future communal exhibitions:[173]

> The committee will organize on the national and international scale... Through the word, the paintbrush, the crayon, the popular reproduction of masterpieces, by the intelligent and moral images that can be spread widely and exhibited in the town halls of the smallest communes of

> France, the committee will assist in our regeneration, the inauguration of luxury for the whole community and the splendors of the future and the universal republic.[174]

Cultural change for the masses operated on several levels. One sign was a shift in forms of address from *Monsieur* (whose origin was *mon seigneur*—"my lord") and *Madame* to the term *citizen* that came from the 1790s.[175] Another was the opening of the Tuileries imperial palace and gardens. One section was made into a military hospital while the gardens and reception rooms became visitor attractions. On the walls were banners that said: "People, the gold that exudes from these walls is your sweat!" and "Today the Revolution has made you free, you now own what you have created."[176]

The Comédie Française theater company put on daily performances and when conscription took away the male actors women filled their roles.[177] Packed concerts and gala performances took place right up until the end. Indeed, one of these was going on at the very moment the Versailles forces invaded the city. One insurgent captured the spirit that the Commune embodied:

> Neither winter, nor the siege, nor treason nor hunger, nor black pox, nor the bombardment accepted as the normal state of affairs, nor the pang of defeat, nor the civil war, nor the savage executions, nor the threats for the future, nothing has been able to prevail against the serenity of the ancient Capital... Paris fights and Paris sings! Paris is on the eve of being assailed by an unrelenting and enraged army and Paris laughs! Paris bristles with fortresses, entrenchments and breastworks, and at the same time Paris preserves within its formidable enclosures places where one can laugh.[178]

"A Gigantic Liberation of the Word"[179]

Let's claim henceforth the earth for workers

The question of how to create real democracy and avoid bureaucratic degeneration is a perennial political issue in popular revolutions, with the example of Stalinism in the twentieth century as a warning of what can happen. Paris in 1871 solved this conundrum by creating an institution that was not a bureaucratic imposition on society from above, but an embodiment of society itself. In January 1871 a "red poster" first raised the idea of a Commune and gave a sense of the unity of both concepts: "Make way for the people! Make way for the Commune!"[180] More than any plans or strategies of the organized revolutionary left, mass self-activity would be decisive in shaping the new institution.

The spirit of mass involvement that was developing in Paris even before March 18 was encapsulated in this anti-communard's description: "From Rue Druout right up to the Montmartre district the boulevards had become a permanent public meeting or club where the crowd, divided into groups, had filled not only the pavements but also the road to the point of blocking the way to traffic. They formed a myriad of public assemblies where war and peace were hotly debated."[181]

How did this mass movement link with the overall Commune structure after March 18? There were interactions at three levels. The Communal Council sitting in the Hôtel de Ville was the first. The "sections"—organized bodies, including groupings such as the Women's Union, International, trade unions and local borough administrations—formed the second.[182] The third level was the Parisian population itself which, after the exodus of the wealthy, consisted of the middle and working classes. If the Commune was to be radically different from all previous states, evidence for it would be found at this third level, through the involvement of the Parisian populace.

Prominent insurgents encouraged mass involvement in the life of the new government and saw themselves as mandated delegates. Parisel stated: "We are here as representatives of the people and we must know how to obey its wishes." Urbain agreed: "From the moment a project is generally supported it acquires an importance which means the Commune cannot refuse to discuss it... When a project has general sympathy, it must have ours too." Jourde had a different opinion: "The public is not the judge of the questions posed here," but Parisel retorted, "Not only is it indeed the judge, but I believe it is the sovereign judge!"[183] Many of the insurgents had fought previous dictatorships and suffered imprisonment and exile for this. They had been committed to universal suffrage and individual freedom, which they saw as a step forward compared to the feudal past. But the revolution of March 18 opened up a new vista that went much further, and the communards had no doubt of the limitations of suffrage operating where capitalist economics was dominant. The points made by the revolutionary press remain valid, such as this statement in the *L'Avant-Garde* newspaper: "What does it matter to the worker that the press is free, that universal suffrage exists, if the laws of the economy remove from him the greater part of his labor and rivet him eternally to the chains of the proletariat."[184]

L'Affranchi agreed:

> In effect, though the people have the illusory right of putting their votes in the electoral urn, they nevertheless remain crushed under the pressure of a type of slavery, the slavery of poverty which bends the great army of proletarians under a yoke of iron and forces them, in the face of the hunger which grips them and their families, to return each day to the master who agrees to rent their labor for an insufficient salary... So, while there remains the issue of practical social emancipation of the poor classes who produce the abundance but who vegetate in poverty and destitution, the revolution is not over.[185]

Politicians may pay lip service to democracy but they seek to anesthetize people with their words. By contrast the communards sought to mobilize them. How did Commune democracy differ? It encouraged:

> The permanent intervention of citizens in communal affairs, by the free manifestation of their ideas and the free defense of their interests... It is more essential than ever that you maintain an interest in public affairs. You should meet, organize, reconstitute in some way the Districts, the primary assemblies to which the 1789 Revolution owed part of its strength. By the efforts of everyone we will achieve the great principle of social renewal: the emancipation of the workers by the workers themselves.[186]

This sentiment was reciprocated at the base and took various forms. A brief newspaper item from early April indicated both the widespread involvement and the anti-hierarchical attitude of the insurgents: "We are receiving many letters addressed to the President of the Commune. We do not have and will not have a President. Please address letters to the members of the Commune, Hôtel de Ville."[187] Indeed, the Commune had no single "leader"—no Cromwell, Robespierre or Lenin (though, as we shall see, a lack of leadership would produce problems in itself). When the council was inaugurated on March 26, Charles Beslay was selected to speak for it simply because he was the doyen or oldest member.

The Commune welcomed input from outside bodies but was overwhelmed by it: "Every day we receive verbally or in writing a great number of proposals... These propositions are often excellent... It is urgent that a commission is nominated to examine these proposals from which the Commune can gain great benefit."[188]

As time passed the sheer volume of suggestions created difficulties and, with civil war raging, the Hôtel de Ville found it hard to cope with the stream of people who crammed into the offices. The *Journal Officiel* complained: "Every day and at all times, the offices are invaded by numerous citizens who come here to satisfy their legitimate demands but who get very overwrought. All requests should henceforth be submitted in writing. It is a way of economizing on the time of everyone, and releasing the officials from too much of a burden."[189]

Rather than individual petitioners, however, the main living link between the mass movement and the Communal Council was the clubs. In later workers' revolutions workplaces became the centers of mass debate. However, in Paris this was precluded by the minuscule size of most production units and the fact that many were closed anyway. There were some 36 to 50 clubs meeting daily, though they tended to be concentrated in the working-class areas.[190] Some meetings were huge. One, held in the 3rd arrondissement on May 1, had 5,000 in attendance. The figure climbed to 6,000 later in the month.[191]

The clubs' very meeting places had radical significance. They moved from local halls to take over churches, an initiative spearheaded by the "Communal Club of the 3rd arrondissement, Nicolas-des-Champs." ("Saint" had been dropped from the name, which was the general practice):[192] "A great revolutionary act has just been accomplished. To educate the people politically, the population of the 3rd arrondissement has finally taken possession of a monument that until now only served a caste of people who were sworn enemies of all progress."[193] This takeover is a good example of the positive interplay of the various "levels" of the Commune. It was the decision of the Hôtel de Ville to bring churches under communal ownership that made this relocation of the clubs possible.

Churches now performed an extraordinary dual function: "In the morning the mass, baptisms, marriages, confession and burials. When night fell the side chapels were shut, the bronze candlesticks, the crucifixes remained on the altars and the flowers in front of the Virgin and Saint Joseph. All stayed in place. Only the bench of the churchwardens looked different: the statue of Christ above it was holding a red flag."[194]

Women formed a large proportion of the audiences[195] and Lissagaray gives a sense of the atmosphere of the meetings:

> The Revolution mounts the pulpits. In the old quarter of the Gravilliers, Saint Nicolas-des-Champs is filling with the powerful murmur of many voices. A few gas-burners hardly light up the swarming crowd; and at the farther end, almost hidden by the shadow of the vaults, hangs the figure of Christ draped in the popular oriflamme. The only luminous center is the reading-desk, facing the pulpit, hung with red. The organ and the people chant the "Marseillaise." The orator, overexcited by these fantastic surroundings, launches forth into ecstatic declamations, which the echo repeats like a menace. The people discuss the events of the day, the means of defense; the members of the Commune are severely censured, and vigorous resolutions are voted to be presented to the Hôtel de Ville the next day.[196]

Along with such subject matter there was a great variety of other items that reflected this moment of transition for the socialist movement. Here are some examples. A 500-strong assembly in the 1st arrondissement proposed the right of divorce. Giant meetings at Nicolas-des-Champs called for new communal elections (to replace delegates who had resigned), a stronger leadership through a Committee of Public Safety, improvements in the state of barricades, expulsion of the wives of those men who had joined Versailles, and a review of the rents decree.[197] A meeting of 3,000 at the Club de la Révolution on May 13 unanimously called for the abolition of magistrates, the ending of religious ceremonies and immediate arrest of priests, changes to the decree on pawnshops, the banning of brothels, all communal work to be undertaken by workers' corporations and the execution of a hostage every 24 hours until political prisoners of Versailles were released.[198] The president of the Club Saint-Séverin wrote to the Commune to ask it to "finish off the bourgeoisie in one blow [and] take over the Banque de France..."[199] The "Free Thinkers' Club" demanded full equality for women.[200]

Relations with the Communal Council, or assembly, were often discussed. The ever-creative Nicolas-des-Champs issued a manifesto affirming "the sovereignty of the people above everything. They must never abandon the right of supervision of the acts of their representatives. People, govern yourselves through public meetings, through your press; lean on those who represent you."[201] Nicolas-des-Champs was among the 11 clubs that established a federation to channel proposals into the Hôtel de Ville and produce a regular bulletin for the public.[202] The Club Ambroise unanimously voted to demand "the presence at each meeting of a delegate of the Commune, with whom one can reach accord on the decisions taken at its sessions, gain inspiration from the council and permanently establish a direct rapport with the Commune."[203] In the 1st arrondissement consultative councils were organized to maintain permanent contact between the local population and the elected Commune members.[204] In the 4th arrondissement giant public meetings were organized where council members were summoned to account for their actions.

How successful was the Commune in forging a new kind of state? If we use the idea of the three levels once more, it is clear that the links between the first level (the Hôtel de Ville) and the second (the "sections") were strong and reciprocal. In education, for example, much of the momentum came not from the Commune's commission but from preexisting bodies of educators such as the Société des Amis de l'Enseignement.[205] The Labor Commission's work was shaped by, and depended absolutely on, the Women's Union and the trade unions/workers' corporations, which in turn were empowered by the commission.

The relationship neither glorified the state (in Stalinist fashion) nor ignored it (anarchist-style), but inextricably linked change from below and the state. Other important second-level bodies were the local *mairies*, the borough administrations:

> It is there, at the base, that communal work was accomplished above all and where the communal revolution lived from day to day. For it was not simply a matter of carrying out banal functions such as registering marriages, births and deaths. They dealt with social questions, unemployment, the regeneration and organization of production, basic provisioning, canteens and soup kitchens, public assistance, the secular reform of education, the maintenance, arming and discipline of the National Guard...[206]

Relations between the Commune and the "third level"—the clubs and the mass meetings—are harder to measure. It is not surprising to find that in the midst of civil war "the Commune, with the possible exception of its Commission for Labor, Industry and Trade, did not answer most of the numerous reports and letters it received..."[207] Once the fighting began, the principle of instant recall was not consistently implemented, though it did operate in some areas.[208] While the Commune encouraged clubs and individuals to submit proposals "the motions piled up at the Hôtel de Ville, in the offices of the secretariat, without [the Commune] even discussing them for the most part in plenary sessions."[209]

However, despite the mounting chaos of civil war, elected delegates consulted their electors in detail over issues such as bills of exchange. Bakery workers went to the Commune and it did their bidding.[210] Council members appeared at mass meetings to account for their actions and ask for a renewal of popular confidence. One example was on May 20, just days before the end, when 2,000 people assembled in the 4th arrondissement.[211] And, as we have seen, the life of the Commune did not start and stop in the council chamber. The mass of Parisians were living in a new way, whether it was in forms of address, relations with their landlords and employers or their schooling.

Even if we confine our focus to the Communal Council itself, the change was still undeniable. Democracy cannot be judged solely on the basis of formal institutional arrangements. Establishment politicians under capitalism claim to embody democracy and serve the electorate. This is false because even if they are honest this ignores the environment in which the state operates. A million golden threads bind the state to the capitalist system, whatever the official version given. Given the brief life of the Commune and the fact that it was embroiled in a vicious civil war from the moment of birth, the formal development of popular sovereignty, important as it was, could not be fully worked out. So we must look at the underlying relations of power to find the substance of the Commune state as a radical alternative.

The contemporary state acts abroad and at home as defender of big business. Toward the poor and oppressed it is a form of external coercion (either directly through armies, police, prisons and so on, or indirectly, through ideological pressure, social policies, etc). Under the Commune force was fundamentally different because of the role of the National Guard. This turned the very principles of the state upside down because "it gives to the city a national militia that defends the citizens against power, instead of an army that defends the state from the citizens..."[212]

The National Guard's internal democracy guaranteed that coercive force belonged to the mass of the people, instead of being used against it. This could be seen on the streets, but also at the summit of power:

> In the military arena the people under arms exercised their right of recall over the members of the Commune and removed individuals put in charge of military affairs. The National Guard removed Cluseret and Rossel [successive military delegates in charge of the war effort]...

> Therefore a right of recall of delegates operated in the short period of communard government...[213]

The Commune was surrounded by hostile forces and could not function at the national level. But what did it have to say about this wider arena? Many people are rightly suspicious of bureaucracy given the terrible legacy of Stalinism, which used the language of "socialism" and "communism" but operated a centralized dictatorship of one man. The Commune insisted that power must come from below and so aimed to "break the alien system of centralization and thus destroy the only weapon that the privileged classes possess."[214] The goal was "Free Paris—that is the Paris Commune. Free France, that is communal France in federal form."[215] This would allow the population to be directly involved in accessible power structures. The implications were enormous, as one Communal Council member explained:

> This programme was so clear, so radical, so moderate in form that, if accepted and understood and imposed by France on its government it would have put an end to all conflicts and all struggles. It would have allowed the solution, in detail, step by step, without violent shocks, of all social and political questions by breaking *unitarism* and *centralization*, in other words despotism of either one man or one assembly... The triumph of the communal idea is, in other words, the social revolution.[216]

There would be a major debate about whether, given conditions of civil war, power could be decentralized immediately (and this will be dealt with in a later chapter) but former proponents of centralization were open to new ideas. Delescluze, the Jacobin leader, wrote that "Paris, always held in bondage by previous governments, has at last fully won its absolute autonomy. It is going to be able to run things in the way it wants and take control of its internal affairs. This is justice..."[217] Even the Blanquists, a current that was most insistent on the need for centralized organization to defeat the enemy, rejoiced that "the communal constitution will have restored to the social body the forces until now absorbed by the parasitic state..."[218]

The Proclamation

The soaring hopes aroused by the Commune were demonstrated in spectacular fashion on March 28, the day when the names of those elected to the Communal Council were read out at the Hôtel de Ville. There are many, many accounts of that day. It seems that everyone with literary talent felt moved to chronicle the emotions they felt. Both friends and foes were carried away by the dazzling spectacle. Catulle Mendès, a bitter enemy of the Commune, wrote:

> I was in the square in front of the Hôtel de Ville at the moment that the names of the members of the Commune were declared, and I write these lines still full of emotion.
>
> How many people were there? One hundred thousand perhaps. Where did they come from? From every corner of the city. Armed men spilled out of every nearby street, and the sharp points of the bayonets, glittering in the sun, made the place seem like a field of lightning… The music playing was "The Marseillaise," a song taken up by fifty thousand resolute voices: this thunder shook all the people, and the great song, out of fashion from defeats, recovered for a moment its former energy.
>
> Suddenly the cannons fired. The song redoubled in its awesome volume; an immense sea of banners, bayonets and caps, surging forward, drifting back, undulating, breaking against the stage. The cannons still thundered, but they were heard only in intervals between the singing. Then all the sounds merged into a single cheer, the universal voice of the countless multitude, and *all these people had but one heart just as they had but one voice.*[219]

Whether it concerned workers' control of production, women's emancipation, education, internationalism, law or democracy from below, the Paris Commune had planted the seeds of a new social world and opened the way toward the liberation of all humanity. In the words of the Paris section of the International:

> By affirming its principles, the communal revolution removes all causes of future conflict… The independence of the Commune is the commitment to a contract whose clauses will be freely debated and will bring to an end class conflict and guarantee social equality. We have demanded the emancipation of the workers, and the setting up of a Commune is its guarantee… You are masters of your destiny.[220]

The Central Committee of the National Guard was more eloquent:

> Workers, do not be deceived: it is the great struggle: parasitism and labor, exploitation and production are at death-grips. If you are sick or vegetating in ignorance and squatting in the muck; if you want your children to be men gaining the reward of their labor, not a sort of animal trained for the workshop and for war, fertilizing with its sweat the fortune of an

exploiter, or pouring out its blood for a despot; if you want the daughters whom you cannot bring up and watch over as you would, to be no longer instruments of pleasure in the arms of the aristocracy of wealth; if you want debauch and poverty no longer to drive men to the police and women to prostitution; if, finally, you desire the reign of justice, workers, be intelligent, arise! And let your stout hands fling beneath your feet the foul reaction!

...Long live the Republic! Long live the Commune![221]

Barricades after the attack,
Rue Saint-Maur, June 26, 1848

Two

The Capital of the Human Race

The Place

Servile masses arise, arise

There are many alternative ideas about how to deal with the greed of capitalism and the destruction it causes, but for a different society to amount to more than an abstract blueprint, there must be a means of making it a reality. This can only occur when mass social forces, with the strength and the will to struggle for a new world in the face of opposition from the old, see it as relevant and embrace it as their own. The communal experience was an example. The revolution of March 18, 1871, was not the result of some pet project of an individual political thinker or small group, but came from a groundswell of mass action from below. The historical and material roots of the Commune lay in the Parisian working class. The next chapter looks at how its mass base developed.

In the nineteenth century the French capital was much more than an agglomeration of people. While the mills of Manchester had transformed the world economically through an industrial revolution, Paris had shaped it politically. For the novelist Victor Hugo, Paris was "the capital of the human race" and the "city of cities."[1] It gained this reputation because its working people had fought the power of wealth and privilege with an unparalleled intensity. A pattern was set during the Great French Revolution of 1789–94 that had an enormous influence on Parisians in the century that followed.

This event was precipitated by a government financial crisis. Extravagant spending on personal luxuries and war left royal coffers empty, and in May 1789 Louis XVI was forced to recall the Estates General (a parliament) for the first time in a century and a half. His attempts to bully this body into voting in new taxation failed, and it set itself up as an independent National Assembly. In July 1789 Parisians feared that the king was about to repress the growing democratic movement. To preempt this they stormed the fortress prison of the Bastille located in the heart of the capital. Their action, on July 14, 1789, fatally undermined the authority of the ancien regime, the old state system.

Until this point the revolution consisted largely of a dispute between the monarchy and the relatively privileged layer of middle- and upper-class representatives who sat in the National Assembly. The intervention of the Parisian crowd transformed the revolution's character from words to physical confrontation and propelled it in a far more radical direction. In the summer of 1789, as peasants burned down the aristocratic chateaus, feudal privileges were abolished, a Declaration of the Rights of Man was introduced and the motto of "Liberty, Equality, Fraternity" was adopted.

In 1792 war broke out between revolutionary France and its neighbors. The monarchs of Europe united to crush this mortal threat to their authority. The French king was discovered to be secretly collaborating with the enemy and the country suffered a series of reverses. When the Duke of Brunswick advanced toward Paris and threatened to massacre its citizens, the ordinary people of the city—the sansculottes—swung into action once again. Under their pressure an emergency city government, the Revolutionary Commune, was established in August 1792, and in September the First Republic was proclaimed.

By now the National Assembly had been replaced by a Convention, and with the outcome of the war still hanging in the balance, a fierce debate developed within its walls over how to proceed. Although the

Convention was middle class in composition, it contained political currents that were prepared to take radical measures to protect the gains of the revolution. The Jacobin Club, whose leaders included Robespierre and Marat, proposed strong and daring action to reorganize the war effort. They advocated a centralized and efficient command structure, the use of what they called the Terror (severe repression of internal enemies), and daring social measures that would engage the popular enthusiasm of the French people, especially the Parisian sansculottes. Their opponents, the Girondins, disapproved of centralised state intervention and resented concessions to the sansculottes as an infringement on the rights of private property. With the backing of the Parisian crowd, the Jacobins won the argument and in 1793 they established a Committee of Public Safety along with a Law of Maximum limiting the rights of business to impose price increases.

Their vigorous new policies began to bear fruit and French armies triumphed against opponents of the revolution both at home and abroad. The middle-class Jacobin leadership now had less need of the revolutionary enthusiasm of the sansculottes. The Law of Maximum was now applied to wages, which led to falling incomes for the sansculottes. Robespierre also turned against the *enragés,* a faction that wished to push the revolution toward a full-scale assault on property. After a failed demonstration in March 1783 *enragé* leaders were arrested and executed. Other sans culottes leaders followed them to the guillotine soon afterward. However, the Jacobins were weakening their base of popular support by attacking the sansculottes. So, when France's military success eased the pressures of war, the Convention began to regard the Jacobins and their authoritarian interventionist methods as too radical and no longer necessary. In July 1794 the Jacobins were overthrown and the revolutionary period came to an end.

With feudalism abolished, the French middle class had now secured favorable conditions for the development of capitalism, with all the consequences that entailed. The mass popular involvement and democratic structures of the earlier period were no longer essential. It was in this climate that, a decade later, Napoleon Bonaparte crowned himself emperor and installed the First Empire. He was finally defeated at Waterloo in 1815, whereupon the monarchy was restored. In spite of this, the hold of the ancien regime as a social system would never be fully reconstituted.

The world-historic impact of the Great Revolution cannot be underestimated. It invented the basic vocabulary of modern politics. For example, the terms "left wing" and "right wing" come from the seating arrangements of the Convention in which the moderate Girondins were on the benches to the right, while the radical Jacobins were on the left wing. Furthermore they were among the first modern political parties because political issues were now no longer the exclusive domain of a small group surrounding the monarch. The revolution popularized ideas of democracy and civil rights that are the common currency of political discourse throughout the world today.

Naturally, such a momentous event strongly influenced later insurgencies. In March 1871 the first edition of the Paris Commune's official newspaper, the *Journal Officiel de la République Française sous la Commune* described the Commune as "the Child of the Republic upon whose emblem is written that great word—Fraternity."[2] Just before the communal movement was smashed, another paper saw the Commune as completing the Great Revolution's unfinished business: "The struggle that has been going on in France for 80 years against the old world is reaching its dénouement."[3] Indeed, the Commune's labor commissioner, Frankel, who as a foreigner may have had a bit more detachment from 1789 than his fellow communards, was so exasperated by their constant references to it that he complained of his comrades "sleeping with and waking up with the *Moniteur* newspaper of 1793."[4]

What were the key ideas from the Great Revolution that were taken up by the insurgents of 1871? For some it was the sense that action by ordinary people makes a difference. In 1792 an enragé leader expressed this when he wrote, "On July 14, [1789], liberty emerged shining from the debris of the infamous Bastille... Our sovereignty was not an illusion; we were free and without restrictions."[5] During 1871 this aspect of popular self-activity was emphasized by the Proudhonists. For others the chief legacy of the Great Revolution was a belief in the efficacy of centralized authority. In 1871 they remembered how the original Jacobins had retrieved the military situation against all the odds:

> In 1792 the rights that had been won by the people were in danger of being lost. The men who at that time were devoted to the cause of our class had recourse to the extreme measure of delegating all the active force of the revolution to a few citizens. Armed with unlimited powers,

> these citizens were able, through the energy and decisiveness of their action, to save our rights.[6]

In 1871 neo-Jacobins promoted this approach within the Commune. Yet other insurgents focused on the importance of revolution as a means of achieving total social transformation. This theme was taken up by the Blanquists in 1871. Each of these movements will be discussed later.

The tidal currents stirred up by the Great Revolution remained active in the period between 1789 and 1871, showing just how deeply the spirit of insubordination and rebellion was ingrained. One historian has identified some 137 "major violent events," including 37 "insurrections/rebellions," in the Paris region between 1830 and 1869 alone.[7] In 1830, for example, the restored Bourbon monarchy was toppled by three days of mass protest. Though the revolution succeeded in removing one king, another—from the Orleanist line—was installed to replace him. The human costs of the 1830 revolution were high, with 1,800 insurgents and 200 soldiers dead. The new king soon faced opposition on the streets of Paris. In 1832 fighting cost the lives of 80 insurgents and 70 soldiers, with 490 wounded.[8] Two years later the minister of the interior, Adolphe Thiers, ordered 40,000 troops into Paris to crush a rebellion. During this operation the notorious massacre of the Rue Transnonain took place—the unprovoked killing of 12 unarmed inhabitants. This presaged the brutality Thiers would employ against the 1871 Commune.

Revolutionary Paris scaled new heights in February 1848 when the Orleanist king, Louis Phillippe, was overthrown and monarchy finally banished from France. This event sparked a wave of revolt that spread swiftly across Europe, engulfing Germany, the Austrian Empire and Italy in a matter of weeks.[9] The February 1848 Revolution was supported by both the republican middle class and the working class, and unlike previous revolutions, it seemed that both sections might benefit as a result. The newly formed Second Republic made an important concession to the mass of ordinary Parisians by establishing national workshops for the unemployed.[10]

However, peace was short-lived. In June the workshops were closed down, and workers rose up in what Marx described as a:

> gigantic insurrection, in which the first great battle was fought between the two great classes which divide modern society... The workers, with unheard-of bravery and ingenuity, without leaders, without a common plan, without supplies, and for the most part lacking weapons, held in check

> the army, the Mobile Guard, the Paris National Guard and the National Guard which streamed in from the provinces, for five days. It is well known how the bourgeoisie sought compensation for the mortal terror it had suffered in outrageous brutality, massacring over 3,000 prisoners.[11]

Bitter feelings were added to by a further 15,000 arrests and 3,400 deportations.[12] This created a deep gulf between middle-class proponents of a republic as a purely political institution, but which did not touch capitalism, and those who wanted a "social republic" that delivered serious reforms for ordinary people. The hostility engendered by the events of June 1848 would influence the civil war in 1871. The defeat of the workers in 1848 cast a shadow over the Republic. In December 1851 the elected president, Louis Bonaparte—the great-nephew of Napoleon Bonaparte—used this to his advantage. He declared himself hereditary emperor. Protests against the coup were smashed and repression endured until the Second Empire was itself overthrown in 1870.

As this brief history of Parisian revolt makes clear, the numerous upheavals in the capital had a huge political impact, and this was out of proportion to the number of people involved. The reason was the long tradition of state centralization begun by monarchs even before 1789, which meant events in the capital shook society as a whole.[13] Population concentration accentuated the city's importance. At over 1.7 million inhabitants in 1860[14] it was the world's biggest city after London. (Comparable capitals were Berlin with 548,000, Moscow with 352,000, Vienna with 476,000 and Amsterdam with 244,000).[15] Within France itself no other city came close. Paris had a larger population than the other 14 large towns combined.[16]

The presence of a revolutionary tradition, combined with political and demographic weight, meant that Paris was not run like other cities. While the tiniest French hamlet had its "commune," its unit of local government, Paris was ruled directly by prefects—the equivalent of provincial governors. The capital's 20 arrondissements (small boroughs, or districts) had their own mayors, but no central organization or municipal council was permitted. Only Lyons shared this dubious distinction because it had its own tradition of workers' uprisings.

When Louis Bonaparte came to power in 1851 (and called himself Emperor Napoleon III) he wanted to go beyond simply restraining the city. He ordered radical surgery to cut out the revolutionary heart of these urban centers: "The whole problem is to find a way of reducing the number of malcontents from Lyons to Paris."[17] The architect (almost literally) of this process in the capital would be Baron Georges Haussmann, prefect of the Seine, and so the appointed head of local government. He was acutely aware of the importance of his task:

> Everything ends up at Paris: the main roads, railways and telegraphs. Everything comes out of Paris: laws, decrees, decisions and government emissaries. These energetic forms of centralization which have been organized century after century by successive governments have made of the city the "head and the heart" of France... Paris is the very essence of centralization.[18]

Haussmann concluded that as a consequence "law and order in this queen of cities is one of the first conditions for general security...and public peace."[19]

The baron ordered a total physical transformation of the place. Public pronouncements dwelled on the provision of more space, a better environment and modern amenities,[20] but class fear was a stronger motive. To banish insurrection, the erection of barricades had to be made more difficult. The capital was to be reshaped house by house, street by street. The aim was "to establish routes which secured broad, direct and straightforward lines of communication between the key points of the capital and the military establishment charged with protecting them."[21] The old narrow streets, ideal for barricades, were swept away by broad, straight boulevards.

Social engineering went further. The "malcontents" who had so often held a dagger to the heart of the establishment were driven from strategic locations. The language used was warlike: "We have to attack the old neighborhoods head on...we have to force the population away from the center..."[22] Under Haussmann 20,000 houses were demolished and 800 km of broad new roads (20 to 35 meters wide) were constructed.[23] The result was that in the third of a century after 1861 the population of the central arrondissements grew by just 7 percent, whereas overall population grew by 50 percent, and the peripheral arrondissements added 103 percent.[24] Open spaces where crowds might congregate were swept away and (prefiguring fascist architecture) open views were built to direct one's gaze toward imposing monuments.[25] Civic buildings were also disengaged from their surroundings to be more secure from assault.[26]

When demolition failed, rent increases did the trick.[27] In a town where 19 out of 20 were tenants, city center rents doubled in just 6 years.[28] During 1871 one writer described how he was crippled by municipal taxes to "enable Mr. Haussmann to create a palace of the town where I could no longer stay because of the high cost of living and rents." Workers were forced to live further away, but their workplaces clung on in the center, and since public transport was expensive (a single journey costing a quarter of the daily wage) they had to commute on foot.[29]

Haussmann's central Paris became a haven for the rich, a "Babylon," a nineteenth-century theme park known "for its carnival flash, a crazy tinsel circus of all fleshly pleasures and all earthly magnificence." Gautier, who would be a fierce critic of the Commune, recognized that "the religion of money is the only one today that has no unbelievers." Thomas Carlyle said of Paris, "I think there never was a more corrupt, abominable city, nothing but a brothel and a gambling hall."[30] By contrast working-class districts like Montmartre and Belleville "were dismal half-finished urban wastes of railway yards, factories, quarries, building sites, workshops and jerry-built housing, short of schools, churches, transport services and urban facilities of all kinds, even water."[31]

The exceptional history of Paris explains why the Commune began there. This city was the structure into which the explosive charge of mass discontent would be inserted. When that charge was detonated all the precautions and plans of Bonaparte and Haussmann came to naught.

The Power: Second Empire

On our flesh long has fed the raven

History is littered with radical currents that set out to change the world but foundered on the rock of the state machine, the British Labour Party being one example. These movements thought they could use the existing power structure to bring about the changes they wanted. They tinkered with established institutions but did not abolish them. The originality of the Commune lay in its determination to found a new type of state. Where did this resolve come from? The communards' response was based on their experience of previous French governments, the most recent being Louis Bonaparte's Second Empire, which lasted from 1851 to September 1870.

In a Europe still dominated by monarchies it was unique in claiming authority from the people rather than the "divine right of kings." Long before he came to power Louis recognized that "one can govern only with the masses." Yet he was haunted by fear of class struggle and so insisted the masses must be "disciplined so that they may be directed."[32] His regime has been described as the prototype of fascism because of its combination of populism and authoritarianism. Bonaparte indeed owed his position to the masses. The February 1848 Revolution had increased the electorate from 250,000 to 9 million, sweeping him to the presidency of the Second Republic on a tide of peasant votes.[33] In 1851 he expressed his gratitude by overthrowing the Republic, and that day declared "the era of revolutions closed."[34]

This was mere wish fulfillment, as the Second Empire had to rely on repression from the beginning. During the 1851 coup 380 civilians were shot, 26,000 arrested and thousands driven into exile.[35] Later on workers were forced to carry a booklet obtained from the Prefecture of Police testifying to their behavior[36] and unions were illegal; 4,000 workers were convicted between 1853 and 1866 under anti-combination laws.[37] All this was enforced by a police force doubled in size.[38]

For a time economic growth bought off discontent, but in the 1860s the contradictions began to unravel. A foreign policy adventure in Mexico ended in disaster with the public execution of the French-installed puppet ruler, Maximilian. Voices of dissent grew louder. In successive parliamentary elections antigovernment votes tripled and then almost doubled again.[39] Parisians led the way in the last election, with 234,000 opposition votes to the Bonapartists' 77,000.[40] The conclusion was clear to Bonaparte's leading minister. There were now "only two forces: the emperor and democracy. The forces of democracy are growing all the time; they must be placated if we are not to be carried off by them."[41] Repression was not working, so the emperor was advised to "forestall the day when concessions would no longer be voluntary."[42]

The result was the so-called Liberal Empire of the late 1860s. Ministers could now be questioned in parliament and public meetings were allowed, provided they were under police supervision. But the new line still followed the Bonapartist motto, "Progress towards liberty through dictatorship."[43] Despite Bonaparte's intentions the protesters were not appeased and his reforms simply allowed expressions of discontent to be aired. Of the 150 newspapers founded in 1869, 120 were hostile to the emperor, the most well known being edited by Rochefort, who famously said that, instead of citizens, "France has 36 million subjects, not counting the subjects of discontent."[44]

The Liberal Empire failed because its reforms were obviously the result of pure opportunism.[45] An ironic proof of this was the May 1870 referendum in which the electorate was given the "choice" of voting for or against limited liberalization. Not surprisingly the result was a massive 7.4 million "yes" votes to 1.5 million "noes." This victory was hollow, for just four months later the empire was overthrown, unlamented.

The catalyst was France's crushing defeat in war with Prussia. An army's military prowess might seem more related to tactics and technology than class struggle. However, in the words of one historian of war, "the military system of a nation is not an independent section of the social system but an aspect of it in its totality."[46] Louis, of all people, might have been expected to make success on the battlefield his absolute priority, since his main, indeed only, claim to fame was his link to Napoleon I, the first emperor of France. His 1848 manifesto said, "There is one name which is a symbol of order, of glory and of patriotism... [Vote for] the man who bears it today."[47] So why did the Second Empire fail to repeat the illustrious feats of the first?

In 1793 the French had faced the concerted onslaught of Europe's aristocratic states. The Jacobin government turned to mass recruitment to construct its army (the *levée en masse*), fusing battalions of eager new recruits with professional soldiers and providing "the purest historical expression of the nation-in-arms."[48] Napoleon I used the energy and enthusiasm generated by the Great Revolution to launch his continental conquests. His opponents, composed of mercenaries and professionals fighting for monarchs and princes, were no match. In the revolutionary levée en masse lay the secret of military success, but also risks.[49] Arming the people was a strategy that could turn against a government, especially an unpopular and repressive one.[50] "It was not safe to place a gun on the shoulder of every Socialist," said Thiers.[51] Indeed it was Napoleon I who disposed of the levée en masse (while Prussia would adopt it).

The regime that followed, the restored Bourbon monarchy of 1815–30, opted for the opposite strategy: "Politically reliable troops could be formed only of men broken into unquestioning obedience through long years of service."[52] Such extended duty was not attractive to the rich and privileged. National pride was all very well, and the right wing was perfectly happy to bang the jingoist drum, but let someone else (from the poor and underprivileged classes, of course) bear the burden of actually serving. A system was introduced whereby those liable for military service could hire a substitute to take their place. Naturally the rich could afford to hire, while the poorest could be induced to serve. Louis Bonaparte took this process to its logical conclusion. Instead of individual rich people having to find substitutes, they could pay the government to release them. Now the thinning ranks of the army were composed only of those unfortunate enough not to be able to afford their own freedom.

Louis would not be complacent for long. Unlike the previous Bourbon and Orleanist monarchs, who were regarded as legitimate by the surrounding powers, he was seen as an upstart. His feelings of insecurity intensified in 1866 when Prussia humiliated the Austrians in a short war. Bismarck had created a redoubtable mass army and Louis felt compelled to duplicate this process by introducing universal short-term military service. However, his plans for expansion were scuppered by the growing left opposition. A new military law was enacted but war came too quickly for the plan to bear fruit and the new Garde Mobile turned out to be a mixed blessing. Its officers were appointed by the emperor's prefects, but the rank and file, drawn from the region around Paris, were too insubordinate: "To organize the Garde Mobile will simply be to prepare an army for insurrection against the government and society."[53] General Trochu, who would shortly be running Paris, foresaw the disintegration of the army, years before it faced its great test: "Today colonels, generals, the highest ranking military personnel make no impression when they appear before the troops... The greatly prized cohesive force of the army, which I call its *hierarchical spirit*, is disappearing...just as the principal and habit of *respect* is in decline within French society as a whole."[54]

When war came in the summer of 1870 the French ruling class was more afraid of its own working class than of Prussia. This fact was underlined by every phase of that disastrous campaign. Despite his army's numerical weakness Louis entered the war because he needed a foreign success to overcome rising domestic tensions. The French theoretically had 370,000 soldiers (of which 66,000 were committed abroad in Algeria and Italy), but the Germans had half a million at their immediate disposal, with

160,000 reserves and 190,000 in the territorials.[55] As Dombrowski, the Polish emigré who became the Commune's leading general observed, it was the Germans who were now using the levée en masse against the French:

> The Prussian army is nothing other than the nation-in-arms... animated by a great idea, the idea of German unification. The German army's enthusiasm and popular organization gives it a great moral force and massive numerical strength... France opposes this army with a much smaller force, without reserves and under the command of generals and senior officers who are as arrogant as they are stupid. It fights not in the name of the country, liberty or humanity, but in the name of the emperor and conquest.[56]

France had been promised easy victories and a rapid advance into enemy territory. Officers did not even bother to carry maps of France, only maps of Germany! Yet it very soon became clear that the fighting would take place on French land. In August 1870 Marshall Bazaine's forces became isolated in the advanced position of Metz. Military common sense dictated that they be abandoned and that the remaining army withdraw to the country's heartlands around the well-fortified city of Paris. The emperor's instinct was for retreat, but the Council of Ministers told him, "it was...an imperative duty for us to avoid any act which might bring about a revolutionary movement."[57] The War Ministry weighed in: "If you abandon General Bazaine there will be a revolution in Paris."[58] Finally, in a comment reflecting a typical royal marriage, the empress herself added this endearing advice: the emperor "must not return. It would be better that he were killed."[59]

Emile Zola's novel *La Débâcle* describes in agonizing detail how many thousands of troops tramped backwards and forwards, day after day, as military and political considerations fought their own battle in the minds of the government. Eventually the emperor set off in one last attempt to reach Metz with his army. One of Zola's characters says, "Ah! This desperate and doomed army that was being sent to a certain crushing defeat, for the salvation of a dynasty."[60] Louis never arrived, because he was captured at Sedan, along with 84,000 men. In an anonymous pamphlet attributed to Louis Napoleon himself, we read the following: "It is true that the struggle was disproportionate; but the outcome could have been more strongly disputed and less disastrous militarily if army operations had not been continually subordinated to political considerations."[61]

The Second Empire contributed to the Commune in two main ways. Firstly, its brand of populism and dictatorship bred a healthy distrust of repressive state systems and phoney claims to represent the people. Secondly, the utterly disastrous Franco-Prussian War, which left the bulk of soldiers as prisoners of war in Germany and disillusioned the remainder, prepared the way for mutiny on the Montmartre heights. The communards would strive to construct the very opposite sort of state to the Second Empire. It would be one in which mass democracy, internationalism and anti-imperialism were paramount.

The People

Each at the forge must do their duty

Reflecting social development during the nineteenth century the Commune differed from earlier Parisian revolts in explicitly espousing socialism and workers' liberation. It was under the Second Empire that France underwent "take-off" into an industrial revolution of major proportions. A few statistics illustrate this. In 1850 French steam engines delivered 17,000 horsepower. On the eve of the Commune the figure stood at 341,000.[62] Over that same period coal production tripled and steel output grew nine-fold, as did the length of railway tracks.[63] Capitalism was booming, with the number of limited companies being established rising from an average 15 per year to 223 in 1870.[64]

The economic transformation was paralleled by an increase in numbers of the working class. By 1866 11 million people, or 29 percent of the population, were dependent on industry.[65] Half the population in the Seine region (which included Paris) were workers, making it the second most advanced area after Lille (where the proportion of workers stood at 52 percent).[66] This must been seen in perspective, however. Although the French economy was industrializing rapidly, the process was far from complete.[67] Agriculture still employed considerably more people nationally.[68]

Alongside the rapid accumulation of vast wealth there was appalling poverty. It is true that Paris was a relatively high wage city for workers,[69] which made it a magnet for migrants from rural France, but:

> The general picture was depressing. Apart from a minority of workers who were relatively well paid...the mass of the working class lived in misery...

> The scale of this chronic poverty can be gleaned from some statistics... The death rate in the poorer arrondissements was double that of the bourgeois quarters where life expectancy was higher. 60 percent of those who died had no funeral, even of the cheapest kind. They were simply transported to the cemetery by the local administration and thrown into the common pit...
>
> There were more than 100,000 officially registered paupers in 1866, or 7 percent of the total population of Paris. But it is estimated that a quarter of the total, which means the majority of the working class, had occasion to require assistance. Indeed Haussmann, in his *Memoirs*, suggested that in 1862 it would have been appropriate, and non-controversial, to distribute bread to some 1 million Parisians.[70]

Paradoxically, despite rapid population growth and economic expansion, Paris itself was not at the leading edge of industrial change. It was the case that 70 percent of the capital's population relied on industry or commerce for their income.[71] At 900,000 the workers were by far the largest group, with the middle and upper bourgeoisie at 150,000 and the petty bourgeoisie at 400,000.[72] However, Haussmann's restructuring of Paris deliberately worked against the growth of large-scale industry. For example, when Napoleon III learned that a railway company planned to build workshops in Paris he insisted that "all means must be used to delay this."[73] That is not to say that large industrial units were entirely absent. To the north east of the city the 2,800-strong workforce of Cail produced steam engines and locomotives, and this factory would play an important role in the Paris Commune.[74] But it was the exception.

Older forms of production predominated, with the proportion of smaller enterprises actually increasing under the influence of Haussmann. Workshops employing more than ten people were just 7 percent of the total, while 31 percent of units had two to ten employees. Fully 62 percent included just two workers.[75] What was the nature of the work they performed? There were some 126,000 in textiles, 40,000 construction workers, 36,000 furniture makers, 25,000 in small-scale metal trades, 17,000 in jewelry and 6,000 working leather.[76] Many tens of thousands toiled in food production, there being 4,000 greengrocers' shops, 1,900 butchers' shops and 1,300 bakeries.[77]

Did the prevalence of artisans and handicraft production mean that the Paris Commune could have nothing to teach our world of global corporations and mass production? The answer is no. The social dynamism of a movement is not dependent on the level of technical development. Countries that are not in the economic forefront such as Russia in 1917, China in 1927, or Ecuador and Venezuela today, can generate powerful revolutionary currents that are at a higher level than those in modern economies like the USA or Japan.[78] The small boss is often as exploitative and bullying as the big boss. So artisan production was not an automatic brake on the communards' ideas and aspirations for a different kind of society. The nature of production did have an influence on the organizational structure of the 1871 movement, however. Trade union action was difficult to mount and broad activities could not easily be built from tiny workplaces. Such units of production could not provide a collective focus for the working class. Instead that came from the National Guard and the clubs that offered a framework for collective expression and organization.

The trajectory of the labor movement under the Second Empire was one of growing confidence, though from a low base. Severe repression following the December 1851 coup led to many workers becoming apolitical, avoiding conflict with the state or employers. An 1861 workers' pamphlet expressed this mood when it called for "new corporations" to be made up of equal numbers of workers and employers representatives under which "there would be no strikes or industrial crises."[79]

Though Louis did like to pose as the workers' friend, such pleas were ignored. However, he did allow a 200-strong workers' delegation to attend the 1862 Exhibition in London. There they encountered British trade unionists for the first time and were deeply impressed by their organizations. A sign of new thinking was the 1864 "Manifesto of the Sixty," a declaration announcing the rebirth of an independent labor movement in France: "We are told there are no longer any classes. But we who own nothing but the strength of our own arms and are always under the arbitrary or legally enforced conditions of capital...find it very difficult to believe this."[80] That same year French delegates attended the founding of the International Working Men's Association.

Neither repression nor paternalism could hold back the French labor movement forever, and a rising tide of strikes developed as the 1860s wore on. In these struggles vital lessons were to be learned. One of the most important struggles came in 1867 when Parisian bronze workers struck over pay. The 5,000 locked-out workers faced starvation,[81] but they won due to financial support from international members in France itself, Britain, Switzerland and Germany. This was a lesson in working-class solidarity that was not quickly forgotten:[82]

> Strikes may raise our wages but they also require us to set aside some of the rise itself to help toward our emancipation... The greedy capitalists want to rob us of the fruits of our labor. This must make us unite in a great effort for a new goal... We have given a great example to workers whose dignity is threatened. So let us go forward toward complete emancipation, which is found through *unity*.[83]

The bronze workers' example was infectious. Parisian tailors soon demanded and won a rise, followed by Lyons's textile workers, and engravers and cloth printers further afield.[84]

The repressive role of the state was underlined in 1869 when 15,000 miners walked out in the Loire region.[85] Troops intervened, killing 13 strikers and wounding nine others at Ricamarie. At the Aubin pit the figures were 14 dead and 20 wounded.[86] An official commission of inquiry investigated whether these strikes "were purely social and industrial or whether they were political in motivation." It concluded that "the political events and troubles in Paris and electoral agitation in the country were responsible for the menacing explosion."[87]

In this industrial ferment backward attitudes toward women were also challenged. The sort of beliefs expressed by one prominent member of the First International, that "women should stay indoors and avoid the physical and moral dangers of workshops," became untenable after fighting between miners' wives and gendarmes during the Le Creusot strike of 1870. Now many working-class men realized that women should gain independence through work and "will march alongside us in the exercise of democratic and social cooperation."[88] The workers' movement was maturing rapidly.

The Politics

We'll change forthwith the old tradition

Three main left groupings influenced the popular movement in Paris, although the distinctions between them were not hard and fast. They were the Proudhonists, Jacobins and Blanquists. Although they have no direct modern descendants, because many of the challenges are the same today, they are nevertheless recognizable as archetypes of tendencies in our movement. The capitalist system may have grown older, but the questions of how to overcome the poverty, oppression and wars that it creates are still with us.

Proudhon and Proudhonism

The ideas of Pierre-Joseph Proudhon (1809–65) were very influential in the Parisian working class. He was an anarchist made famous by his aphorism, "What is property? It is theft."[89] This phrase must be set alongside the other parts of his analysis for a true understanding of his outlook. Proudhon's criticisms of the failings of capitalist society were sharp and won him many converts, but he did not reject the market system as such.

Proudhon regarded exchange of commodities through a market system as fundamentally fair, believing that "a commercial operation is necessarily free from inequality, for no free man knowingly makes a deal by which he is the loser..."[90] It followed that, since the selling of labor was itself a form of commercial operation, when employees went to work for the bosses they were not being exploited, because "any man's labor can buy the value it represents."[91] This put a limit on the degree to which Proudhon rejected the capitalist system as such.

If the bosses became rich while workers stayed poor, if their property was gained through theft but the crime did not occur in the labor process, how was it perpetrated? It must come from outside of commercial or capitalist relations, through force and fraud, through "the multitude of unearned increments, premiums, tithes, interest, domestic agricultural and industrial rents; dividends..."[92] In other words, the evils of industrial society were a by-product, a side effect of capitalism, not a direct consequence of it. The theft arose through activities peripheral to regular capitalism, through external impositions on an essentially healthy system of market relations. So the cure was to remove external interference.

In Britain this idea was given a French name—*laissez-faire*—and was easily recognizable as the precursor of neoliberal economics today. But Proudhon's ideas were located in a different context and so took a far more radical form when adopted by the male artisan class.

Karl Marx, who studied Proudhon's work carefully, had a very different analysis that located exploitation at the very heart of the capitalist production process. Callinicos sums it up like this:

> The worker will normally create during a working day more value than the daily wages with which the capitalist purchased his or her labor power... In other words, the capitalist does not gain his profit by cheating the worker... Exploitation...is a typical outcome of the regular workings of the capitalist mode of production. It arises from the difference between the value created by labor power once it is put to work, and the value of labor power itself.[93]

These economic arguments may seem a little obscure and abstract, but they had profound practical consequences. Proudhon's approach made his ideas especially attractive to artisans undergoing the rigors of an industrial revolution. In earlier times a handicraft worker expected to progress from training as an apprentice to working for a small employer as a journeyman. Later on, after accumulating the funds to buy tools and premises, he would become a master craftsman in his own right. He would in turn train apprentices and employ a few journeymen. Thus the cycle would repeat. Now, as the nineteenth century progressed, large-scale production disrupted the pattern, threatening artisans with ruin and relegation to the working class. They were being deprived of all but the ability to sell their labor power to an employer, or worse:

> In the old days an intelligent, honest and hard-working worker could hope to emancipate himself, and it was not uncommon to see a worker become a master in his turn and then retire with a reasonable pension for his old age. With a few rare exceptions this is quite impossible today, no matter how good the worker. When old age is reached this worker will have saved nothing due to the high cost of basic necessities and is forced to end his days begging on the streets for a crust of bread.[94]

From the craftsman's point of view the lower working class, unskilled, poorly paid and used to undercut traditional trades, might be perceived to be as much a threat to his economic security as the rich. Proudhon voiced that fear: "The spirit of rapine and greed is the true characteristic of the modern epoch: the poor exploit the rich, the workers their employers, the tenant his landlord, the company promoter his shareholders, no less than the capitalist exploits and puts pressure on the industrialist, the industrialist his workers and the landlord his tenants."[95]

To counter this fate Proudhon wanted to return society to an earlier golden age: "It must be understood that henceforth the labels of worker and boss, like those of apprentice and journeyman, will no longer be class distinctions, but simply different roles during the career of the producer... *[We stand for]* the solidarity of interests between journeyman and master, for the guarantee that the worker will in his turn become master and bourgeois."[96]

How could this utopia be reached? "Force" (the state) and "fraud" (the big capitalists) were simply to be excluded from the commodity production system by being ignored. Proudhon's position led toward anarchism and, in this sense, elements of Proudhonism are alive in sections of today's anticapitalist movement. While his disciple, Mikhail Bakunin, made abolition of the state his central tenet, Proudhon's approach was to focus on economics alone.

Alas, in real life the state will not allow itself to be overlooked, so whenever faced with serious political issues Proudhon was unprepared. Take his reaction to the February 1848 Revolution: "I fled before the democratic and social monster whose riddle I could not answer. An inexpressible terror froze my soul and paralyzed my mind."[97] Since the state was to be disregarded, the idea of any working-class political involvement enraged him: "All this democracy disgusts me... What would I not give to sail into this mob with my clenched fists!"[98] In May 1848, at a time when the Parisian working class was fed up with the Republic's lack of progress, a demonstration led by Auguste Blanqui stormed the parliament. Proudhon wrote, "The people, impatient with the slowness of parliamentarism, invaded the Assembly, disturbing representatives in their innocent deliberations... Is it the policy of the government that infuriates you? Leave the government to its tribulations and the National Assembly to its fears. They have more to complain about than you." So what should the workers do? "Well, the social question can only be resolved by you, by you alone, without the assistance of power... Leave eternal political questions to follow their constitutional course... and maintain strict neutrality vis-à-vis power."[99]

Neutrality is impossible to maintain in the midst of revolution and great power struggles. When Proudhon was compelled to consider the December 1851 coup his conclusion was bizarre.[100] This anarchist counseled republicans and socialists to rally to Bonaparte, who was publicly committed to "efficiently protect family, religion and *property*"![101] Proudhon wrote a pamphlet with the extraordinary title *The Social Revolution Demonstrated by the Coup d'État*! This predicted that "one way or another [Bonaparte will] introduce all the reforms demanded by socialism."[102]

So, for all his penetrating criticisms of contemporary society, Proudhon fell down in terms of offering solutions to pressing political issues. Alas, the same difficulties would apply to his economic program. Turning to the question of big capitalists, Proudhon believed they could be excluded from commodity production through mutualism, or workers' cooperatives. He was pleased that after the massacre of June 1848 the working class turned its back on "the utopia of a workers' state" and toward "the principle of mutuality."[103]

Proudhon thought that if cheap credit was available individual workers or small workshops could compete with the capitalists "value for value, service for service, credit for credit, guarantee for guarantee."[104] Thus the transformation would be achieved "without confiscation...without common ownership, without state intervention and without the abolition of inheritance."[105] In 1848 he actually set up a People's Bank, lending at low interest, because "reduction of interest rates to vanishing point is in itself a revolutionary act, since it is destructive of capitalism."[106] Although the bank quickly failed, further attempts to establish one were made right up to the eve of the Commune.[107]

How would a Proudhonist society have been organized? Rejecting the centralized state, the many tiny economic units would federate together, making agreements to provide each other with services, products, and so on. These federations would group into local communes or parishes and then upwards into regional and finally national federations. Communes would be "self-governing, self-administrating, self-taxing."[108] The communes would make central power irrelevant and so "the idea of groups limiting the power of the state was a waste of time..."[109]

Proudhon's ideas had an enormous influence. Practically all the leading worker militants who took part in the Commune were convinced Proudhonists and they were the backbone of labor organization. However, in the years after his death in 1865 the labor movement had to confront an increasingly politicized situation. The strengths of Proudhon's approach—his anti-authoritarianism and stress on self-organization by the working class—were adapted to meet the rapidly changing climate. By the time the Commune arrived it was necessary, as a recent commentary puts it, "to distinguish between Proudhon's ideas...and Proudhonism."[110]

In sum, Proudhon's legacy was complex. Like many thinkers of the anticapitalist movement today, he provided a biting critique of the existing state and society, their corruption and injustice, and so his group became a rallying point for many thousands of Parisian workers. However, there was also a limitation to his achievement. He focused on the symptoms of the disease but held back from dealing with the core of the system—the exploitation at the heart of the capitalist-worker relationship, and the state that exists to protect that exploitative process. When the communal revolution took place on March 18, 1871, his followers turned criticism of the old system into active struggle to create a new one, but gaps in Proudhon's analysis left them unprepared for many of the problems that would occur.

Blanquism

Like the Proudhonists, the followers of Auguste Blanqui were supporters of the Paris Commune, but they were at the opposite end of the spectrum when it came to policy and strategy. Where Proudhonists ignored politics and emphasized grassroots workers' self-activity, Blanqui was obsessed by the need to take state power through revolution. The Blanquists were small in number but they had a huge impact. Da Costa, who was active in 1871, wrote, "All those who have read [the history of the Commune], even in the works that are the most hostile to this insurrection, are obliged to recognize that the Blanquists are the instigators and the executors of all the truly revolutionary and effective measures."[111] The key to their importance was organizational cohesion. They came closest to having a revolutionary party.

Blanqui was a veteran agitator, "the phantom of the insurrection...the cold mathematician of revolt who seemed to hold the balance of the suffering and rights of the people between his frail fingers."[112] He had risen to prominence in uprisings as far back as 1839 and 1848, spending 36 years in jail and earning the nickname *l'enfermé*—"the imprisoned one." Blanqui was credited with inventing the term "class war" as well as "dictatorship of the proletariat." As early as 1832 he declared, before a court, "I am accused of having said to 30 million French people, proletarians like myself, that they have the right to live... Yes, there is a war between the rich and the poor, but the rich brought it on themselves because they are the aggressors... These privileged people live in luxury from the sweat of the proletariat."[113]

Blanqui's ideas came from Gracchus Babeuf who, in 1796, through the Conspiracy of the Equals, attempted a revolution to institute the common ownership and distribution of goods.[114] He was executed as a result. The program of Blanqui's party was summed up as "Atheism, Communism and Revolution."[115] In stressing atheism he expressed the classic enlightenment view that religious mysticism was the enemy of rational thought upon which social progress depended. Blanqui summed up his vision of a communist society like this:

> In the intellectual sphere, no other principle than science, the sole benefactor of humanity. In the moral sphere, no other principle than justice, that is to say equality and solidarity. In the social sphere, no rights except the rights of those who work. In the political sphere, no other goal but the triumph, at any price, of the three great laws of society—labor, science and justice.[116]

What about the third concept—revolution? There can be no doubt of Blanqui's dedication to the cause of workers' liberation. He spent most of his life in jail for that. But while he welcomed strikes[117] he doubted the revolution could come through workers' self-activity because "the great majority are mired in ignorance."[118] So the action of an educated minority would be required: "There is no durable revolution without light! Liberty means instruction! Equality means instruction! Fraternity means instruction! Teachers, books, the printing press, these are the true revolutionary agencies."[119]

Workers lacked "instruction" unlike the middle class. So an enlightened section of that class must act on their behalf:

> The bourgeoisie includes an *elite* minority, an indissoluble group, highly-strung, ardent and full of zeal; it is the essence, the soul, the life of the revolution. It is the incandescent source from which spring incessantly ideas of reconstruction, stirring and exciting the masses. Who has planted the flag of the proletariat? Who has rallied it after its defeats? Who are the promulgators, the apostles of doctrines of equality? Who leads the people to battle against the bourgeoisie? The bourgeoisie itself. They will cease only after having led the revolution to the victory of equality. But what is the device on its banner? Democracy? No—the proletariat. For its soldiers are workers though the leaders are not.[120]

Blanqui believed that workers would need to be educated into communism over a period of time because "the working class, accustomed to the yoke by long years of oppression and misery [is led] by their masters like blind beasts..."[121] Through the revolution the elite minority would construct a revolutionary dictatorship "on behalf of the general interest and human progress."[122]

Blanquism should not be understood primarily as a theoretical movement. Blanqui spent little time on ideas despite his many years of enforced idleness. He was, above all, a man of action and, unlike the other major currents involved in the Commune, his faction was consciously revolutionary. He wanted to overthrow the current political system rather than ignore it (as the Proudhonists wanted) or reform it (as the Jacobins desired). He mobilized to that end. Solid organization and clear leadership were distinguishing features of the Blanquists.

If Proudhon's anarchism led to the ignoring of politics in favor of economic struggle, Blanqui went in the opposite direction. There was a great deal of heroism and self-sacrifice needed to conduct a revolutionary conspiracy, but it also required isolation from the mass of ordinary people. Inevitably the "*elite* minority" of revolutionaries was very small. In 1866, after some 30 years of tireless activity, he wrote with pride, "Things are going well with us insofar as young people are joining. There are now 25 of them who are determined atheists and socialists, plus 25 fellow travellers."[123] In total the Blanquist party has been estimated at 250 adherents in 1867 and perhaps 800 in 1868. It was limited exclusively to Paris.[124]

A sign of numerical weakness was the fact that the Blanquists could not sustain a regular newspaper. *La Patrie en Danger*, which ran for only a few issues and appeared in the autumn of 1870 during the Franco-Prussian War, was the only newspaper Blanqui was ever able to produce. By December it failed due to lack of funds.[125] This was at a time when almost every journalist (hack or otherwise) produced their own individual newspapers, which literally deluged the streets of Paris.[126]

The Blanquists' ardent desire for a different society, plus impatience with the movement of ordinary people, are traits shared by some in the anticapitalist movement today. The pitfalls were demonstrated in August 1870 when Blanquists attempted an uprising. The plot was hatched by Granger, who spent a 10,000 franc inheritance on 300 revolvers and 400 daggers. He convinced Blanqui to return from hiding in Belgium, because the war crisis meant that the moment was right. To his credit the old campaigner insisted that the workers must be ready to join in, if it were to succeed. Objectively the situation was more than ripe. The military effort was going disastrously for Napoleon and the government had lost all credibility. But the Blanquists could know very little of the subjective mood of the working class because they lacked any links with it.

The plan was to seize an armory on the outskirts of Paris as a prelude to a general rising. On a sunny Sunday afternoon, August 14, 1870, some 100 men assembled under cover of a crowd watching a juggler and at 3:30pm they stormed a garrison at La Villette. Blanqui begged the men there to join the insurrection and distribute their arms to overthrow the empire, but they obstinately refused. The plan frustrated, the Blanquists burst onto the streets of the staunchly working-class district of Belleville, an area that later proved to be one of the strongest centers of communard activity. Blanqui's own account of the debacle is painfully honest:

> The population appeared dumbstruck. Attracted by curiosity, but held back by fear, they stood, immobile and silent, backed up against the houses. The boulevard that the insurgents were on was completely deserted. In vain did they appeal to the onlookers by shouting, "Long live the Republic! Death to Prussians! To arms!" Not a word, not a gesture was given in response to this agitation... The fact is that, in this very revolutionary district of Belleville, the uprising did not attract a single recruit.

Blanqui finally concluded, "We have no guns and as you see no one will join us. We can do nothing without the people!" So they dispersed.[127]

It was ironic that exactly three weeks later Paris underwent a mass revolt that toppled Bonapartism. The problem on August 14 was not that the working class was apathetic or passive, far from it. But a minority that is not linked organically to the wider movement through daily participation, through sharing the ups and downs of day-to-day struggle, through debating and battling for leadership, cannot expect an instant mass following. The Blanquists on the streets of Belleville that day were seen as strangers, and who would automatically trust a stranger to lead an action that could potentially result in death? As one historian who is sympathetic to Blanquism recently put it:

> It is not enough that a group of militants is perfectly organized and trained. It is not enough even to have thousands of demonstrators. With that, you may possibly succeed in an insurrection, according to circumstances, but not in a revolution. For this to happen it is necessary that the masses are touched in their essential interests; not just the men but all the women must be involved.[128]

There was a further bitter twist to Blanqui's story. He was arrested on March 17, 1871, putting him out of action one day before the communal insurrection! This had serious consequences, for his particular talents were sorely missed by the insurgents. It was Blanqui who spent a lifetime studying "armament and organization," which he regarded as "the decisive agencies of progress."[129] It was precisely in these tactical spheres that the Commune proved woefully lacking. Dommanget argues plausibly that if Blanqui had been at the helm some of the most disastrous errors of the Commune's military campaign would have been avoided.[130] Thiers probably realized this when he refused to exchange Blanqui for the Archbishop of Paris who had been taken hostage by the Commune.[131] To have freed him might "give the Commune a leader," as Marx put it.[132]

The Neo-Jacobins

The Jacobins were the most influential leadership element in the 1871 Paris Commune. They took their name from the Jacobins of the Great Revolution and its heroic 1793–94 period. At that time Maximilien Robespierre led the French Republic in a desperate fight against a coalition of the monarchies of Europe and domestic reactionary forces dedicated to wiping out the gains that ordinary people had made.

The new Jacobins regarded the Great Revolution as unfinished business. Its motto—"Liberty, equality and fraternity"—was still to be achieved. France might have changed considerably since the fall of Robespierre in 1794, but apart from the brief interlude of the Second Republic (1848–51) governments had been no more than a succession of kings and dictators. Although the new generation of Jacobins did not consider themselves socialists, they were aware that the economy might have prospered, but the benefits were unequally shared. Perhaps those who gained the most, the new capitalist class, sympathized with "liberty, equality and fraternity," but they preferred to see the policeman's boot on the neck of the workers.

The neo-Jacobins came to national prominence when they opposed Louis's assault on the Republic in 1851. For their principled stand many endured prison, exile and penury, and so won widespread respect. They tended to come from middle-class backgrounds. Charles Delescluze, their best known figure, was a former law student, while Felix Pyat was a journalist and Paschal Grousset a doctor.[133]

Jacobinism had no single program, but in 1870, during the last days of the empire, Delescluze issued a manifesto that can be regarded as typical. He criticized high taxation and foreign imperialist adventures. Delescluze was opposed to the conscription system that "took the best seven years of life" from so many young men, but complained that it left too small an army when "we need at least 1.3 million armed men to win France respect abroad, rather than to repress those at home." His only mention of the working class was in a passage that talked of "the unfortunate workers of France who demand justice and bread."[134] If there was one slogan that united the Jacobins, it was the cry of "The Republic." For some this was the "Republic, one and indivisible" as enunciated by Robespierre,[135] which focused on the need for a strong state to carry society forward. More left-wing Jacobins preferred the slogan of "The social and democratic Republic.'[136]

Just as Proudhonism evolved in the period leading up to 1871, so did many Jacobins. It is perhaps going too far to argue, as one writer does, that, "far from being static, Jacobinism evolved with the preoccupations of the different generations of Parisians, and in 1871 instituted a social movement consecrated *above all* to promoting the interests of the workers..."[137] Nevertheless, when the Commune arrived, with some exceptions, the Jacobins joined it. Delescluze and others were ready to go along with the socialist vision of the Commune and sacrifice themselves heroically on its altar.

Despite his anarchism, which made him a natural opponent of the statist Jacobins, Bakunin wrote just after the Commune:

> Let us make it clear, there are Jacobins and Jacobins. There are Jacobin lawyers and doctrinaires, like Mr. Gambetta... And there are Jacobins who are frankly revolutionaries, the heroes, the last sincere representatives of the democratic faith of 1793; able to sacrifice both their well-armed unity and authority rather than submit their conscience to the insolence of the reaction. These magnanimous Jacobins led naturally by Delescluze, a great soul and a great character, desire the triumph of the revolution above everything else; and since there is no revolution without the masses, and since the masses nowadays reveal an instinct for socialism and can only make an economic and social revolution, the Jacobins of good faith, letting themselves be impelled increasingly by the logic of the revolutionary movement, will end up becoming socialists in spite of themselves. This is precisely the situation in which the Jacobins who participated in the Paris Commune found themselves.[138]

The International Working Men's Association

The First International was an organization that played a special role on the Parisian left. It linked up many varied national political traditions in a common cause. Its headquarters were in London where Karl Marx played a significant role. This does not mean, however, that the French section was full of Marxists. Here the Proudhonists were the most influential current and they could see the International in entirely their own terms. "[It] aimed to group together all the workers of Europe in solidarity in order to win the abolition of wage labor. This would be achieved by the peaceful purchase of the means of production which is the creative principle of general association and federalism."[139]

There were perhaps only two "Marxists" in the Commune—Frankel at the Labor Commission and Dmitrieff in the Women's Union. She arrived in Paris nine days after the March 18 revolution.[140]

The International brought the Proudhonists into contact with different tendencies and this contributed to their evolution. The organization was founded after a mass meeting in London to support the 1863 Polish uprising for national independence. At that time the issue of Poland was the focus of international solidarity in the way that Palestine is now. However, Proudhon himself regarded actions in support of Polish independence as political, and therefore "puerile."[141] Nevertheless, French Proudhonist workers were in attendance at the 1863 London mass meeting.

They were not the only French citizens involved in the First International. The latter had also ignored their leader's advice by becoming involved. Blanquists attended the 1866 Geneva Congress (though their hostility to the Proudhonists led to violent rows and their forcible ejection).[142] In the last days of the Second Empire Blanqui's followers merged into the Paris section of the International and controlled its Left Bank branches.[143] Despite the difficulties, the barriers between Proudhon's avoidance of politics and Blanquist dismissal of workers' self-organization began to break down. Unfortunately, there would not be sufficient time for this process of synthesis to develop fully.

Through its membership the International was able to bring together seemingly incompatible elements because it was not an artificial creation or a forced marriage. Its foundation in London in September 1864 did not simply reflect the wishes of the individuals present, but deeper processes. The idea was grounded in both theoretical and practical considerations. Capitalism was, and is, a world system that seeks to divide ordinary people, one from another. It can only be overcome by international unity. Hence the motto of *The Communist Manifesto*—"Workers of the world, unite!" But a genuine international could not simply be willed. The First International grew by stressing basic working-class solidarity. Like globalization today, the nineteenth-century industrial revolution was creating massive discontent across continents and generating a mass of people who were becoming aware that their common interests transcended national boundaries.[144]

The founding documents of the International—Marx's *Provisional Rules* and *Inaugural Address*—transcended the limitations of Proudhonism and Blanquism in crucial ways. The *Rules*'s famous first statement, "That the emancipation of the working classes must be conquered by the working classes themselves"[145] was acceptable to Proudhon, but anathema to Blanqui. However, a key passage in the *Address* says, "To conquer political power has therefore become the great duty of the working classes..."[146] Proudhon rejected this notion while Blanquists applauded it.[147] Synthesizing both concepts within a practical workers' movement represented a major step forward.

We have already seen how the International was important in assisting the Parisian bronze workers in their dispute.[148] After years of illegality French trade unions were initially weaker than their British counterparts, and so appreciated the sort of solidarity they, and workers in other countries, could offer. But the French movement was more developed in other ways. Class struggle was far more ideological and revolutionary in character. Proudhonism had deep roots in the working-class movement and laid stress on action from below. Blanquism was politically organized and committed to revolution. The banner of the International attracted both elements and challenged their weaknesses.

Eugène Varlin showed what could be achieved. A Parisian bookbinder, he was an organizer of the French section under the Second Empire and later a key figure in the Commune itself. Born in 1839, Varlin was prominent in a successful strike of bookbinders in 1864 and joined the International a year later. Though from a Proudhonist background, through these experiences he became critical of Proudhon's rejection of strikes, opposition to working women's equality and promotion of joint worker/employer associations.[149]

Varlin and the International were heavily involved in organizing "chambres fédérales"—federal councils that represented a cross between trade unions and trades councils. The success of the movement was shown at many levels: 60 percent of bronze workers were organized into unions, as were one-third of engineers and two-thirds of painters. In all 54 associations with 40,000 members joined the "chambres fédérales" and in Paris the International had 20 branches with 50 to 100 members per branch.[150]

Varlin's method gives an insight into the nature of the French section. International supporters were encouraged to set up branches that in turn created "corporate syndicates" (local craft bodies halfway towards trade unions). These in turn would send delegates to the International's federal council.[151] This was a hybrid organization—part political party, part trades council, part trade union. On this basis the International grew rapidly in spite of government attempts to suppress it through arrests and a series of show trials. By the third trial of its leaders, in 1870, both the prosecution and defense estimated that across France the International had 245,000 supporters.[152]

A key moment in the left's development was the funeral of Victor Noir. Noir was a radical journalist of the *Marseillaise* newspaper whose editor, Henri Rochefort, was a leading republican. Noir was assassinated by Prince Pierre Bonaparte of the imperial family. Astonishingly, the prince was exonerated, while Rochefort was sent to jail for sedition! On January 12, 1870, a huge demonstration of at least 100,000 attended Noir's funeral,[153] and there was serious discussion among its leaders about overthrowing the emperor there and then. It did not happen, but it helped Varlin and others realize that Proudhonist disregard of political questions was a hindrance:

> The Federal Council has only just been established. To tell the truth it is barely constituted in reality, and it has not, as yet, occupied itself with the idea or the practical issue of a political movement. Yet it is a fact that all the delegates to the Council met up at the funeral of Victor Noir without having discussed it together in advance. Some had gone to Paris ready to give battle. Others, more circumspect, wanted the demonstration to retain its peaceful character. Indeed, these two alternative viewpoints split the crowd throughout the day.
>
> We were shaken by this situation and the next day the meeting of the Federal Council was completely given over to discussion of what we should do if similar circumstances arose again... Henceforth, we will consult and act together...[154]

Answering a friend who accused him of abandoning "socialism" by taking up politics, he wrote:

> You are wrong to believe for an instant that I am ignoring the socialist movement for the political movement. No, it is entirely from a socialist perspective that I pursue revolutionary work... If in the current circumstances the socialist party allows itself to be put to sleep by abstract scientific sociology [such as Proudhonism], we might well wake up one fine day to find ourselves under new even more dangerous masters, because they will be newer and consequently more vigorous and powerful.[155]

Although many Proudhonists remained wedded to their old positions[156] Varlin showed the creative potential unleashed by the International, and the progress that some were making toward understanding the link between economic and political struggles.

The Commune, for all its daring and forward-looking ideas, was not written on a blank sheet. The physical structure of the city, the regime of the Second Empire, a growing working class, and the intense ideological debates—all these meant that the left-wing movement in Paris was very advanced before 1871. These elements were not, however, sufficient to create the Paris Commune. It would only appear when the demand for radical change was enthusiastically embraced by the mass of ordinary Parisians, when the desire for a radically different state and society became a fundamental life-and-death issue for them. It would take the hammer blows of war and a protracted siege to bring about this transformation.

A balloon attempts to break the siege,
Place Saint-Pierre-de-Montmartre, 1870

Three

War and Siege

From Republic to Commune

On the tyrants only we'll make war

In our society we are supposed to have democratic choice, but in reality accumulated wealth dominates the formation of state policy. The ultimate expression of this is shown in the United States where, in nominally free elections, corporate power virtually dictates the outcome. The illusion is sustained because the establishment relies heavily on apathy, on convincing people that there is no alternative to this state of affairs, that no other world is possible. The Paris Commune was completely different and revolutionary because at its base was a living mass movement. This unique combination of people and power, which was therefore truly representative, was the fruit of the broadest activism. How had such a movement been aroused and why had the people of Paris been so deeply stirred?

The answer is to be found in the impact of the Franco-Prussian War that began on July 19, 1870. The path that led from this event to the March 18, 1871, revolution was a very twisted one. Unlike the invasion of Iraq in 2003, which quickly led to a huge antiwar, anti-imperialist movement, in 1870–71 French public opinion veered wildly from initial opposition to war to fervent support and finally to revolution. The speed and intensity of these abrupt shifts confirmed the well-known aphorism that war is concentrated politics.

When the threat of conflict loomed between France and Prussia (the major German state that was seeking to unify the others under its crown) there were peace protests in both countries. The French section of the International issued this statement:

> Workers of France, Germany and Spain, let us denounce this war with one voice. In reply to bellicose statements from those who demand a tax in blood, or use public misfortune as a new source of speculation, *we protest. We demand Peace, Labor and Liberty*... To our German brothers we say: do not listen to the paid, servile lackeys who want to mislead you as to the real sentiments in France... Workers of all countries: whatever the outcome of our common efforts, we, members of the *International Working Men's Association* who do not recognize frontiers, we give you our commitment of unbreakable solidarity and greetings from the workers of France.[1]

The German left had the same attitude. It denounced:

> this war which serves only dynastic interests and satisfies the ambition of a few powerful individuals by playing with the lives of hundreds of thousands, and the well-being of millions. The meeting greatly welcomes the stand of French democracy and the socialist workers in particular. It is in full agreement with their efforts against the war and expects that German democracy and the German workers will raise voices of opposition in the same way.[2]

Alas, antiwar demonstrations in Paris could not restrain the government.[3] The French pretext for war was that "Prussia is a challenge to the influence that we are entitled to in Europe."[4] So France began as the aggressor, but by August it was clear that the character of the conflict had changed. French armies were sent spinning into chaotic retreat after a series of catastrophic defeats at Wissembourg, Froeschwiller and Gravelotte. Now the country was defending itself from an invading army bent on conquest and booty.[5] This did not mean the population rallied behind Napoleon. As long as the war was understood to be for the glory of the Second Empire it was almost impossible to recruit volunteers to fight. Only 4,000 signed up in July; but nine times as many Frenchmen did so when national defense became the issue in August.[6] In Marseilles and Lyons mass demonstrations called for the abdication of the emperor alongside the arming of the population.[7]

The September 4 Revolution

When news arrived of the defeat and capture of Napoleon and his army at Sedan, Paris exploded. *L'Illustration*, a right-wing paper, described the revolution that occurred:

> Paris rose with but a single thought: To the Legislative Body [Corps Législatif]! From all the districts, on all the boulevards, from every quarter, torrents of people growing ever more numerous, National Guards, various army corps, and the workers, all descended on the Place de la Concorde and around the Legislative Body… And how can you shut a gate when 20,000 bodies are pressing forward against it? Impossible! The flood of people passed through, and one minute later they suddenly appeared in the parliamentary chamber.[8]

The Second Empire was overthrown and a republic, led by the "Government of National Defense" chosen from Parisian deputies was put in its place pending a general election.[9]

Those who came to power as a result of the revolution of September 4, 1870, had very little sympathy with the crowd who put them there. The new president was General Jules Trochu who had been Napoleon's military governor of Paris. On the very day of the revolution he told the empress, "I will stay at my post, and I will not abandon you." His own account shows he only changed his mind after becoming trapped in a mass demonstration: "Ten times sinister-looking men threw themselves on my horse, seizing the bridle and shouting at me: 'Long live the Social Republic!'"[10] He knew then that he had lost control: "In reality I am in command of nothing… Stop half a million people marching on the Assembly? It is absolutely impossible."[11] However, Trochu insisted that he would only head a new government "if you promise that nothing will be done against god, the family and property."[12]

In fact Trochu was more right wing and less typical of the post-September government than figures like the "three Jules"—Jules Favre, Jules Ferry and Jules Simon, republicans who had opposed Napoleon.[13] There was a clear difference between such people and the old right composed of royalists and

Bonapartists. But given the choice between maintaining "law and order" under the empire or popular power these liberals had no doubt which side they were on.[14]

After the September revolution made him foreign minister Favre admitted his "indefatigable self-denial in having begged the [legislative] chamber for a month to take power *to prevent a revolution*."[15] On September 4 itself he had been ready to give up calling for the removal of the emperor[16] and only came forward when "a noisy and agitated crowd filled the [parliamentary] benches, blocked the passageways and came down into the semi-circular floor…shouting 'Sack the emperor! Sack him! Long live the Republic!'."[17] In retrospect Favre saw the revolution as "the ultimate disaster."[18] Jules Ferry agreed: "The last thing we were thinking of was an act of violence" on September 4.[19]

The September 4 revolution threw up a central contradiction—between those who made the revolution and those who profited from it in spite of their anti-revolutionary views. The Parisian masses would soon discover this fact.

The Government of National Defense

Paradoxically victory on September 4 threw the left into a deep crisis as the rhetoric of national unity to resist Germany carried all before it. Léon Gambetta, once a Jacobin but now the interior minister, appealed for harmony: "Our new Republic is not a government which has any political disagreements or pointless quarrels… Unite all our wills together so that, in an immense and unanimous effort, France will be saved thanks to the patriotism of all its children."[20]

Favre too emphasized the "solemn embrace sealed by patriotism and liberty. This alliance makes us invincible."[21]

The Proudhonists' distrust of politics left them with little experience in dealing with such arguments. Arnould, later a leading communard and prominent Proudhonist, described how he and his comrades were bowled over: "The radical republicans and socialists resolutely set to work and, silencing their most legitimate criticisms, their most justified feelings of mistrust, offered the government of national defense their loyal support, asking nothing from it politically, and only asking for one thing—the defense of the country."[22]

They would be denied that "one thing."

The Jacobin tradition, based on the memory of the defense of France during the Great Revolution, needed little encouragement to express fervent nationalism, which was at its most blatant in Pyat's new paper, *Le Combat*: "People of Paris, on September 4 you took back liberty! Well done! Now retake France from the foreigner, the enemy who exists in Paris as well as Metz... No more Corsican emperors, Spanish regents, Italian diplomats or Greeks and Turks as generals. No more foreigners carrying the flag of France! Barbarians cannot carry the flag of civilization!"[23]

The Blanquists crumpled too:

> In the face of the enemy, no more parties, no more differences... The government that came out of the great movement of September 4 represents the republican idea and the national defense. That is sufficient. All opposition, all dissent must give way to the common safety. Henceforth there is only one enemy, the Prussian... The undersigned, putting aside their particular views, offer the provisional government their full and energetic cooperation without any reservations or conditions except the maintenance of the Republic...[24]

Even the International was cowed. Serraillier, the envoy sent from the General Council in London, reported that "if they had adopted any other tone they would be sent packing."[25] Varlin realized that there was a problem, though as yet he had no solution: "This is not a favorable time for [socialist] propaganda. Everyone is fixated by this somber drama that is being played out on the plains of Lorraine and Champagne. Everybody anxiously awaits the outcome of this bloody struggle and the social question is quite forgotten."[26]

Succumbing to pleas for national unity behind the new government meant that the left was now swimming with mainstream opinion (or rather swept along in its flood tide). This did not win it popularity, but inhibited criticism of the Government of National Defense instead.

War fever and the illusion of a harmony of interests in the all-embracing nation hypnotized the working class, but not forever. Six months after September 1870 the "solemn embrace" became strangulation when, to smash the Commune, government "patriots" turned on the people of Paris and massacred them in a bloody civil war, exhibiting a zeal and enthusiasm never shown against the Prussians, a fact recognized even by the right-wing press.[27]

Contradictions of Wartime Politics

The Franco-Prussian War did not raise complex issues for the left alone. The government had its own problems to resolve. In the competitive system we live in both business corporations and states confront each other as rivals. In extreme circumstances this can lead to wars. At the same time they share a common interest in maintaining the profit-making system from hostile forces. They are thus "a band of hostile brothers." The members of the Government of National Defense were in this ambiguous position. They may have wanted to fight Prussia, but they were also afraid of the popular power shown on the streets of Paris during the September 4, 1870, revolution. Over the next six months they would choose their priority.

Imperialist powers frequently use wars, racism and xenophobia to divert and weaken radical movements (their failure to stop the recent movement against the Iraq war being a notable exception). In the days following the overthrow of the Second Empire the Parisian left proved vulnerable to this allure of national unity. However, there was a highly unusual twist in the French situation. The left was pro-war and the right was antiwar. This was because the current conflict with Prussia was seen through the prism of the Great Revolution, the time in the 1790s when the first French Republic fought against the assembled reactionaries of Europe. That earlier crisis led to all-out mobilization of the sansculottes, the coming to power of the Jacobins, and a series of very radical measures of state intervention. It was generally expected that the same scenario would be repeated in 1870. The longer the war continued the more left-wing government policy would have to become. Conversely, the quicker it ended, the fewer the inroads into the rights of property.

A typical left-wing expression of this view was put at a public meeting in November 1870, when one speaker told his audience that a cease-fire between France and Prussia would mean "a monarchy will be imposed on you. (…*From all sides*: No monarchy. We don't want it)."[28] Similar sentiments were expressed elsewhere: "Armistice leads to peace, and peace to an Orleanist restoration."[29] So if peace equaled reaction, continuing the war equaled revolution.

Curiously, the right agreed. It too thought further war might radicalize the domestic front and shift politics to the left. So the right was pacifist, with royalists, Bonapartists and capitalists in favor of ending the war as soon as possible. The peasants also wanted a return to stability through peace.[30] Therefore, the first concern of the Government of National Defense was not national defense at all. Its primary motive was protection of profit-making and property by quelling the radical movement in Paris. That this should be so was no surprise given the track record of its key figures.

Take the "three Jules"—Favre, Simon and Ferry. In 1848 Favre had instituted a press law that silenced all attacks on property. Simon's book on *Freedom* insisted that "there will always be poverty."[31] He considered that "one overturns aristocracy, which is a privilege... One does not overturn the bourgeoisie; one attains it."[32] Ferry opposed any measure that reduced economic inequality because "the only real inequality left was the inequality of education."[33] Adolphe Thiers, at that time the chief diplomat of the Government of National Defense, summed up his philosophy in a book called *On Property*: "Considering human nature, in all countries, at all times, and in all degrees of civilization, everywhere I find property to be a general and universal fact which suffers no exception."[34] It followed that economic inequality was 'necessary and incontestable.'[35]

A conflict between Paris and the Government of National Defense was bound to occur as the contradiction between the expectations of the people and the real intentions of the state unfolded. Vigorous measures from the Government of National Defense against Prussia were awaited but were not forthcoming. It was much more concerned with ensuring public order. It refused, for example, to dismantle the Bonapartist establishment. As Arnould put it, "Once they were in charge they had only one preoccupation, to preserve all the mechanisms and the agents of the empire knowing that this machine was wonderfully effective in crushing the people."[36] Glaring evidence of this approach was the appointment of a Bonapartist, Count de Kératry, as head of the hated Prefecture of Police. He was therefore responsible for "law and order" in Paris.

By contrast, the government seemed less than wholehearted about organizing the defense. Gambetta alone put any energy into this. The others, as laissez-faire liberals (today they would be called neoliberals), rejected any state-directed mobilization of national resources, although that alone stood any chance of succeeding. The all-important railway system escaped regulation, notwithstanding the fact that the private railway companies had shown their "patriotism" by shipping most of their rolling stock to Switzerland for safekeeping. They were not touched because the minister was "convinced that the government's chief support lay with business interests and that nothing should be allowed to alienate this support."[37]

The Siege

Arise ye prisoners of want

The myth of national unity, that all the French shared a common interest, began disintegrating at the first shock. On September 19, just two weeks after the revolution, the Prussians laid siege to the capital. In that short interlude some 100,000 rich Parisians had abandoned the city. At the same time 230,000 refugees from areas near Paris arrived along with 200,000 regular soldiers.[38] But the departing rich did not make their empty apartments available to the new arrivals and sealed them up instead.[39]

The siege instantly wrecked the Parisian economy, causing not only mass unemployment for the working class, but financial ruin for many in the middle class. In this desperate situation membership of the volunteer militia, the National Guard, turned out to be a lifeline. During 1848 National Guard membership had been restricted and it had acted as a middle-class bulwark to crush workers' revolt. Now its composition and role were changed drastically. True to its laissez-faire principles, the Government of National Defense did not wish to be seen handing out welfare. However, with many French soldiers in Prussian captivity, only the National Guard could defend Paris. So under cover of military necessity the threat of further revolution was bought off. This was akin to the situation in 1848 when the new republican government placated revolutionary workers with national workshops. In both cases the government handed out what amounted to a dole and kept busy the workers who would otherwise have endured enforced idleness with all the dangers that involved.

Guardsmen were paid 1.50 francs per day, with 0.75 francs for wives and 0.25 francs for "legitimate" children. They were also issued guns, like a regular army. In a short time 340,000 Parisian men were enrolled. Not everyone received even this pittance. By December 1870 almost 500,000 people were registered as paupers and dependent on municipal charity to survive.[40]

Another feature of siege life was that food supplies to Paris were stopped. The wealthy, however, did not intend to do without, and class distinctions of the stomach soon emerged. Resourceful butchers turned to the zoo for their supplies. Two popular elephants—Castor and Pollux—went on sale in Boulevard Haussmann along with kangaroos, yaks and buffaloes.[41] At meetings ordinary Parisians complained that "the elephants were sold for vast sums to the restauranteurs of the Palais-Royal... Everyone knows the war was declared in the interest of the swindlers who earned immense fortunes by supplying goods and who now enrich themselves by starving us."[42]

When the zoo ran out, other sources of sustenance were tried, as this imaginative menu for a gala dinner for Paris notables demonstrates:

> *Consommé of horse with millet*
> *Dog liver brochettes au maître d'hôtel*
> *Minced back of cat with mayonnaise*
> *Filleted shoulder of dog with peas*
> *Rat salami à la Robert*
> *Dog gigot with baby rats*
> *Begonia in juice*
> *Plum pudding in juice with horse marrow*
> *Dessert and wine*[43]

Ingredients like this might seem disgusting to our tastes, but even these "delicacies" were well beyond the typical working-class family income of 2.25 francs a day. Cats cost 6 francs, rats 1 franc and dog 1.50 francs a pound.[44] Still, for the right price the best food was available throughout the siege. There was, for example:

> a fabulous dinner in the Rue de Ponthieu, given by a French naval captain just two weeks before the capitulation to celebrate the installation of a new mistress. Domestics in breeches and silk hose served up *foies gras truffés*, fillets of steak of real beef—no [zoo] hippopotamus—enormous Argenteuil asparagus, grapes from Thomery that had escaped Prussian surveillance, and bucketfuls of the finest champagne.[45]

The government was unwilling to alleviate inequalities in food supply because, despite the rhetoric of unity, it rejected interference with the market in food on liberal economic grounds. Against this, at a meeting chaired by Blanqui it was the unanimous view that "all basic goods should be rationed and distributed according to the need of each family. It is only fair that all, whether rich or poor, bear their share of the suffering of the siege..."[46] When the state was eventually forced into a grudging acceptance of rationing[47] it was of little avail to many people. Goods were not distributed free and so families had to:

> buy heating and coal, which was nowhere to be found anyway, and pay for the insufficient ration of meat and bread, distributed on set days in

> each arrondissement through the municipalities. It was so derisory, so impossible, that many working-class women sold their meat ration cards to rich people, who found that they could acquire supplementary rations at rock bottom prices.[48]

Complaints about shortages and long queues were a recurring theme of popular meetings at this time. In November 1870 one speaker told the meeting, "Today 1,500 women appeared at the borough hall of the 20th arrondissement to demand bread. There are people who are gorging themselves while others lack everything."[49] Two months later things life had not improved: "This morning, by 8 o'clock, there was no more bread to be had in any bakers in the 12th arrondissement. (A woman's voice: It's true! We'd been queuing for five hours.) And when you get bread it's more like eating plaster than bread... We have to queue for meat; then we queue for wood, and then for bread."[50]

Speculators used this crisis to amass profits.[51] Here was a class issue where capitalist methods came into direct conflict with the common interest. At mass meetings some speakers even saw a speculative influence behind talk of peace with the Prussians: "Now that they have sold everything and there are no more profits to be made, they have begun to talk about giving in."[52] Not everything had been sold, however. When the siege finally ended a few weeks later, it was reported that: "Game, fish, fresh meat, fowl, delights hitherto squirrelled away in hidden places, reappeared simultaneously on the shelves. The women, the National Guards, and the working class cried out that the people had been cheated. Paris had enough food after all. The government had betrayed us."[53]

Even the right-wing papers were enraged: "The decree requisitioning potatoes had barely been lifted before bags full of these precious tubers flooded on to indoor market stalls. The first note on the armistice had barely been published before the pavilions were replete with all sorts of merchandise."[54]

That day the crowd reacted with fury and violently looted what they could.

Along with hunger came the cold of an exceptionally harsh winter[55] during which the Seine froze solid for three weeks.[56] This combination was deadly. In a single week smallpox and typhoid carried off 203 people. Over the course of the siege 64,154 deaths were recorded. During the same period of the previous year the figure was 21,978.[57] During the four months and 12 days of siege mortality tripled.[58] Workers suffered disproportionately, their death rate being twice that of the upper class.[59]

After January 5, 1871, came the additional threat of German bombardment. In relative terms the victims of between 200 and 500 shells daily were few, but the effect was still deeply shocking.[60] In the three last days of January 31 children, 22 women and 52 men were killed and even more wounded.[61] Yet the revelries continued for the rich: "while artillery shells rained down on the left bank, these gentlemen, feeling very secure on the right bank, demanded champagne, the corks flying up to the ceiling. So began a joyous bombardment which continued amidst peals of laughter and witty discussion... You don't forget such things. The heart may lose its memory, but the stomach never."[62]

Every day the gulf between the classes widened, as the siege cut through the rhetoric of national unity. The importance of this fact in the development of the Commune should not be underestimated. It meant that the dreams that the left had about social transformation were to acquire a level of mass support powerful enough to challenge big business and its state machine. The good intentions of a minority armed with radical theories and personal dedication were not enough. Only a mass of people united by a common interest in opposing capitalism could turn the Commune into reality. The Commune's program of women's liberation, enlightened education and culture for all would offer a new world to all humanity, but the driving force that made that new world possible was the working class. The sufferings of the siege gave it many grievances, and the National Guard marshaled it into an organization.

In addition to these factors was the pressing political question of the conduct of war. To repel the invaders, the far left had suspended its opposition, and the mass of Parisians had tolerated mass unemployment, hunger, cold and epidemics without weakening in their resolve. All that they asked of the Government of National Defense was energetic resistance. President Trochu certainly gave the impression that the city would fight valiantly to the very end:

> Europe has been struck by the unexpected spectacle that we have given it, of the close union between rich and poor in devotion and sacrifice... The world would not understand that the population and the army of Paris, after having so energetically prepared itself for all sacrifices,

> did not know how to progress, that is to say to suffer and combat until it is no longer capable of suffering and fighting any more.[63]

Alas, there was no action to match his high-flown nationalist rhetoric. The military situation was difficult. There were few regular troops left to oppose an occupying force of 400,000 backed by 700,000 reserves, and it soon became clear that Paris could not expect outside assistance.[64] On the other hand, as Friedrich Engels wrote, Paris was a "colossal entrenched camp" whose fortifications "form the hugest complex of military engineering works ever constructed."[65] Within this powerful defensive network of forts and walls there were up to 450,000 fighters.[66]

And yet month after month the grand promises of an armed response came to nothing. The streets were full of rumors about a "Trochu plan" for an offensive but it obstinately failed to materialize. Engels, an astute observer of military affairs, was perplexed: "It is impossible to explain why... Trochu has done nothing to take advantage of the chance thus offered."[67] Finally, a "great breakout" was announced at the end of November. General Ducrot made this inspiring speech to the troops: "As for myself I have made up my mind, and I swear before you and the entire nation: I shall only reenter Paris dead or victorious. You may see me fall, but you will not see me yield ground."[68]

Ducrot did not die heroically on the battlefield, although approximately 12,000 did.[69] He later returned to play his part in an even greater massacre—the Bloody Week offensive against the Commune. His heroic words only became deeds when fighting the class enemy. The breakout failed because the political and military leaders had no intention of fighting to the finish despite their public oratory. Just two days after the September 4 revolution they were privately arguing that to defend Paris was a "ridiculous folly."[70] As time went by, more and more government figures expressed such opinions behind closed doors. Trochu said, "The resistance is a heroic madness," and Picard, "We shall defend ourselves for honor's sake, but all hope is chimerical," and Crémieux, "The Prussians will enter Paris like a knife goes into butter."[71]

The government and its military advisers took this view for political reasons. Dombrowski, a future communard general, pointed out that "Trochu can make no use of the immense resources he has at his disposal... It will not be the *chassepot* rifle or the machine gun, or special weapons that will give victory, but ideas..."[72] To win, Trochu would have to inspire the masses by giving them a reason to fight. In 1793 the promise of liberty, equality and fraternity had transformed the military situation in favor of the Republic. To rally the working class of Paris in 1871 required the right wing to promise a better society, something it would not countenance because that threatened their coveted property rights. Without popular mobilization France was certainly defeated. Yet the government dared not admit it too soon, because the people who had so recently made the September 4 revolution, and who were now organized in the National Guard, could rise again. So the mythical Trochu plan continued to be peddled.[73]

The real government policy, and one which had been pursued from the very start of the siege, was for a peace settlement on almost any terms. Once again public rhetoric said the opposite. Jules Favre led the negotiations for the French side. He had famously asserted, "We will not give up one inch of territory or one stone of our fortresses."[74] Even as he said this he was meeting Bismarck secretly to discuss capitulation. Prussia's terms were an irritation, but the Parisian population were a greater one. Ducrot blurted out the truth: "Virtually the whole defense revolved around a single thing! *Fear of a rebellion*."[75] How could this fear be overcome?

The answer was perhaps the most grotesque plan ever concocted by a military high command. Here is a contemporary right-wing account of it:

> In the meeting of January 10, 1871, General Trochu said: "If 20,000 or 25,000 men are left on the ground after a major battle under the walls of Paris it will give in." Voices of protest were raised. He returned to the theme: "The National Guard will only accept peace if it loses 10,000 men." A general [Ducrot] replied: "It's not that easy to get 10,000 National Guards killed."[76]

Finally another general declared, "These loud-mouth National Guards really want their heads smashed in. We'll help them achieve that."[77] The officers wanted as many of their own side to be killed by the enemy as possible! So another "breakout" was organized for January 19, but the battle beneath the walls left only 3,000 dead, which was insufficient blood. Trochu then resigned and was replaced by the Bonapartist General Vinoy.

Despite government efforts to hide its true intentions, Parisian workers were shedding the illusions of September 4, 1870. The Government of National Defense (*Gouvernement de la Défense Nationale*) was nicknamed the *Gouvernement de la Dépense Nationale* (Government of National

Waste)[78] or *de la Défaite Nationale* (of National Defeat).[79] The government rather than the Prussians was blamed for the terrible sufferings of Paris. National Guards could now see behind the bold rhetoric: "Our generals don't want to precipitate events; they want hunger to lead to capitulation. People concluded that their inertia must be part of a deliberate plan. They want to use the situation to wear the people down."[80] A telling piece of evidence was the fact that while many thousands died of preventable disease and privation, and others died in poorly planned breakouts, not a single general or senior officer had been killed during the siege.[81]

The Idea of a Commune

Peasants, artisans and others
Enrol'd in the party of toil

It was in this climate that support for the idea of the Paris Commune would blossom. It is interesting to note that the Commune had been a topic of left discussions before the war,[82] but no one had conceived of the body that would emerge in 1871. This reinforces the argument that it was truly the product of a mass movement.

All those who discussed the Commune before 1871 saw its role as limited to acting as a Parisian local government with restricted powers.[83] Indeed, immediately after the September 4 revolution the mayor of Paris promised that "in a short time, circumstances permitting, the citizens will be called to elect their municipal government."[84] However, this promise was not carried out once it became clear that Parisians regarded self-government as something more than the powerless hot air chamber that the government planned.

For the Jacobins and Blanquists, the future Commune would be a return to the glory days of the Great Revolution. Pyat's *Le Combat* wanted the Commune "revived like in 1792."[85] By contrast, Proudhonists gave a more anarchist and anti-state slant: "What did Paris intend when it proclaimed communal autonomy?... In a word, the Commune wanted to break centralization." It was the embodiment of "the federation of communes" that would replace the state, as Proudhon had envisaged.[86]

Important though these views were, for most people they remained abstract. None of them adequately captured the imagination of the communal mass movement that developed. The Commune had to be the mechanism that would address practical day to day concerns, and bring power down into every street and every workshop. This shift of emphasis began as a reaction to government inaction during the siege. Laissez-faire liberal attitudes meant that body did virtually nothing to address the suffering of beleaguered Parisians. In the vacuum local bodies—the mairies (borough or local town halls) of the 20 Paris arrondissements—acquired a crucial, indeed life-saving, role. *L'Illustration* reported that by early November the town halls had taken responsibility for "(1) equipping the National Guard; (2) establishing soup kitchens; (3) distributing handouts to the destitute; (4) returning for free clothing and bedding that had had to be pawned."[87] Other functions included housing the homeless, regulating markets, distribution of fuel and flour, control of municipal butchers' shops, the supply of ration cards, and organizing the work of thousands of seamstresses to supply clothing to the National Guard.[88]

The siege encouraged the formation of the Commune in another way. Along with unemployment came a government order closing all theaters. People who had ample time for political discussion now found they had spaces available to hold it.[89] The result was the setting up of "Red Clubs" which, when there was no lighting or fuel at home, became a refuge for entire families and forum for debate and argument. These popular assemblies had been legalized in 1868 under the "Liberal Empire" but were forbidden to discuss religion or politics, an injunction enforced by a policeman who had to be in attendance.[90] This changed after the September 4 revolution. Illumined by a few flickering candles (the only lighting obtainable under the siege), the Commune of 1871 took shape. The clubs transformed politics from a distant, obscure craft indulged in by professional talkers (almost all drawn from the middle and upper classes), into a daily and tangible reality for masses of people. The establishment hated that. Vinoy, for example, complained that people actually dared to speak their views:

> Public expression was now fully liberated so that the most exaggerated and often the most criminal opinions were aired. The clubs met in permanent session and there were even discussions in the street, with numerous meetings of citizens *[in]* a perilous and unwarranted growth of public opinion.[91]

A new force was in gestation—the people grasping toward power for themselves. That alternative vision, which burst onto the world stage after

March 18, 1871, first developed at the molecular level of club discussion. During the siege some 30 clubs operated on a daily basis. Many were presided over by well-known political figures such as Blanqui. Their subject matter could range from socialism and communism to the price of food (rats, cats and dogs included), the nature of the family institution, military strategy and the need for a commune. The clubs were also the focus for organization, deciding who should stand in elections, what demonstrations should be held, and so on.

The range of opinion expressed in these genuine and free discussions was inevitably vast. Such mass meetings were not won overnight to the idea of overthrowing the government, or of the need for radical social change. At first many speakers defended Thiers, Favre and Co., but the experience of siege conditions compelled a change of heart. The shift in opinion was not linear, but moved backward and forward with the ebb and flow of events. An example of how varied views could be, and how minds could be changed, was this speech against the prevailing anti-German chauvinism:

> These men who we fight, and who we must battle against to the bitter end, are our brothers and we mustn't forget that even in the heat of struggle. They are not the authors of this horrible war and they suffer like us. *[Some protests are heard but the orator returns to his theme with redoubled energy.]* Yes, we must never forget that fraternity is written on the emblem of the Republic, and when I see a wounded man on the battlefield, a man writhing in agony, even if he is a Prussian, I'm moved to pity. *[Applause is heard from all sides.]*[92]

The butchers of the Commune during Bloody Week would not share such humanity in May 1871 when they murdered the Parisian working class.

The (literal) bread and butter issue of solving food shortages, unequal distribution and government treachery, became inextricably linked to the concept of all power to the "people's Commune." Adopted as an idea in these rank-and-file assemblies, it would be a million miles away from the sort of municipal government advocated by some middle-class Parisians. However, it was not always so. The idea evolved. On November 1, for example, a speaker could still draw vigorous applause when he argued that any municipal government "must stay within the confines of its remit and abstain from interfering with the tasks and powers of the government."[93]

One month later the mood was changing: "The government must be held responsible for the high price of coal and the poor quality of the fat. With 'the Commune' we will have coal in abundance, and soon butter will replace the candle grease." The report adds that not everyone was convinced.[94] By mid-December the Commune had become a "profession of faith," the aim being "the universal Republic...the means being the revolution and the Commune."[95] Now meetings were becoming impatient and there were moves to nominate a Commune there and then.

Why the transformation? Political and social issues were becoming fused. The government was blamed for both military failure and the continuing siege conditions with all the suffering they entailed. It was hoped that the Commune could break out of this vicious circle: "We ourselves need to choose 80 pure republicans who will form the Commune and save the Republic, as was done in 1793. (Yes! Yes! That's it! The revolutionary Commune.)"[96] Pyat's paper carried an article in which every line began, "Ah! If we had the Commune, then..." This list followed:

> Ah! If we had the Commune, then...the generals would have all the troops they need; the wounded would not die from cold and the lack of ambulances and doctors; a cabbage would not cost 100 sous; the town halls would not be weighed down by the poor.[97]

By the end of 1870 the vision of a Commune as a complete alternative to the existing power was emerging from club discussions. An account of a club meeting shows the audience believed a workers' government would, for example, seize the wealth of the churches and use it to buy cannons, and:

> It will place its contracts with workers' associations which will replace the big bosses, the great companies (railway companies in particular...and other parasites). In short, the "real" Commune... will chase away the Prussians and organize the democratic and social Republic. The meeting ended as it had begun, with the cry *Vive la Commune*![98]

How did the left react to this developing situation? Although initially swamped by the rhetoric of national unity, after September 4 it gradually recovered its independent stance. The government had clearly exposed itself and not done the one thing that all sections had asked of it in return for suspending opposition. It would not fight the war effectively and was more an enemy of ordinary Parisians than the Prussians. The supposed victorious revolt on September 4, 1870, had turned out to be a chimera. The left wing was in transition from uncritically backing the war effort to propounding its own social demands. This could sometimes lead to contradictory language. Thus a First International poster simultaneously called on supporters to "put aside our demands so as not to put any obstacle in the way of *National Defense* [and the] honor of France," and demanded "*land for the peasant* who cultivates it, the mines for the miners who work them, the factory for the workers who make them prosper [because the struggle] between socialism and feudalism has already begun."[99]

The international went on to argue two practical policies. People should mobilize behind locally organized bodies called Vigilance Committees, and strengthen the National Guard as their independent armed force. A circular signed by prominent members of the International made these proposals clear: "Since the Republic was proclaimed this horrible war has changed its meaning. It is now a struggle to the death between feudal monarchism and democratic republicanism... In this sense we are organizing vigilance committees in all areas and are pushing for the formation of district organizations such as were so useful in 1793..."

These would:

> (1) use every means to stir up patriotism to save revolutionary France;
> (2) take energetic measures against bourgeois and Bonapartist reaction and push for acceptance of major defensive measures by organizing republican committees, first elements of future revolutionary communes. Our revolution has not yet been made.[100]

The vigilance committees were composed of groups of 25 to 30 republican activists[101] elected from public meetings.[102] The plan was to have at least one for every Paris arrondissement (though there were actually two in Montmartre, one for women the other for men).[103] The committees hoped that the local mayors would officially recognize their role, but this happened only in the minority of cases where the mayor was sympathetic.[104] Each vigilance committee sent four or five delegates to a Central Committee of the Twenty Arrondissements meeting at a place called La Corderie. It would become very important because all the key components of the left movement would eventually assemble at this location. As one writer put it: "The revolution was sitting there on the benches, leaning against the walls, its elbows resting on the platform. The revolution in workers' clothes! It was here that the International Workingmen's Association held its sessions and the Federation of Workers' Unions had its meetings."[105]

In March 1871 these organizations would be joined by the most important one of all—the Central Committee of the National Guard.

The first major statement of the vigilance committee movement was its "red poster" (named for the color of the ink), which called for the election of a Commune.[106] There was no doubting the radical intent of some of the committee members: "Every member of a Vigilance Committee declares his adherence to the Revolutionary Socialist Party. Consequently, it demands and seeks to obtain the elimination of the privileges of the bourgeoisie by all means possible, its downfall as a governing caste, and the rise of the workers to political power. In a word: social equality..."[107]

The Proudhonists, the main force behind the vigilance committee movement, tended to focus on the practical concerns of Parisians under the siege and social measures to alleviate the crisis. Essential as these were, they paid less attention to political policy or the government. Therefore the vigilance committees undertook tasks like searching out provisions[108] and distributing them equitably,[109] as well as registering and paying National Guards.[110]

There was a difficulty here, and a recent account pinpoints the problem: "The Central Committee did not know what role to choose in the face of the provisional government. Should it be the concerned friend, the moderate opponent or the resolute adversary?"[111] Unclear as to the answer, the vigilance committees "were quite simply 'domesticated' by the mayors into performing menial tasks useful to local administration, but of no real import."[112] By November 1870 very little was left of the ambitious aims of the vigilance committee project. In confronting the question of how much effort should go to immediate campaigns, and how much to the bigger challenge of posing an alternative political vision, the Proudhonists emphasized the former at the expense of the latter.

There was another strategy on offer that took the opposite approach. This emanated from the Blanquist/Jacobin tradition. They believed in initiating full-scale insurrection out of mass demonstrations. The first time that this was attempted was on October 31, 1870, when news reached Paris of the loss of nearby Le Bourget. That same day the capture of a vast army at Metz was confirmed and the existence of ongoing negotiations for an armistice admitted. All this was widely interpreted as proof of government treason. In the mid-afternoon a demonstration of 300 to 400 marched on the Hôtel de Ville (City Hall), and sections of the National Guard led by left-wing commanders moved in to occupy it. In doing so they captured several members of the Government of National Defense.

What happened next became a tragic farce. Gustave Flourens was a fiercely courageous but utterly romantic revolutionary. He led his contingent of sharpshooters from the working-class district of Belleville to where members of the Government of National Defense were now sitting, and then, "brandishing his sword, he jumped onto the table and proceeded to march up and down it, tearing the green baize with his spurs... Inevitably Flourens had his list for a Commune, or, as he seems to have preferred to call it, Committee of Public Safety."[113] Blanqui arrived in the early evening to find that he too was a member of the new government. He promptly set to work issuing proclamations, one of which stated, "The population of Paris has judged it necessary to replace the government which has gravely compromised the Republic."[114] Unfortunately, "the population of Paris" had not been consulted. They were deeply discontented at this time, but that is not the same as saying that they were ready for a new revolt. This left the occupiers of the Hôtel de Ville vulnerable.

It was not long before National Guard battalions still loyal to the Government of National Defense massed outside. Inside confusion reigned. In one room Flourens and others were planning their revolutionary dictatorship but were unable to finalize the exact ministerial lists. In another room Jacobins like Delescluze and Pyat were proposing a new government to be chosen by regular election. In a third room discussions with the captive government representatives were taking place. After hours of tortuous negotiation the insurgents in this last room extracted a promise of formal preliminaries for the election of the Commune, and voting for a provisional government to follow soon after.[115] Millière, a socialist who reluctantly became involved in the insurrection, recounts that:

> Written commitments were demanded, especially from Generals Trochu and Tamisier. But Messieurs Jules Favre, Jules Simon and Garnier-Pagès vigorously protested against the outrageous idea that one suspected their sincerity. They had promised elections and were indignant at the very thought that one might believe them capable of breaking their word of honor.[116]

Eventually this proposal was put to the assembled revolutionaries, who rejected it.

Millière continues:

> Those citizens who so violently rejected the deal...had lost their political senses or were ignorant of the real state of affairs. They had the pretension of dictating conditions, of imposing their will, just as if their new government was uncontested master of the situation. They did not want to see how the situation worsened as each minute passed. I could not make them understand that while at the beginning of the negotiations the previous evening we were as strong as our opponents, now, at 4am in the morning, reaction had regained its superior strength, and it was now our turn to be prisoners of those who still seemed to be in our power.[117]

Soon after this a group of right-wing National Guardsmen gained access to the interior of the Hôtel de Ville by an underground passageway. They found everyone totally exhausted and the revolutionaries were driven out.

Of course the solemn pledges of Favre and Co. were not honored. When people began arriving to vote in the promised municipal ballot they were met with a poster signed by none other than Favre canceling it! Instead there was a referendum on whether or not the population of Paris supported the Government of National Defense. The result was catastrophic for the left: 557,900 said yes; 65,000 voted no.[118] However, abstention by 300,000 electors showed the government had lost much popular support, even if the left had not gained it.[119] The failed October 31 insurrection led to a major setback. It gave the government a free hand to repress opposition, and leading figures such as Flourens were arrested. Others were forced into hiding.

Following a third and final failed "breakout" from Paris the left attempted another showdown. Many suspected the authorities wanted to surrender and had deliberately sabotaged the military effort. Indeed, the armistice was just five days away. On January 22 a crowd released Flourens from captivity, and once more demonstrators descended on the Hôtel de Ville. Their exact numbers are unknown, but they appear to have been limited, the most important contingent being 150 National Guards who stationed themselves before the Hôtel de Ville, crying "Down with Trochu!" and "Long live the Commune!"[120] This time the building was well defended by Breton Mobile Guards. A shot rang out. Then:

> as in the grand scene of a melodrama, the windows and the great door of the Hôtel de Ville were flung open, and two lines of Mobile Guards disclosed themselves, the front rank kneeling, the second standing, all levelling their muskets and prepared to fire, which they did in a volley, spreading terror amidst the crowd of people... The insurgents, during this mad flight of men, women and children, answered their attack.[121]

Five people died and 18 were wounded, including women and children.

The consequences have been described as follows: "In fact the January 22 uprising had been no full-scale attempt at revolution; the numbers of the insurgents were far fewer than on October 31... But the shooting changed everything, and Paris hardened into two irreconcilable camps... After the January 22 uprising, 'civil war was a few yards away,' Jules Favre wrote in retrospect."[122]

The repression that had followed October 31 returned with redoubled fury. Radical newspapers like *Le Combat* were banned, all the clubs were shut down,[123] and 83 people, including Delescluze, were arrested. Then came the armistice and the bitter feeling that all the suffering and sacrifices of the siege had been in vain.

While the vigilance committee movement had failed to bring about the Commune because it focused only on immediate issues and became lost in the minutiae, the Jacobins and Blanquists had failed because they attempted to institute the Commune by a sheer act of will. Without mass support they could not succeed. The Commune could not be gifted by the action of a minority, no matter how heroic and dedicated.

The left was in a parlous state even before January 22. The International's internal minutes reveal just how bad things had become: "The sections are ruined, their members dispersed. If the public knew all of this they would realize how weak we are and the association would collapse."[124] Now, wrote one Russian eyewitness:

> The newspapers, which the International depended on, had to close because of lack of money. The capitulation of Paris sent everyone into a state of depression. There was not even the means of publishing a pamphlet on the events of January 22. At the meeting of the Federal Chamber on January 26 it was said, "The people will not support us." Frankel believed that "the delegates' speeches expressed utter hopelessness."[125]

Frankel went on to suggest that the International should give up intervention and retreat into reorganizing itself and study.[126]

The depths were reached with a national general election held on February 8, 1871. The rural population formed the majority of the electorate and their verdict could not have been more demoralizing for the Parisian left. One historian has written that the peasantry:

> obeyed an atavistic reflex. Facing national disarray, the collapse of administration and the political structures, and the momentary rupture of national unity resulting from the occupation and the battle fronts, it turned toward the hereditary guardians of tradition, descendants of the noble families, the offspring of the lords of the manor... Never had an elected chamber counted such a high proportion of representatives of the ancient nobility, not even the Estates General *[of 1789]*.[127]

Fully 230 deputies—one third of the total—came directly from the aristocracy! 250 others were landowners and 100 were former army officers.

There were a number of reasons for this staggering result. During the siege the voice of Paris had been gagged and right-wing influence in the countryside could not be challenged. The peasants also wanted a return to peace and normality so that they could get on with farming undisturbed. Finally, as small property owners they feared the socialistic tendencies of the working class.[128] The urban vote was rather different. Republicans did well, and the larger the size of a town's population the higher the percentage of republican votes cast. However, only 80 republicans such as Favre and Ferry were elected. Socialists were still fewer in number. Some 40, of the least radical, won seats.[129]

Despite its revolutionary tradition Paris cast its votes in a similar fashion to other French towns, although Parisians showed no love for the government. Demoralization with official politics led to a 40 percent abstention rate and, only seven of the 43 seats went to the peace party.[130] However, the capital's votes did not go to the far left, even though it had pooled its meager resources. A common list representing the International, the Central Committee of the Twenty Arrondissements, the Federal Chamber and elements of the National Guard was presented. To its credit, the electoral slate included the leading German socialist Wilhelm Liebknecht. When the ballots were counted even major figures like Varlin, Blanqui and Flourens came in at the very bottom of the poll.[131] With only around one in five votes the revolutionaries' weakness was palpable.

A New Type of Mass Power

No saviour from on high delivers

Given this situation it was all the more surprising that the Paris Commune should emerge just weeks after the February general election. The change in fortune was brought about because of the bungled attempt by the French government to seize the National Guard cannons at Montmartre. These arms were an open challenge to the French state that aimed, like all other states, at holding the monopoly of force within its territory. Why had the Government of National Defense become terrified of the Parisian militia, its own creation? The guard had only been intended to give the impression of resisting the Prussians, and act as a form of dole. But the government seriously misjudged the situation because the National Guard increasingly escaped official control as time passed.

Curiously, not only had the government underestimated the new force, but so had the left.[132] The militia was too closely identified with the state and the exercise of power to attract the Proudhonists. Yet it was too broad and amorphous an organization to interest the Jacobins or Blanquists. Another impediment was the memory of 1848, when the National Guard had been composed of wealthy volunteers who readily butchered the workers. Furthermore, there was nothing overtly radical in the usual routine and unexciting activities of a guardsman. Typically companies would assemble at 9am. An hour later they would set off for guard duties on fortifications, or undertake military exercises lasting up to six hours per day.[133] Some guards had backed the risings on October 31 and January 22, but they played the role of foot soldiers and did not act on their own account.

However, the National Guard was changing. Firstly, the social balance within it shifted dramatically now membership had been widened from the middle class to all male citizens between the ages of 25 and 35.[134] The 340,000 men in the ranks constituted around three quarters of the eligible male population of Paris[135] and they controlled some 200,000 guns.

Widespread unemployment and the lure of a salary, though minimal, encouraged workers to join in disproportionate numbers. Thus in the working-class districts of Belleville and Montmartre there were ten instead of the normal eight guards companies. Each numbered from 2,000 to 2,500 men. By contrast, in the wealthier west, instead of the stipulated 1,500 per company there could be as few as 360 guardsmen.[136] The armistice at the end of January 1870 exaggerated this tendency still further, because it gave the rich another opportunity to escape Paris. In the period between January 30 and the communal revolution in March another 150,000 left, cutting numbers of right-wing guardsmen even more.[137]

While this was going on, the relative military weight of the National Guard was also increasing. Generals like Vinoy were desperate to have enough regular troops "to maintain internal security in Paris"[138] but the bulk of the French army was in captivity. Prussia, which had now created a united Germany, wanted the army dissolved entirely, but in the end it relented and permitted Vinoy just a few thousand regular soldiers. On the other hand, as a mark of its power and independent position, the Parisian National Guard was left untouched under the terms of the armistice.

One National Guard tradition was maintained from the past, though in the context of 1870/71 it gained an utterly new significance. Unlike a regular army, all officers (except the government-appointed commander in chief) were elected. This was because, ever since the Great Revolution of 1789, the guard: "expressed the idea of a national militia... The National Guardsman is a citizen-soldier. In an emergency he sets off to rejoin his district battalion under the command of officers that he has chosen, along with his comrades, by means of direct election. The officer is therefore not only a soldier, but also a mandated representative."[139]

The election of officers was originally designed to bind and enthuse the rich in the defense of their class interests. In the hands of the working class such democracy would grow into the powerful tool of a new type of state.

This evolution began during the siege and operated on both political and organizational planes. When new battalions formed, it became common for prominent left leaders like Blanqui, Granger and Longuet to be chosen as company commanders.[140] The existing officer group also came to reflect the changing popular mood because of the system of recall. Its composition was subject to constant modification through successive elections.[141] Varlin gives a sense of how this mechanism worked, describing his nomination to the 193rd batallion: "I was in competition with a citizen who had a much longer history of service to the republican cause than I. However, as an artilleryman in the National Guard this citizen had attacked the people in June 1848... It was because I promised to never lead my battalion into fighting against republicans that I was elected."[142]

Of course instant recall could work the other way. For example, after the debacle of October 31, 1870, Millière was sacked as commander of the 208th.[143]

The National Guard developed organizationally too. Company delegates who met to elect the higher ranking officers were supposed to disperse once their choice was made, but gradually and to the government's alarm, they formed permanent delegate committees that aimed to exert control over the high command and direct the administration.[144] At the end of 1870 the government ordered these committees to dissolve, but it was ignored.[145] The guards' political role developed further after January 22, 1871, when the clubs were shut down and public meetings banned. As one participant wrote, this "did not prevent citizens from meeting and discussing political affairs, as they wished. After all, was not every National Guard company a permanent public meeting?"[146]

This grassroots organization was politicized by the February 8 general election. A National Guard delegate meeting put its name to a joint left list, "presented in the name of a new world, by the party of the disinherited." The candidates stood for the "organization of a Republic [and] political freedom through social equality."[147] Further meetings, with up to 2,000 delegates in attendance,[148] created a Federation of the National Guard (which is why the fighting forces of the Commune were called "Federals"). At its first meeting, on February 15, there were 7,200 delegates[149] representing 1,325 companies, and 215 out of the 260 battalions.[150] On February 24 a formal structure was agreed upon based on fortnightly meetings of elected delegates at all levels, from Company Circles to Battalion Circles and finally the Central Committee.[151]

The federation's statutes formally incorporated the principle of recall: "The National Guard has the absolute right to choose its officers and to recall them as soon as they lose the confidence of those who elected them..."[152] The constitution, as one writer puts it: "provided an elective body, at once rigid and flexible, completely democratic, and, most important, completely in opposition to the official organization with its officers appointed by the government and responsible not to their men, but to the Minister for Internal Affairs."[153]

It is important to note that the Central Committee members received no special payment for service. They earned the same as other guardsmen of an equivalent rank. These principles of instant recall and payment of representatives tied to workers' wages were carried over, in modified form, into the Paris Commune.

Soon after the formation of the National Guard Federation momentous decisions were taken. The first was proposed by Varlin on February 24 and adopted unanimously: "The entire National Guard must obey the orders of the Central Committee. If the military leaders issue a contrary order, the High Command must be arrested."[154] This simple statement was a absolute challenge to the authority of the government. As one National Guard put it, this meant "there were two powers in operation" in Paris.[155]

The February 24 meeting followed up with an extraordinary resolution: "The National Guard must henceforth replace permanent armies, which have only ever been instruments of despotism and which inevitably bring the fatal ruin of the country... The national citizen militia is the only national force, to the exclusion of any other..."[156] This decision led directly toward an entirely new form of the state that, in its utter novelty, owed nothing to either Proudhon's anarchist rejection of the state, or Blanqui's veneration of elitist dictatorship. The federation wanted to replace the permanent army with a workers' militia loyal to their own class, which constituted the majority of the people. That completely subverted the idea of the state as something imposing its will upon society from above, because it was not only composed of the workers, but also controlled by them, through democratic structures.

Instant recall did not automatically give the socialist or revolutionary left a predominant influence. The federation, as a democratic body, was bound to reflect the current state of political consciousness, and as yet many were unconvinced by or unfamiliar with the far left's arguments. According to Lissagaray, in the first Central Committee there was "not a known name among them. All those elected were men of the middle classes, shopkeepers, employees, strangers to the coteries, till now for the most part strangers even to politics."[157] Why had such people been chosen, if they were atypical? "The companies preferred delegates who were small masters, shopkeepers and white-collar employees—men of the liberal professions who knew how to read, write, keep accounts, and above all, make good speeches when the occasion demanded it."[158]

The left was therefore initially suspicious of the Central Committee, and on March 1 a row blew up at the International over participation:

> Varlin put forward the proposition: "It is absolutely necessary that members of the International use all possible means to be elected as delegates and become part of the Central Committee..." Frankel disagreed, arguing that involvement in the Central Committee would be "a concession to the bourgeoisie." He added, "We are internationalists; we dare not depart from that." Pindy feared that "the International would be compromised"... Varlin countered: "If we remain apart from such a powerful body at present, our influence will evaporate. But if we join the committee we will be making a meaningful step toward the future society."[159]

To have remained outside would have been utterly sectarian. To have joined but hidden their left-wing politics would have been equally flawed. In the end a compromise was reached. Four observers were sent, but they were "expressly forbidden from committing the International" to the committee's actions.[160] Such caution was quickly thrust aside, and by mid-March not only were 16 of the Central Committee's 38 members of the International, but it had set up its HQ at La Corderie.[161] The turnaround came when the Central Committee, showing its inexperience, almost made a fatal blunder and had to be saved by the prompt intervention of the International.

The French government wished to offer proof of its commitment to the peace treaty by permitting 30,000 German troops to parade in triumph through Paris.[162] The procession was set for March 1. After Paris had resisted the invader for so long, the Central Committee was furious with this humiliation and planned to physically prevent it. Lissagaray is certain that if that had been attempted, "catastrophe was inevitable." It would have "exposed the people to the blows of the enemies of the revolution, who would drown all social demands in a sea of blood."[163] In other words, the militant population of Paris might well have been put to the Prussian sword. All the other organizations at La Corderie—the International, the Central Committee of the Twenty Arrondissements and the Federal Syndical Chamber—threw themselves into dissuading the National Guard from this perilous action. The Central Committee was eventually convinced, and what might have been its worst decision became a great show of its power and influence.

It ordered that "barricades will be established all round the quarters to be occupied by the enemy, so he will parade in a camp shut out from our town."[164] Shops were shut, their signs saying "Closed for national mourning."[165] Even opponents were impressed by the level of discipline demonstrated:

> From the morning on, public buildings (including the Stock Exchange), the shops, cafes, the boutiques, all were shut, by the river, on the boulevards, even in the most out of the way places. Everywhere the tricolor flags had black crepe added, there were black sheets at the windows and black crepe in the hats of passers-by; even black veils over the heads of statues on the Place de la Concorde![166]

The National Assembly versus Paris

The symbolic cementing of the peace treaty on March 1 closed an important historical phase. Nothing would bring back the 150,000 Frenchmen who had died in the Franco-Prussian War (the equivalent German losses being 28,000),[167] but at least it was over. Until now the left had been hindered by the tricky problem of how to support the war effort but oppose the Government of National Defense. That obstacle disappeared on March 1, but a new challenge arose in its stead. The government had decided to settle old scores and punish the Parisians and their National Guard for insubordination. Favre, the architect of the peace treaty, admitted that "the armistice was only the means of resolving the fundamental questions..."[168] For him the class war could now commence in earnest.

The Central Committee of the National Guard also sensed the change. When the working class of Paris moved from initial faith in the Government of National Defense to a suspicion that it was intent on selling out, it created an independent National Guard. The federation expressed organized mistrust of the establishment but did not yet stand for a new society in opposition to the existing one. However, after the armistice a new socially radical tone was evident in Central Committee statements:

> No more oppression, or slavery, or dictatorship of any kind; instead the sovereign nation of free citizens will govern as they desire. In a word, kings, masters, and leaders will impose themselves no more. Henceforth we will have representatives at all levels of power that are permanently accountable and subject to recall. And then no longer will the sublime slogan of *Liberty, Equality, Fraternity* be uttered in vain.[169]

The Central Committee was consciously challenging capitalism and its state structure.

The government was thoroughly alarmed and the mainstream press unleashed a barrage of abuse against this "clandestine" organization whose "anonymous" members had the affrontery to deny the dominance of the rich and famous. The Central Committee replied that a body freely elected by hundreds of thousands of men, in over 200 battalions, could not be regarded as anonymous.[170] Its reply reflected the widespread suspicion that an attempt to restore the monarchy was afoot: "That which we are, events have made us. The reiterated attacks of a press hostile to democracy have proved it; the menaces of the government have confirmed it: we are the inexorable barrier raised against any attempt at the overthrow of the Republic."[171]

It was now that the issue of the cannons came to the fore. The National Guards owned 2,000 or so of these.[172] They dated back to mid-November 1870 when the population, frustrated by the inactivity of Trochu,[173] funded the forging of artillery pieces by public subscription.[174] The route offered to the Germans for their procession of March 1 took them near many of these cannons, and the government was suspected of wanting to give them to the enemy. So guardsmen hauled the guns away to safety. Although usually drawn by large teams of horses, 200 of these giant weapons were dragged up the steep ascent to Montmartre, in the working-class northeast of Paris, and far away from Haussmann's remodelled central area.[175] The government was outraged but could do nothing about it. A despondent General Clément-Thomas, government-appointed commander of the National Guard, bemoaned the fact that every day power was slipping from his hands "without having the means to triumph over the constant threat of uprising."[176] In early March he resigned.

The situation at the end of February 1871 and in early March was described by one eyewitness as follows: "There was no government in Paris…only an anonymous power, the power of Mr. Everyman. At that moment, and it's something that cannot be stressed enough and which seems not to have been noticed, *the Commune was effectively already in existence*, in the sense that Paris was in charge of itself…"[177]

So even before March 18 the alternative power that was the Commune was flexing its muscles. It did not only include the National Guard, or its Central Committee, important though these were. The Red Club movement repressed after January 22 now revived and people took to the streets in lively demonstrations once more.

The most important of these processions was held on February 24, the day the Central Committee was set up, and also the anniversary of the 1848 Revolution. A republican newspaper, *Le Rappel*, described the spontaneous demonstration of tens of thousands at Place de la Bastille:

> Battalions of the National Guard, delegations from the clubs, from the International, from all the workers' societies and corporations, came to affirm their republican faith. The flags which fluttered, the patriotic tunes played by military bands, the immense multitude, the swirling tide of humanity, the decorated column, the windows filled with people, made it clear to anyone who may have doubted it, just what a festival Paris makes of the anniversary of the Republic. When night fell the spectacle became still more moving. The column was illuminated. The bright light lit the funeral wreaths and black flag on the plinth and was a physical representation of both consolation and promise, like the shining beams of the future on the mournful present...[178]

Such displays became an almost daily occurrence from then on.[179] Soldiers who were sent to disperse the crowd ended up fraternizing with the demonstrators. General Vinoy realized that he must "withdraw all troops who were mixing with the population, because of the dangerous effect this had."[180]

Although the issue of the cannons sparked off the communal revolution, people would not have risked their lives for weapons alone. These lumps of inert metal symbolized a power struggle between the two types of state—a National Assembly elected by universal suffrage but dominated by wealth versus direct democracy based on instant recall, working-class mobilization and self-activity.

As we have seen, the February 8 election produced an assembly with a deeply reactionary majority of so-called rurals. It first met on February 13 in Bordeaux, far out of reach of the German army. The first measure taken was for the Government of National Defense to cede authority to an administration headed by Thiers who took over most of the former government's personnel. In other words, the government that would butcher the Commune included many middle-class republicans of long standing. The assembly very quickly made its intentions clear. It ratified the peace treaty handing Alsace-Lorraine and its 1.6 million inhabitants to Germany, and agreed to pay reparations of 500 million francs.[181] Who would have to pay this particular bill? "Where would the money come from if not the pockets of the poor? ...Once again it is labor, and labor alone which will shoulder the costs of the Empire," wrote one contemporary.[182]

Next the government imposed a new National Guard commander in chief, the Bonapartist general Aurelles de Paladines, whose declared program was "to ensure the maintenance of order and respect for the law and for property."[183] Republican Paris was being deliberately snubbed: "Two senators, Vinoy and D'Aurelles, two Bonapartists, at the head of republican Paris—this was too much," wrote Lissagaray.[184] Thus only 30 of the 260 battalion commanders turned up when Aurelles summoned them to meet him.[185]

More provocative acts followed. With the war over, the assembly decided on March 10 to return to the north. However, it would not relocate to Paris but Versailles, where the king of Prussia had recently been crowned as German kaiser. Even the right-wing press admitted the reasoning behind this move: "It is a matter of putting the assembly far from the reach of the uprising."[186] *Le Vengeur*, edited by the Jacobin Pyat, expressed popular disgust with this "decapitalization": Versailles "is still warm from the Prussians. Where better could one go? The traitors who have delivered France can find nowhere more appropriate than the palace of Louis XVI."[187] A blizzard of punitive assembly decisions followed. On March 12 *Le Vengeur* together with five other republican papers was banned. To this was added an injunction against "the publishing of political, social or economic material."[188] Then Blanqui and Flourens were sentenced to death for their role in the October 31 insurrection.[189]

Vindictive decrees also touched the lives of ordinary Parisians, uniting the middle and working classes in common outrage. On March 13 it was decided to end the moratorium on debt repayments. Bills of exchange (a sort of post-dated check) were a widely used form of credit in Paris. When the war and siege had wrecked the city's economy payment of these debts had been suspended. Now, long before trade had had a chance to revive, the debts would have to be paid regardless of the ability to do so:

> Two or three hundred thousand women, shopkeepers, model makers, small manufacturers, working in their own lodgings, who had spent their little stock of money and could not yet earn any more, all business being at a standstill, were thus thrown upon the tender mercies of the landlord, of hunger and bankruptcy. From the 13th to the 17th of March 150,000 bills were dishonored.[190]

While this hit small businesses worst, other decisions struck at the poorest sections. One required the payment of back rent to landlords, something else that had been suspended during the siege. Finally, the peace treaty was the excuse needed to stop the National Guard salary. Vinoy was for halting these payments to the mass of unemployed Parisians immediately,[191] but Thiers convinced him to "retain for a few weeks the subsidy on which they depend to live."[192] This dire threat now hung over the hundreds of thousands whose livelihood depended on the payments.[193]

In Lissagaray's words, the National Assembly was "calling forth the Commune" and "despair was to supply it with an army."[194] Why was it being so provocative? After all, the failure of insurrections on August 14, October 31 and January 22 indicated that only a minority of Parisians wanted outright revolution. This government did not want merely to rule, it wanted to humiliate the capital and crush the resistance of its inhabitants to exploitation. Louis XVI had failed. So had Charles X in 1830, Louis Philippe in 1848 and, despite all Haussmann's efforts—Napoleon III. Now financiers threatened to withhold the loans the government needed to pay off the Germans[195] unless something was done to tame what they saw as this "monstrous agglomeration that must be liquidated for the peace of France and of all Europe."[196]

When the National Guard tried to find a compromise over the cannons, the government "maintained a scornful silence... Thiers was not interested only in regaining control of the cannons. He wanted to slaughter the working classes of Paris and the entire socialist and revolutionary sections."[197] The capital had to be smashed before the Assembly reopened at Versailles on March 20. After an early attempt to seize cannons was repulsed, March 18 was chosen.

The basis for the Commune had been laid. Hundreds of thousands of Parisians had been galvanized into political participation by the war and government provocation. It was this that made the achievements of the Commune possible.

Barricade at the entrance of Faubourg du Temple (above);
Barricade at Place Vendôme (below)

Four

Fighting the Civil War

We are but naught; we shall be all

Inspired by the March 18 revolution, the Parisian masses set out to remake society from top to bottom. However, the new world was being built in the midst of the old one, and in open defiance of it. It followed that the Commune would be bitterly opposed by the establishment. This created a dilemma that confronts any movement for progress. How can the desire to advance toward human liberation be balanced against the need to confront the enemy of that goal? How can a movement that wants to end violence and repression combat an adversary that employs violence and repression? How, in winning freedom for the mass of the population, can opponents be prevented from using that freedom to destroy the gains that are being made? In 1871 these were very practical and immediate questions, as the foe was camped just outside the city walls.

On March 31 the first skirmishes took place between the troops of Versailles and Parisian National Guards. Thiers had launched the civil war. This was unexpected: "At the report of the cannon all Paris started. No one believed in an attack."[1] A few days later, with the memory of Prussian cannonades still fresh, the capital was bombarded by Versailles shells. In response a giant protest demonstration assembled. Many people brought their guns, and all demanded action.[2] On April 6 the funeral of the first victims took place:

> Three immense catafalques, each containing 35 coffins, covered with black crepe, adorned with red flags, drawn by eight horses each, slowly rolled toward the great boulevards, preceded by trumpets and the Vengeurs de Paris. Delescluze and five members of the Commune, with their red scarves on and bare-headed, walked as chief mourners. Behind them followed the relations of the victims, the widows of today supported by those of tomorrow. Thousands upon thousands, men, women and children, silent, solemn, marched to the sound of the muffled drums. At intervals subdued strains of music burst forth like the spontaneous mutterings of sorrow too long retained. On the great boulevards we numbered 200,000, and 100,000 pale faces looked down upon us from the windows… Delescluze exclaimed in ecstasy, "What an admirable people! Will they say that we are a handful of malcontents?"[3]

After this no one could doubt that survival for the Commune rested on winning a titanic struggle with Versailles. Its outcome depended both on the level of external support Paris could attract, and on its own actions.

Beyond the Walls

The prospects for outside assistance were initially good, for the capital was by no means the only center of radical activity. The first demonstrations against the Empire occurred in Lyons during August 1870,[4] while on August 8, 1870, Marseilles witnessed the first attempt to create a Commune.[5]

Provincial communes could vary dramatically. On September 28, 1870, one was declared in Lyons in the name of "a revolutionary federation of Communes." Signatories to its manifesto included the Russian anarchist Mikhail Bakunin:

> (1) The governmental and administrative machine of the state, having become impotent, is abolished.
> (2) All criminal and civil courts are suspended and replaced by people's justice.
> (3) The payment of taxes is suspended…
> *To arms!*[6]

The limits of this approach were illustrated when, on the very day the state was declared abolished, it returned in the shape of 40,000 National

Guards loyal to the French government. Bakunin and his supporters were unceremoniously ejected.[7] In spite of this setback there were more disturbances at Lyons on November 3, December 20 and February 3, 1871.[8]

The commune briefly installed in Marseilles on November 1, 1870, took a much more moderate approach. Its goal was "the salvation of the French Republic, one and indivisible." After this classic Jacobin formula the declaration rounded off with Favre's famous words, "Not an inch of our soil, not a stone from our fortresses."[9] With a program that differed little from the government's professed aim of national defense, the Marseilles Commune lacked a strong reason to exist and soon ran out of steam.

Despite these setbacks, the fact remains that the Parisian movement lagged behind the provinces. How can this relative backwardness before March 18, 1871, be explained? One reason is that the great city was a large body to shift. Revolutionaries there had to contend with the presence of the leading politicians and government ministries. In the capital a commune meant overthrowing the national government in the midst of a war. These factors worked in the opposite direction after March 18. The provincial communes, unable to shake the state machine to its foundations, were easily defeated and never established themselves securely. By contrast, when Paris finally moved, the very centralization of the French state gave it an immense advantage.[10]

As March 18 approached yet other factors came into play. A key element marking Paris out from the provinces was the siege. This generated a mass working-class National Guard, while the gross inequality in suffering between rich and poor discredited the politics of national unity. Sharpened class issues tore through the veil of class collaboration. Such political radicalization was not easily exported to the rest of France. Paschal Grousset, who was to become the Commune's representative for external relations, explained why. He wrote that it was difficult to imagine "how much the blockade had separated us from the rest of the world, and how far the provinces on one side, and Paris on the other, were ignorant of each other's respective histories for five months. The isolation was complete."[11] The sole contact with the outside during this entire time was via hot air balloons and carrier pigeons. A dramatic example of this came on October 7, 1870, when Léon Gambetta took a perilous flight out of Paris to organize resistance armies in the south. In all 65 balloons were launched. Lacking the ability to navigate, many ended up in Belgium, Holland, Germany, Norway, behind enemy lines or in the sea.[12] Of the 302 carrier pigeons released only 59 got through: "The remainder were taken by birds of prey, died of cold and hunger, or ended in Prussian pies."[13]

Paris resumed external contacts after the truce with Germany, but its natural sympathizers in the provinces were still unsure how to interpret the situation there. The Paris Commune was such a novel type of body that they had difficulty making sense of it.[14] This does not mean there was much support for Versailles instead. In municipal ballots at the end of April and early May 1871 some 8,000 councillors were elected who backed Versailles, against 290,000 who did not.[15] The new representatives went so far as to call a meeting in Bordeaux that was to act as a "counter-assembly" to Versailles. However, Thiers successfully banned it.[16] Provincial towns may have wanted the civil war against Paris to end, but the majority were not prepared to challenge Versailles to bring this about.

Parisian events did, however, stimulate a rash of risings across the country.[17] On March 23, 1871, Lyons and Marseilles again established communes. The next day they were followed by Creusot, Narbonne and St. Etienne, and on March 25 by Toulouse. In Paris the *Journal Officiel* even carried an excited report of a commune in Algeria, although precise details were lacking.[18] Alas, these communes were weaker than the one in Paris.

The March 18 revolution had been provoked by the issue of rents, the threat to the National Guard salary and so on. Provincial communes lacked such internal drives and were created primarily out of sympathy for Paris. One example was Marseilles, whose commune lasted 13 days—the longest provincial commune of all. A recent account states:

> The factor that launched the movement was Adolphe Thiers's declaration of...March 22 announcing the departure of the government to Versailles and the reorganization of the army to "conquer" the Parisians. The republicans of Marseilles thought it was madness for Frenchmen to fight each other, and it seemed strange to them that it was now possible to constitute an army when they had not been able to do so against the Prussians.[19]

Toulouse was even more timid, its spokesperson insisting that "in reality the proclamation of the Commune at Toulouse was in no way part of a communalist movement..."[20] Its leadership promised to "be faithful to the program of order, liberty and conciliation..."[21] This was not full backing for Paris, but an appeal for arbitration.

Some provincial communes showed more mettle. Narbonne, for example, was led by Digeon, who had socialist sympathies. Its founding statement sent solidarity to Paris for standing against "those who seek to restore the throne, that has been broken by the anger of the people three times already."[22] Against this can be set St. Etienne. Despite being in an area of mining villages, its leader declared its commune to stand for no more than "municipal independence for Saint-Etienne alone, with liberty and security for all citizens."[23]

There was one last attempt at establishing a commune in Lyons. An uprising on April 30, 1871, expressed full solidarity with Paris, and framed its language in revolutionary and socialist terms:

> Citizens, the hour has come for the city of Lyons. It was the first, on September 4, to demand the rights of the Commune, and can no longer stand by while our sister, the heroic city of Paris, is slaughtered. The traitors of Versailles have exceeded their mandate. After having accepted without discussion all the conditions the enemy foisted on France, they want to impose a new constitution on us that will be the first step toward royal restoration... Long live the democratic, social and universal republic.[24]

Alas, the insurrection never extended beyond a suburb of the city—La Guillotière—where 30 people died. Paris had to fight on alone.

The provincial Communes did not emulate the success of Paris on March 18, 1871, because they lacked the key element of mass power that it possessed—a mass National Guard under working-class control. The provinces saw no defections or mutinies of troops such as occurred on the Montmartre heights on March 18.[25] Outside the capital the movements were headed either by middle-class groupings (whose moderation led them to emphasize the purely political issue of maintaining the Republic, and conciliation between Versailles and Paris) or by socialists and anarchists (whose ideas were much more radical but who lacked a mass following). In Paris the pressure cooker conditions of the siege had brought together political, economic and social issues in a genuine mass revolutionary movement.

This does not mean that the provincial movement had no impact at all. Thiers would later confess that he had had to offer huge concessions to prevent the regions linking up with the capital, even to the point of maintaining the Republic rather than returning to his cherished idea of a monarchy:

> How could anyone imagine that I, old monarchist that I am, did not spend some time hesitating before deciding for the Republic. However, numerous delegates from the regions came to warn me that if I did not formally commit myself to it, they would imitate Paris and establish communes themselves... I had to make promises that today are impossible for me to escape from.[26]

Just how finely balanced the situation was is revealed by Thiers's admission that "if we had had to detach 15 to 20 thousand men from the army of Versailles to contain Lyons, Marseilles, Toulouse, Bordeaux, we would never have got into Paris.'[27]

What Is to Be Done About Versailles? March 19–31

If salvation was not to come from outside the capital, then everything depended on its own actions. The Commune represented a mass movement of working people groping for answers on how to change society. Spontaneity had carried them a long way. The action of the women of Montmartre had been vital on March 18 when the National Guard was caught unawares by the Versailles coup. The enormous scale of working-class mobilization on that day brought victory, in contrast to Blanqui's meticulously planned but minority effort in August 1870. However, fighting the civil war required complex political judgements with regard to strategy and tactics, and to the balance of military needs and social reforms. There were no spontaneous solutions for these difficult questions. The general revolutionary goal had been laid out by the uprising of March 18, 1871, but the fine detail of how to reach that goal required careful thought and deliberation.

The Commune could not avoid the issue of leadership. For many people this term has, for quite understandable reasons, become a dirty word after the experience of Stalinism in Russia and Eastern Europe. Where that system prevailed, the language of socialism, democracy and social emancipation was perverted by the governing body to justify a dictatorial and exploitative regime. Such a concept of leadership was foreign to the Commune, which would not accept orders imposed by bureaucratic fiat. An effective leadership would have to find and pursue the best strategy as a collective movement embodying the wishes of the insurgents. At the same time it would need to guide and concentrate their efforts, uniting them around a common fight to defeat Versailles and change the world.

It would be difficult to achieve this. Ever since 1871 popular movements can look back to the Paris Commune and learn from that experience. In contrast, the communards were pioneers venturing into uncharted territory. Furthermore, while they shared the aim of a just and equitable society, there was no agreement about how to achieve it. Given time and the opportunity for calm debate consensus might have been found. Alas, neither was available because the era of peace was so painfully brief.

The Blanquists believed that the adversary at Versailles must be defeated before any social transformation could be contemplated. One of them, Da Costa, wrote that even after March 18, 1871:

> the accomplishment of the political and social revolution still lay in the future. And to accomplish it the assembly that had sold us out had to be constrained by force to dissolve. *It had to be fought and nothing but fighting it mattered*... It would not be by striking it with decrees and proclamations that a breach in the Versailles Assembly would be achieved, but by striking it with cannonballs.[28]

A diametrically opposite view was taken by Proudhonists. Versailles could be overcome if Paris set a model of social transformation and democratic freedom that the provinces emulated. Any action that smacked of state power and politics must be avoided, because this would re-create oppression. They rejected the notion that:

> the Commune speaks like a government armed with full powers. *[That would show]* the influence of the old *state* tradition, the old centralizing conception... It is not communalist... We need to formulate briefly the straightforward and well-defined program of communal autonomy, to explain to the population the simple mechanism of direct government by means of natural groupings constituted into federations... All that was needed was to take up the Central Committee program—the abolition of the army and its replacement by the National Guard, municipal administration of the police, judiciary and finance, etc... That deals with internal relations. Externally it is important to declare that Paris did not want to impose its will or supremacy on the rest of the nation in any way...[29]

Which approach would be adopted? The Blanquists stepped forward first. Since Versailles *"had to be fought and nothing but fighting it mattered"*: "on the very night of March 18 to 19 Eudes proposed a march on Versailles.

The next morning, when Duval arrived at the [National Guard Central] Committee, he recommended rapid action instead of elections—the arrest of ministers, the dissolution of the hostile battalions, and action to prevent the retreat of the troops..."[30]

This made tactical sense. Thiers and Co. would never be weaker than in those first hours and days after March 18, 1871. Military discipline had evaporated, and the French army was yet to be buoyed up by prisoners of war released from Germany. So when Vice-Admiral Saisset, who was trying to construct an anti-Commune movement within Paris, begged Thiers for support, the reply he received was: "Neither 5,000, nor 500, nor five; I need the few troops still available—and in whom I don't yet have full confidence—to defend the government and the National Assembly."[31] Even this statement may have exaggerated Thiers's strength. An insurgent who secretly visited Versailles at that time saw only gendarmes on the streets, as regular troops could not even be trusted to patrol the area itself.[32]

The proposal for an immediate offensive was defeated, however. Blanquism's conspiratorial nature had, by necessity, always kept the numbers of adherents very small, and so they were a minority on the Central Committee. The majority did not yet realize that the impending conflict must be a fight to the death between social systems—capitalism or socialism. So they looked for a compromise position. If the Central Committee were unwilling to storm Versailles, they would have to treat with it.

In those early days the mayors of the different arrondissements seemed to offer hope of mediation, and the Central Committee spent several days bargaining with them. The mayors, who represented middle-class republicanism, disliked the monarchist National Assembly but also feared the rule of the working class. They wanted to confine Paris's demands to "the municipal rights which belong to all cities..."[33] Their leaders included local mayors like Georges Clemenceau. A fascinating exchange between the mayors and the committee has been recorded:

> Clemenceau: The government was wrong to unleash its anger on Paris, but Paris must recognize the National Assembly. The [Central] Committee can do only one thing—retire and cede the Hôtel de Ville to the mayors and deputies. They alone can ask for and obtain the recognition of Parisian rights at the assembly... What do you want of the [Versailles] Assembly?
>
> Eudes: That it goes away...

Boursier: There has been talk of social revolution, but our mandate does not include either a federation [of communes], or a declaration of Paris as a free city, or the establishment of the social revolution. (Protests)... Our mission is limited to getting communal elections.

Clemenceau: What are your claims? Do you confine your mandate to asking for a municipal council?

(Many of the Committee: No! No!)

Varlin: We want not only the election of a municipal council, but real municipal liberties, the abolition of the prefecture of police, the right of the National Guard to name its own leaders and to reorganize itself, the proclamation of the Republic as the legal government, the pure and simple remittance of the rents due, an equitable law on overdue bills, and Parisian territory banned to the army.[34]

This discussion raised the issue of legality. The Central Committee wanted to elect "the Commune" (i.e., a communal council or assembly) as soon as possible and set the date for March 22.[35] However, the mayors alone had the legal right to convoke elections. Tridon, a Blanquist, had set out what would be at stake here:

Let there be no misunderstanding or equivocation. There are communes and communes, but they are not all the same. The revolutionary Commune, whose actions on August 10 and September [1792] saved France and led to the republic, was not the product of a regular election, a bourgeois institution that emanated from a herd casting votes into a ballot box. It erupted in a supreme convulsion, like lava ejected from a volcano.

The Commune of '92 was illegality itself, since laws were still unjust. It was forceful and audacious because it was in the right. The revolutionary Commune was directly opposed to the legal Commune, the one elected by *regular* suffrage... The first act of this illegal Commune was to physically eject its predecessor from the windows of the Hôtel de Ville.[36]

Tridon had raised a crucial question. Was this going to be a revolutionary Commune, embodying the principles of collective control and instant recall as embodied in the National Guard, or would the Communal Council be more like a town council?

The mayors wanted to keep the Central Committee talking. The Central Committee wanted to avoid civil war. A deal was finally struck on March 25 to hold legal communal elections, involving male suffrage, the next day.[37]

The Central Committee's desire to both find a way forward for the movement and avoid bloodshed is easily comprehended. However, with hindsight it is clear that the Commune would not be able to win acceptance by using the "legal" framework. The reception the mayors received at Versailles would be revealing:

> As the 14 members of the Paris municipality filed into the hall, wearing their republican sashes, the republican deputies cried "Long live France! Long live the Republic!" The right returned the cheers of "Long live France!" But now the mayors responded shouting "Long live the Republic!" This reply proved explosive. From 40 to 60 deputies from the royalist benches clamored their protest shouting "To order! To order! The assembly is insulted; make them vacate the tribune! They have no right to speak!"[38]

So the very mention of the Republic caused uproar, even though France had nominally been a republic since September 4. The symbolism of monarchy is perhaps a little difficult to grasp today. In 1871 it was a codeword for tradition, reaction and denial of workers' rights. This episode demonstrated that both Thiers and the assembly were intent on civil war and no mediation would be allowed to prevent it, even when proposed by the oh-so-respectable mayors. The Commune would pay dearly for not marching on Versailles and holding municipal elections instead.

The decision to hold elections under the previous framework was significant in other ways too. It meant that after a week of running Paris the Central Committee was abdicating as an organ of political power. "Our mission is completed," it said.[39] Why was the Central Committee stepping back in this way? Although it had played a central role in events leading to the March 18 revolution it was still very inexperienced. The National Guard Federation had been constituted only on February 15 and the Central Committee itself on February 24. Therefore many of its members lacked the confidence to lead and direct a mighty revolution. Such confidence would have come with experience. People like Varlin had gained this through working in the International, the trade union movement and illegal organizations, but the majority within the Central Committee had not. The government's insult—that the Central Committee was composed of anonymous figures—was a backhanded compliment because it meant its members were not career politicians with oversized egos and a history of selling out. However, it was also a handicap.

Even though power fell into its lap on March 18, 1871, when the national government unexpectedly departed for Versailles, the committee still saw its primary role as being "the great family council of the National

Guard"—a sort of guardsmen's trade union.[40] Accordingly it divested itself of government responsibility and handed power to the Communal Council at the Hôtel de Ville.

One consequence of this decision was to reduce the direct influence of the working class in the communal movement. Federation elections had a uniquely democratic character, because battalions met daily, giving ample scope for rank-and-file guardsmen to scrutinize delegates' activities and keep working-class interests at the fore. That was reflected in the social composition of the Central Committee, which by this time had a ratio of manual to non-manual professions of roughly 13 to 2.[41] Compare that with the Communal Council where workers would constitute just over half the membership, and manual workers only one third.

Although the National Guard wanted a diminished role and approved elections under the old voting system to choose a communal council, it had misgivings about the future and gave this advice to voters:

> Do not forget that the men who will serve you best are those you choose from your own ranks, living life alongside you, suffering the same problems as yourself. Do not trust the ambitious or the upstart... Equally you should mistrust talkers who cannot take action... Also avoid those whom fortune has favored, because it is rare for the wealthy to be disposed to regarding the worker as their brother.[42]

In National Guard elections revolutionary direct democracy had been built into the institutional framework. In the "legal" election to the Communal Council such direct democracy could still be expressed, but it was not closely tied in to the structure.

Voting took place on March 26. There had been a great exodus of population during and after the siege, amounting to some 700,000 people or over a third of the city.[43] Only 230,000 of the remaining 485,000 voters participated in the hastily called ballot. A map of electoral participation shows that the middle-class western districts tended to abstain, while the working-class east of Paris voted heavily, and for the most radical elements.[44] Those backing revolution (as opposed to the mayor's legalism) formed 70 percent of the total.[45] Compared with elections held at the end of Napoleon's Second Empire, the proportion of the vote going to the far left was 30 times greater.[46] The working class had not only shaken off the shackles of the old society, but was now committed to establishing a new one.

There were 92 seats in the Communal Council, but due to some multiple candidatures only 85 individuals were elected. It is difficult to precisely categorize their political affiliations, as the situation was fluid. However, one historian has estimated the following distribution: the mayors and their sympathizers numbered 19 and formed the right wing; there were eight or nine Blanquists; the Jacobins had around 40 supporters; and the International had 17, mostly Proudhonists.[47]

Unlike the National Guard Central Committee, the council emerged from a conventional electoral system, where there is no organic link between elector and representative, and voting decisions are influenced by established reputations rather than collective debate. As a consequence the balance in the council reflected the level of support for well-known political tendencies rather than the social composition of the electorate itself. In addition, many council members had been elected on the basis of the reputation they had established in the past, and so did not closely reflect recent developments. Thus the council had five small traders, one owner, two former officers, 25 from the liberal professions, 16 white collar employees, and 21 manual workers.[48]

The Commune had evolved in its first few days. Just affirming its own existence, as a living alternative to the conventional parliamentary government at Versailles, was of cardinal importance. That was why all the participants in the proclamation ceremony of March 28 found it so exhilarating. The power of the masses was being declared before all the world. However, the initial phase of the Commune—its first ten days in which the Central Committee had headed the movement—set it on the defensive. Compromises had been made in a vain attempt to stave off armed conflict, because the Central Committee hoped to carry through a revolution in one city (or federation of cities), without completely overturning the existing state machine in France. The second phase began with the meeting of the Communal Council.

The First Days of the Communal Council

While this body grappled with social issues, it was confronted with civil war, a subject that loomed ever larger in its deliberations. This created a complex situation. The purpose of the March 18 revolution was to create a new society, but there was an immediate threat from outside. Which issue should take precedence?

These questions had been broached in the debate over whether to march on Versailles on March 18/19. They had temporarily receded from view during the negotiations for the Communal Council. Once it began meeting (from March 28 onwards) the Council polarized more and more into different camps. Not only were there Proudhonist and Jacobin/Blanquist groupings, but each of these was internally divided into a left and a right wing.

Arnould, writing from a left Proudhonist/anarchist perspective, described the situation as he saw it:

> Hardly had we met and begun to function, than we noticed an important fact—that these words "Paris Commune" were understood in two different ways by the different members of the Council.
>
> For one side, the Paris Commune expressed and personified the first application of the *anti-governmental* principle. It meant war on the old conceptions of the *unitary state and despotic centralism*. The Commune for them represented both the triumph of the principle of the autonomy of groups freely federated, and the most direct government possible of the people and by the people...
>
> For the others the Paris Commune was, on the contrary, the continuation of the *old* Paris Commune of 1793. It represented, in their eyes, a dictatorship in the name of the people, an enormous concentration of power...[49]

Left Proudhonists emphasized libertarian ideals:

> Paris does not want to rule, but it wants to be free. It has no ambitions for dictatorship other than to conquer through its example. It does not pretend to impose its will, or to renounce it. It shows the nature of the movement by marching forward itself. It prepares the liberty of others by establishing its own. It does not drive anyone violently toward the Republic. It is content to be the first to reach it.[50]

So the role of the Communal Council should be "reduced to a simple organ for executing decisions [and acting as] the real servant of the totality of citizens whose sovereignty is henceforth returned to them..."[51] It was hoped that by these means civil war could be avoided: "By establishing true order, the only durable form, which relies upon the continually reaffirmed support of a frequently consulted majority, [the Communal Council] abolishes all reasons for civil war and revolution by removing the antagonism between popular opinion and the central executive power."[52]

The right Proudhonists laid less emphasis on social change, and argued that by sticking to municipal activities the Communal Council could find a way out of the crisis. Charles Beslay was a right-wing Proudhonist and, as oldest council member or doyen, he was made its first president. He believed that "the Commune only wanted to be a purely municipal movement."[53] Therefore, if "we do not exceed this fixed limit of our program the country and the government will be pleased and proud to applaud this revolution which is so grand and straightforward..."[54] His approach became increasingly untenable when the government did not applaud but fired machine guns.

The Jacobin/Blanquist camp had a diametrically opposed viewpoint, but like the Proudhonists, there were moderate and radical factions, with Jacobins to the right and Blanquists to the left. Delescluze, the foremost Jacobin, wrote: "What does Paris want? Paris wants all the freedoms that arise from full sovereignty within a communal system. It has them today and knows how to defend them against any attack... Treated as an enemy, it has to behave like a government by reestablishing basic services and organizing to fight the war that was declared against it..."[55]

The stress here was on constructing a government, rather than pursuing the social reforms so dear to the left Proudhonists.

The Blanquists wanted to go beyond the Jacobin tactic of defense, and take offensive military action. This position was expressed by Da Costa, a Commune official, who was scathing in his criticism of both the Proudhonists and Jacobins. He accused them all of "extraordinary naivety"!

> The Commune's immediate mission was to organize the inevitable war against the upstarts and conspirators at Versailles. In the end, the reality of the situation could not be ignored. Following the example of the Germans, Thiers had formed an army destined to lay siege to Paris. The choice was either to resign oneself to this and beg for his mercy, or fight. There were no other choices. A communal revolution could have been the fruit of victory, but above all else this victory was still to be won...[56]

All reforms, he believed, were therefore a waste of time:

> Is it possible to imagine anything more incoherent, or above all infantile, than setting the diverse commissions of the Paris Commune to work...at a time when questions should have been limited to the organization and maintenance of an armed offensive... The core of the

> International were so unconscious of the circumstances that they thought it useful to advance their extraordinarily simplistic program by *trying to equalize wages and work*... What candor, what tranquillity, what blindness in a council of men who were already threatened by 100,000 rifles...[57]

The Blanquists went so far as to prepare a motion "adjourning all social and democratic reforms" and "entrusting executive power to a Republican Committee of Salvation," but withdrew it, fearing insufficient support.

These deep divisions meant no one could really be happy with the various resolutions and decrees that were passed by the Council. Even when Proudhonists agreed with the principles underlying the decisions (such as the separation of church and state, or the abolition of conscription), they objected to their form: "These decrees, being presented in traditional format, ran the risk of identifying the Commune with the numerous centralized powers that had followed all our revolutions."[58] They felt that "there is nothing more intolerable than that which *decrees* communism..."[59] From the opposite side, Da Costa wrote in his history:

> Poor, poor Commune Assembly! Without any poetic license or any exaggeration, it is perfectly possible (indeed it is expedient and necessary) to recount the active history of the formidable Parisian insurrection, without pausing to consider the idle chatter of the ranters and dreamers who sat at the Hôtel de Ville for two months during an intense revolutionary episode.[60]

Despite the chasm separating the various sides it would be a mistake to think that such disagreements should have been brushed over. Any real democracy is bound to bring alternative points of view forward, and the wider the level of involvement the more likely different views will be aired. In addition, each faction rightly emphasized important elements in the Commune's overall situation. The Jacobins and Blanquists understood the absolute need to physically maintain the power gained in the March 18 revolution. All hopes of social transformation depended on this. The Proudhonists and socialists understood that the revolution (compared, say, to the debacle of the failed La Villette rising of August 1870) relied on the active involvement of the mass of Parisian workers inspired by a vision of a new society. No dictatorship or committee could substitute for them. The difficulty was how to combine the two insights.

The Federals and Their Opponents

If the Commune was unable to reach a consensus, the same could not be said of its opponents. This does not mean that there were no deep divisions in the ruling class. The monarchist wing of the National Assembly detested the moderate republicans; supporters of the Orleanist royal line hated Legitimists who wanted the Bourbons restored; and the Bonapartists resented having been ousted from power by all the others. However, all factions were absolutely united in their determination to finish off the movement in Paris.

This was to be expected from ruling-class warriors like the royalist Thiers, the Bonapartist General Vinoy, or the right-wing historian du Camp who saw the establishment of the Commune as "an evil act that those who had the misfortune to witness it would never forget, and which history had difficulty in comprehending."[61] Yet liberal republicans, who believed in parliamentary democracy, were not to be outdone in their loathing. As the Commune was drowned in blood by the French army, Ferry wrote, "I may be a liberal, a lawyer and a republican, but to my eyes, watching these reprisals is like watching the sword of the archangel."[62] Historians have been surprised that such unity could exist at Versailles:

> What needs to be underlined is that the responsible authorities in question were not legitimist backwoodsmen but liberals, whether Orleanist liberals like Thiers and Dufaure, or republican liberals like Picard and Simon. And perhaps most shocking of all... was the shame-faced inertia of the *gauche republicaine* [republican left] in the face of Versaillais repression. The left remained silent.[63]

It was clear that the division between Versailles and Paris was over more than whether or not to have municipal rights or state centralism, a republic or a monarchy, parliamentary democracy or dictatorship. The dividing line was an unbridgeable social one—between capitalism and socialism.

While the revolutionaries bent over backward to avoid war, their enemies, as a body, rejected any steps toward compromise. Conciliators, said Dufaure: "are not the enemies of a particular government, but of all human society... You must not hesitate to bring them to justice. Do not be deterred because they make a show of conciliation... It accustoms people to judge on equal terms a legal order and an insurrection..."[64]

The government no longer showed the hesitation it exhibited during the war against Germany. Favre was obsessed by the urgent need to smash the Commune and he fawned, pleaded and begged his German "enemy" to release prisoners of war to help rebuild France's shattered national army. In letters to Bismarck, Germany's Iron Chancellor, Favre offered up the blood of his fellow countrymen: "My intentions and those of the government cannot be doubted for an instant. What we are doing speaks clearly of our determination to finish with the insurrection. Yesterday we attacked Issy [fort], with 48 cannons. We continued all night and all day. We will crush it. We will take Paris by force. Thus we prove our good faith and our energy."[65]

At the end of May, Favre reveled in the knowledge that "the hour of supreme punishment was sounding. This time, the assurances, that I had so often given Mr. von Bismarck of the certainty of our victory, were going to be a reality at last."[66]

The army, which had refused to shoot its sisters on the heights of Montmartre, was gradually remolded by a mixture of terror and greed. Vinoy issued orders on dealing with troops who were over-sympathetic to Paris: "I again request that all soldiers, Mobiles or sailors taken in the ranks of the insurgents are treated according to the laws of war, that is to say, executed immediately by firing squad... These men must be considered as deserters to the enemy and consequently shot on the spot."[67]

Germany returned enough prisoners to be able to rebuild the officer corps and the lower ranks.

What was the balance of forces between Versailles and Paris at this juncture? There were several factors working in favor of Paris. It was well armed, with 1,200 cannons[68] as well as a "formidable system of forts, trenches and ramparts protecting Paris to the south and west...heavy artillery, gunboats and armored trains..."[69] In early March 1871, the National Guard claimed 200,000 armed men, while under the armistice the French government were theoretically only entitled to 12,000, rising to 40,000 by German agreement thereafter.[70] However, these proportions did not remain constant. Versailles's forces climbed while the official number of Federals fell. Half of the National Guard were in put into the reserves[71] while the figure for combat units was 50,000. By Bloody Week at the end of May those who performed active service were no more than 15,000.[73]

There is no doubt that the Commune faced huge technical problems, but the basic difficulty was ideological. Clausewitz, the great military theoretician, famously remarked that "war is politics by other means." Other revolutions in history generated successful military campaigns against overwhelming odds, the most important examples being France after 1789, and Bolshevik Russia during its civil war of 1918 to 1921. In both cases victory depended on fusing popular enthusiasm for the social goals of the revolution with the military campaign itself. In the Paris Commune this fusion was not going to be achieved easily. The Jacobins and Blanquists saw military issues as independent of and taking precedence over the vision of a different society. Conversely, the Proudhonist wing hoped the military questions could be wished away by the "moral power and intellectual influence" that Paris could exert over the rest of France.[74]

Though the issues of social goals and winning the war were linked, they were not identical. Specific military strategies still had to be considered in their own right. For Paris to succeed against Versailles, it had to coordinate the actions of thousands of individuals, and combine them together into an effective force. There was no alternative. Guerrilla-style warfare—a dispersed command structure or autonomous units acting on their own initiative—can sometimes have an impact, especially where there is a lot of space, and hit-and-run operations can be mounted. Guerrilla fighters can merge back into the population or the jungle from whence they came. In the confined conditions of a single city where every working-class person is a target, such tactics could not work. In other words, discipline under a centralized command was absolutely vital to mold a fighting force out of the workers of Paris. This was not some optional extra, or a reprehensible manifestation of "authority." It was literally a matter of life or death.

However, the sort of internal order that was needed should not be confused with the unthinking drilling, bullying and blind obedience used in the national armies we see today. Here young men are trained not to think or question orders. Under the Commune discipline could not come from the rod, but from enthusiasm for the cause, and an understanding that only by acting as a collective force could victory be won.[75] As we shall see, there were many attempts to instill such discipline into Federal forces, but they failed.

The reason for this partly comes down to individuals. Unfortunately, the Central Committee appointed Lullier, who Lissagaray describes as a "crack-brained alcoholic,"[76] as commander in chief. Lullier shared the common expectation that war was unlikely and that preparations for it were therefore unnecessary. He allowed the French army to withdraw its forces to

Versailles unhindered. The chance to spread disaffection in the ranks was ignored. Army commanders were alive to this danger themselves. Such was their fear of revolutionary contagion that any soldiers overheard discussing politics were punished,[77] and rather than risk the slow process of a court-martial they were shipped off to Algeria.[78] In time the Commune's open, direct democracy would have selected more effective leaders from their midst, but it did not survive long enough for this to occur.[79]

Another dangerous omission of Lullier's was his failure to take control of the strategic fortress of Mont Valérien located to the west, halfway to Versailles. Whoever controlled Mont Valérien could launch devastating attacks on their enemy. The fort was empty after March 18, and it was not until the evening of March 21 that Lullier sent Federals to occupy it. They were too late, as Versailles forces had just moved in. It is no exaggeration to say that this transformed the strategic prospects for both sides.

So Paris was on the defensive from the start. The first shots were fired by Versailles in telling circumstances. At 11am on April 2, 1871, Federals encountered two brigades from Versailles at the Neuilly bridge west of Paris. The official account says, "The National Guards, hoping to fraternize, advanced, but were met by a discharge of fire at almost point-blank range."[80] In Paris, Lissagaray tells us, "so completely did all, since the 28th, live in an atmosphere of confidence [that they thought] it was a misunderstanding at the utmost."[81]

When news arrived that Versailles was regularly shooting prisoners of war in cold blood, this sanguine attitude evaporated. The response from Paris demonstrated the extraordinary revolutionary enthusiasm that prevailed, but, alas, also the limitations of enthusiasm without effective coordination. During the night of April 2/3 more than 40,000 people, with few weapons, artillery or supplies, poured out to the west. Ferocious cannon fire from Mont Valérien dented the advance and eventually scattered the insurgent force in panic and confusion. In the rout Flourens, the popular and "irrepressible battle-worn fighter for the liberty of Crete, and hero of the Universal Republic" was captured, and while under guard, had his head cleaved in two by a saber blow.[82] The most notorious butcher to emerge from the civil war was the Versailles general the Marquis de Galliffet. He now warned that "in this war there can be no truce and no pity."[83]

In the capital the need for a well-led military effort was now more widely accepted. Who should organize this? There were two obvious contenders—the National Guard Central Committee, and the Communal Council. A tussle between the two bodies ensued. The National Guard Central Committee felt the civil war was its prerogative, while the Communal Council should deal with civil affairs. Having held authority in the wake of the March 18 revolution, it also regarded itself as the elder partner with rights to oversee the Communal Council, its own creation.[84] For its part, the council thought it should control the military effort as it had been elected to lead the Commune by the wider population.

A complicating factor was the fundamental issue of whether the military campaign should reflect direct democracy from below, or centralized military direction from above. Some saw the Central Committee as representing the former, and the council the latter. Thus Proudhonists like Lefrançais believed the Central Committee was a guarantee "that public power could not become an instrument in the service of those ambitious for power..."[85] Against this, others protested that only the Communal Council, as a supreme authority for all Paris, could organize an effective defense.

Relations had not always been so strained. At the outset the Central Committee had accepted the Communal Council as "the sole legitimate authority" and promised to "act in concert" with it.[86] This harmony broke down when council members proposed the Central Committee be dissolved.[87] In defiance the Central Committee renewed its mandate through new guard elections[88] and imposed General Cluseret as the Commune's War Delegate, despite council doubts.[89] The council retaliated by trying to dissolve the National Guard's locally elected bodies—the Legion Councils. When this move was blocked,[90] a Communal Council member proposed arresting Legion members.[91]

In exasperation at the mess the Central Committee tried to wrest total control of the war effort for itself:

> We have decided, finally, that if the Commune does not give us these things, we will take further steps. We would remind the Council that it is not the government but simply the *communal* (i.e., municipal) *administration*, and that the National Guard, represented by us, is the only rightful resistance force in Paris. In other words, we, the men of March 18, are acting in a revolutionary manner and taking back the revolution that we made.[92]

The final result of this competition for control was deadlock. The Communal Council complained they could find only 6,000 men to fight

Versailles outside the city walls and yet, as one member put it, "the Legion commanders can find 10,000 men to overthrow the Commune. I say that that is an act of treason."[93] Yet it was not the case that the Central Committee had everything in hand, either. It too was far from fully controlling the ranks of the Federals. It confessed that "the [Legions]... act in a very independent manner, and although we have no intention of condoning such behavior...we are completely powerless to stop them."[94]

A terrifying example of the chaotic state of affairs was that, despite strenuous efforts, none of the War Delegates was ever able to bring the Commune's artillery under one command, or even discover the exact number available. Each National Guard Legion claimed exclusive authority over the cannons in its arrondissement.[95] Thus by the end of May it could plausibly be argued that Federal forces were receiving orders from no less than seven different sources—the Communal Council, the Delegate for War, a Military Commission, a variety of civil commissioners and generals (themselves acting with little coordination), General HQ, and the National Guard Central Committee![96] Additionally, many of the units did what they wanted anyway.[97]

Each of the conflicting elements was driven by different imperatives. The rank-and file-guards' outlook was influenced primarily by their own immediate situation. This was a very different starting point to that of the Communal Council, which felt responsible for affairs overall. Equally, there was a difference between civil and military institutions, between immediate economic issues and long-term strategic political aims, and between local democracy and centralism. These differences could not be ignored, but could they be transcended? Could there be a vision that combined the strengths in the situation created after March 18: the self-confidence and mass initiatives from below, and the creation of a working class power at the summit? Alas, a solution could not be found in time.

The War Delegates

It was the unenviable task of the Commune's War Delegates to try and give some sort of coherent shape to its military effort. Like the leading bodies of the Commune, military strategy went through a number of phases. The first was sheer confusion under Lullier. Then followed the brief incumbency of Eudes, after which General Cluseret was appointed.

He had recent experience of senior command supporting the North in the American Civil War. Cluseret's policy was defensive and based on the notion that the Commune could not defeat Versailles, but could hold out long enough to enable the provinces to intervene in favor of a compromise.[98] Later on Rossel would attempt an offensive strategy without success. Finally, Delescluze would summon up popular initiative in a last desperate fight for survival.

Returning to Cluseret, there was a problem with the communal movement adopting his defensive approach. The pitfalls had been outlined by Danton, a leader of the Great Revolution, who famously declared that a successful revolution required "audacity, audacity, and more audacity." Victory therefore depended less on the mathematical counting of people and weapons than on the mass psychology of both sides. In the situation of 1871 offensive action by the communards could have spread uncertainty and disaffection among the still hesitant Versailles forces. At the same time it might have restored self-confidence in the rank-and-file National Guards, and shown the benefits of unified action. The provinces were unlikely to take an active part in supporting Paris unless they were convinced the Commune was a real and serious challenge to Versailles. Caution had the opposite effect. It emboldened the French army generals to order ever more outrageous acts of barbarity against the Federals. It meant individual guard units were less trusting of the centralized leadership, and more unwilling to risk their equipment and their lives to follow its orders. Disorganization and internal disputes therefore tended to grow.[99]

Cluseret tried hard to fashion the National Guard into a conventional force. He began by calling up unmarried men ages 17 to 35 for combat battalions,[100] the rest being put into "sedentary" (reserve) units. The exclusion of older and married men was criticized by some for damaging popular unity: "We could only struggle by relying on popular enthusiasm, on the good will of devoted citizens convinced that they should risk their lives in the communal cause."[101] For the same reason compulsory service proved to be unenforceable as in practice only volunteers would fight.[102] Cluseret had more success in building up a military administration for ammunition and food. He also managed to bring in a layer of officers with combat experience, though at the expense of political activists. He was soon compelled to combat the consequences. In an article entitled "Too Much Braid" Cluseret ridiculed the fashion for fancy uniforms and ribbons: "Do not deny our origins; do not be ashamed of them. Workers we were, workers we are and workers we will stay."[103]

Cluseret was ousted on April 30. Only the day before, he personally led the recapture of Issy Fort, which had been abandoned as a lost cause by its communard governor. Issy was a vital post that had been the center of fierce fighting for weeks. Against the odds Cluseret and a handful of men reached the fort, and when they entered they discovered a weeping boy of about 16 sitting on a powder keg that he expected he would have to ignite when the Versailles troops arrived.[104] As Lissagaray noted, in being dismissed Cluseret paid for the failure of his idea "that firmness and a few weeks of exercises would be enough to transform the National Guard into a regular army... The spirit of this institution was completely in opposition to the rules of ordinary discipline..."[105]

The next War Delegate was Rossel, a junior officer who had fought in the Franco-Prussian war. Rossel's strength was his acute awareness of the problems of disorganization and the need for an offensive policy.[106] Yet his method showed little understanding of the politics of the situation. He admitted he was not a socialist and said, "I am putting myself at the service of the Parisian revolution [because] I support the side which has refused to capitulate to the foreigner."[107] He had a negative view of the National Guards: "They panicked on numerous occasions. It was the most perfect disorder..."[108] Rossel concluded: "Success was impossible as long as the troops were not obedient and could sneak out of their military duties. We had failed to give the National Guard a stable organization, which would have been the best remedy. All that was left to try was repression and it had to be real and swift."[109]

Later on, writing from his cell after being sentenced to death by a Versailles court-martial, Rossel would realize that during his tenure as War Delegate he had expected too much: "The transition was too hurried."[110]

Rossel's appointment coincided with the conflict between the National Guard Central Committee and the Communal Council recounted above. He thought the former "was absolutely incapable of organizing anything"[111] and planned to seize control of the National Guard. The Federals would be housed in barracks, and deserters shot. Conscripts would be press-ganged, and the election of officers abolished. If Rossel had only made enemies of the Central Committee he might have survived for longer. However, he also rebuked the Communal Council for interfering with his running of the war: "Each sphere must stick to its own competence... You cannot have a situation where everyone thinks they are soldiers."[112] He was ready to go further than words, and even considered carrying out a coup against the Communal Council under the slogan "Save the revolution by terminating the Commune."[113]

Rossel's tenure at the war ministry lasted little over a week. On May 9 he sent a letter of resignation to the Communal Council complaining of insurmountable disorder among the Federal forces. He had summoned troops for an offensive, and 12,000 had been promised. In the end only 7,000 turned up, for which he blamed the Legion commanders: "Now I am not a man to step back from repression and yesterday, while the Legion commanders were meeting, a firing squad was waiting for them in the courtyard. But I do not want to take the initiative for such a measure all alone... My predecessor made the mistake of struggling on in the middle of this absurd situation."

The letter hinted at the coup idea, but having backed away from it he now accepted the consequences of his position: "I had two alternatives: either to break through the obstacle blocking my action or resign. I will not break through the obstacle, because the obstacle is you, and I do not want to overthrow popular sovereignty. Therefore I resign and have the honor of requesting a cell at Mazas prison."[114]

His wish was granted.

When this letter was being published news came through that Issy Fort had finally been taken by Versailles. Maury, a rather nonpolitical rank-and-file guardsman, explains the background to the serious loss, and gives us a good picture of the situation inside the Federal forces. He recounts that whenever his battalion was called up "a fair number were missing. So it always fell to the same people to report for duty... Many felt things were being made a mess of, especially those who could manage without the 30 centimes and the welfare handouts. In the end the only ones who marched were the needy, fanatics and curious people like myself."[115] Soon even Maury's commander did not appear: "I was told he had judged it more prudent to stay at home."[116] At the clubs guards were now accused of cowardice for not fighting:

> Many were stung by the accusation and insisted on marching into battle. So the commander was eventually tracked down to obtain precise orders. His reply to us was that, first of all, an entirely new headquarters had to

> be voted in, and once this was done we would be organized to go on the offensive. (What a lot of time was lost in these formalities!)... He promised to lead the battalion out the next day. This did not please me really, as I felt things were going from bad to worse, and it would be futile. So from that moment I took the decision that, with such leadership, I would not bother to report for duty any more... The next day, when the battalion was called up, I didn't budge and let it go off without me.[117]

Maury's unit was marching off to the crucial last battle to defend Issy Fort before it was captured by Versailles.

Commanders with a military background had failed to fashion an effective defense, so Rossel's replacement as War Delegate was a civilian. Charles Delescluze was a veteran Jacobin whose health had been ravaged by long confinement on Devil's Island. A tragic figure who knew he had only a few months to live,[118] he nevertheless accepted the onerous post, out of an overpowering sense of duty. His predecessors had concentrated on discipline, to the exclusion of politics, but Delescluze reversed the equation. This was his acceptance speech:

> You know that the situation is grave. A lot of your generously given blood has already been shed, because of the conspiracy of feudalists and the dregs of royal regimes. I deplore these painful losses and know we may not live to reap what we have sown. Yet, when I think of the sublime future that awaits your children, I enthusiastically salute the March 18 revolution all over again... You know that you are fighting for your liberty, and for social equality, these promises that have eluded you for so long... The whole world is watching you and applauding your great-hearted efforts. It is ready to celebrate your triumph, which means the salvation of all the peoples. Long live the Universal Republic! Long live the Commune![119]

Since discipline could not be established in the short term, Delescluze decided to harness "the power of revolutionary feeling in the Commune to save the country."[120] Alas, Delescluze was no more successful than previous War Delegates, because enthusiasm without organization could be no more effective than organization without enthusiasm.

These awful problems should not be allowed to obscure the real strengths the Federals possessed. Direct democracy was the basis of the communal movement, and it had created an embryonic workers' state, without which the defeat of capitalism and creation of a new society could not have been attempted. A description of the platoon defending the Hôtel de Ville brings out the National Guards' unique qualities: "It was remarkable to see that all the National Guards that I saw were peering at open newspapers and reading them with passion. This first observation alone would be sufficient to prove that these people were not soldiers in the service of authority, but volunteers for the revolution."[121]

What conventional army can boast such a politically literate and involved membership? The Federals may have lost organizational cohesion as time passed, but on March 18 they had held together when the government's army completely fell apart. Numerous commentators also testified to their bravery and heroism on many later occasions.[122] The problem was lack of ideological clarity and absence of good leadership, not lack of commitment.

Indeed, for a long period the forces of Versailles could make little impact on Paris and had to "undertake a slow and tedious siege, digging miles of trenches and bombarding the forts and ramparts."[123] A contemporary eyewitness celebrated the Vengeurs de Flourens, who "for more than a month battled over every inch of the streets of Neuilly, against the ferocious Foreign Legion. Now, these brave youth had an average age of 15 to 18 years." He mentioned "the modest National Guard, Auguste Joulon," of the 177th Batallion who had four young sons serving in the ranks, and who convinced Delescluze to accept his youngest, who had just turned 15.[124] The desperate plight of the Federals made their fight against Versailles all the more heroic. As Lissagaray wrote, they were a "core of men, without cohesion or effective officers, without an HQ, without supplies, without discipline, who stopped the famous army of Mr. Thiers for two months."[125]

The population were not impervious to the problems. One reaction could be a retreat into apathy, as in the case of Maury. Anger was another outcome. At the start of the Commune one left-wing newspaper editorial said, "I give you, citizens of the Commune...an immense unlimited trust." A few issues later the tone had changed: "What a mess! The Commune arrests a commander in chief every week... You are causing disasters."[126] Disillusionment grew ever wider, as this diary entry shows:

> Our National Guards fight for the Commune with an unexpected perseverance, with an astonishing bravery... We, simple citizens, do not know what is going on in the mysterious backrooms and only watch the spectacle as observers. We don't take sides, either for the Central Committee or for the Commune, either for this or for that individual... [But] in such

> a terrible crisis, when the country, indeed more than the country—the idea—is in danger, there must be no petty distractions.[127]

The diary went on to discuss the fighting at Neuilly, just outside the walls of Paris and under heavy Versailles attack:

> For 22 days they have been under cannon-fire and bombardment, suffering under a hail of machine-gun bullets. Their homes have been turned into military posts and barricades. Snipers fire from their windows. Night and day men murder each other, or have their guts ripped out by bayonets. Women, old people and children have their ordinary daily lives disrupted by the intrusion of the civil war. They mostly have to hide in their cellars, and are deafened by the din of the shells that often bring their homes tumbling down upon their heads. They live in the midst of this slaughter. The very air they breathe is that of a charnel house or an abattoir. Sometimes streams of blood run down the stairwells. Entire families have starved to death... Those who have seen this with their own eyes in Paris will no longer speak with a smile about progress, enlightenment, or the triumph of civilization.[128]

The Home Front: Freedom versus Authority

The Communal Council first sat on March 28, and enjoyed only four days of peace. The outbreak of the civil war not only raised the issue of centralized leadership versus democracy from below in the military sphere, but also in relation to the Commune's internal regime. How free should it be? Modern neoliberals, like their nineteenth-century forebears, throw the words "freedom" and "liberty" around like confetti. They want the market system to be free, so that the rich can ride roughshod over the poor. They want liberty for powerful state machines to oppress the weak.

The Commune approached the issue in a quite different way. The revolution had to be protected from the Versailles counterattack, but how far could the Commune constrain its enemies without interfering with the very liberties it stood for? This problem emerged early on in discussions over whether to publish the council's minutes. Current parliamentary democracies are comfortable with open reporting. Such talking shops would lack a reason to exist if no one outside knew what was being said, and anyway the real decisions are made outside of public scrutiny (in boardrooms, stock markets and closed cabinets). However, the Commune was both an executive *and* a representative body, the center of a democratic working-class revolution *and* a war cabinet. This created a real predicament for the Commune.

On one side was the Jacobin/Blanquist view that: "The Commune is, at this moment, not a parliamentary chamber. It is a council of war. In the armed struggle how could we let the enemy into a council of war? How can we discuss in front of them the choice of generals, the resourcing of the army, the plan of attack, etc.?"[129]

Those from the Proudhonist tradition believed that secret sessions denied the concept of "government of the people by the people" and they were "absolutely opposed to this on principle."[130] Without publicity the Commune could not maintain "the enthusiasm of the people."[131] Eventually it was decided not to publish minutes.[132]

The dilemma was that both sides had a point. Openness and mass involvement in political life were vital ingredients for victory, but strategic military discussions and their outcomes could not be aired publicly, as the enemy would learn of them. A middle position—the publishing of all but nonsensitive matters—might have been found if all assembly members had trusted those in charge of military and security measures to be acting in the interests of working-class democracy. Alas, such trust did not exist. The Proudhonists suspected Jacobins/Blanquists of dictatorial ambitions, while the latter suspected the former of rejecting any centralized leadership at all.

The division over whether or not to make public Communal Council proceedings reappeared in regard to press freedom. Even a Proudhonist like Arnould accepted that: "The circumstances were terrible. We were right in the middle of a war and ambushed from all sides. The newspapers (which were almost all in the hands of the bourgeoisie and were organs for Versailles), showed no restraint in calling for the destruction of the Commune. They applauded our defeats and insulted the Federals."[133]

Yet, when certain newspapers were censored, he objected to the infringement of free speech as this "compromised" the Commune.[134] Another Proudhonist demanded that "editors have the greatest liberty to verbally attack the members of the Commune if it suited them."[135] The Proudhonists did put forward alternatives. One was that all papers apart from the *Journal Officiel*, the Commune's official voice, should be banned until the war was won. The problem was this put the extensive revolutionary press on a par with those of Versailles, and would have silenced the very people who needed to be free to discuss and debate the best way forward. The counterblast from Delescluze was simple and direct: "We are criticized for banning papers, but we are at war!"[136]

Who was right? Under capitalism free speech is largely a myth. Before 1871 the capitalists had voiced no objection when left-wing papers were banned. Today, when free speech formally exists, wealthy capitalists like Murdoch control the media and use it to support their system. Equality of expression can only be realized in a society where economic equality exists. In the battle for such a society, the bosses' control of the media and their freedom to use it as a mouthpiece for capitalism must be challenged, along with their economic and political power. In 1871 it was notable that the workers' clubs most clearly demanded strong censorship. So it was right that the Commune eventually acted to silence saboteurs in its midst. The establishment media was directly aiding the murderous forces of Thiers.

The Middle Class under the Commune

How successful was the right-wing press campaign in whipping up anti-communard feeling? Opposition to the Commune within Paris was led by Vice-Admiral Saisset who styled himself the "provisional commander in chief" of the National Guard.[137] Saisset declared, "I will give my life for property."[138] On March 24 he issued a proclamation falsely claiming that all the capital's demands for self-government had been met.[139] He then led a demonstration of "dandies, petty squires, journalists, notorious familiars of the Empire"[140] through Paris under the banner of the Society of the Friends of Order. The fact that this demonstration was permitted emboldened Saisset to hold another march that attracted some 8,000 people.[141] The Commune's indulgence had been interpreted as weakness, and the protesters tried to force their way through to the Hôtel de Ville, killing two National Guards in the process. The latter fought back and a dozen demonstrators died.[142] This was the end of Saisset's campaign.

He did not represent all middle-class Parisians. Workers were not the only people whose imaginations fired were by the March 18 revolution. The middle class is a layer caught between the ruling class and the working class. Squeezed from above, but fearing absorption into the mass of workers below, it can ally itself with one side or the other. In 1789, the middle class backed revolution; in 1930s Germany, it provided the social base for Nazi counterrevolution. During March 1871, however, many middle-class Parisians turned to the Commune.

Thus the grandly titled Republican Union League for the Rights of Paris sternly criticized Versailles for rejecting the capital's demands and spilling blood.[143] More surprising was the stance of the largest business organization, the National Union of Commerce and Industry, which represented 6,000 enterprises. After the events of March 18, 1871, it issued an address acclaiming: "the greatest revolution [Paris] has ever undertaken, for it represents an affirmation of the Republic and of the will to defend it... Why not give these new institutions sanctioned by the votes of our fellow citizens a real chance? Whatever happens, France will never have to pay what the old order of things has just cost us."[144]

The most eloquent gesture was made by Freemasons who ascended the ramparts of the city to plant their masonic standards, despite the risk of being killed by Versailles' cannons. They saluted the Commune:

> In the name of Liberty, Equality and Fraternity—this sacred emblem delivered to the world 80 years ago, whose supporters work for the Revolution and guarantee its triumph. Brothers, let us march! Our flag is now in place. We will defend it! May our throats be cut, and our entrails ripped open, rather than let it be dishonored! With arms in our hands let us obliterate these miserable and perfidious organizations which are killing society, are killing France, and want to kill the revolution.[145]

Socialism is sometimes portrayed as narrow, and only attractive to the manual working class; 1871 showed that the vision of an alternative society without exploitation fired the imaginations of wide layers of the population. Yet, middle class or working class, it mattered little to Thiers. The Freemasons' pleas for peace were met by heavy shelling. A diarist wrote that "never during the siege [by Prussia] was the din of the bombardment so deafening or so ferocious. In the whole population indignation was matched by sorrow."[146]

The Hostage Decree

The issue of freedom versus authority arose in a sharp form over the question of revolutionary violence. On March 18, 1871, the only victims on the Versailles side were two generals who were captured and held at a house on the Rue des Rosiers. Before the Central Committee could assert its authority a crowd entered the house and shot them.[147] General

Clément-Thomas was remembered for butchering workers in the June 1848 uprising. General Lecomte had ordered troops to fire at the people of Montmartre that day. Compared to the bloodshed perpetrated against the working class, the insurgents were right to say that the March 18 uprising would "remain one of the most beautiful pages in our history. It is the first time that the working class has entered the political scene... We must say loud and clear that it was done with less loss of blood than any other revolution."[148] The Paris Commune, that first example of a successful workers' seizure of power, disproves the accusation that revolution means high levels of violence, as it was accomplished with a minimum of bloodshed. As has been the case in every workers' revolution, large-scale killing only occurs when the ruling class retaliates to regain its power.[149]

Nevertheless, when Versailles began routinely slaughtering any Federals taken prisoner,[150] the Commune decided to take counter-measures. A decree was passed whereby those judged by a jury to be "complicitous with the government of Versailles" were to be held hostage and executed if there were any further shootings of Federal prisoners. This seemed to work, as Versailles stopped its massacres after the decree was adopted.[151] The effect wore off when the threat against the hostages proved hollow. In fact, between April 3 and May 23, two days after Versailles' forces began their killing spree inside the walls of Paris, not a single prisoner was executed or hostage harmed.[152]

Did the hostage decree place the Commune on the same level as Versailles? Pacifists see political violence in black and white terms, as an issue of individual morality which makes all aggression, from whatever source, inexcusable. Unfortunately, the ruling class has never used this moral yardstick: its only concern in practice is what best preserves strategic interests and profits. It would not hesitate about employing horrendous violence against the Commune. The revolutionaries' caution in implementing the hostage decree was motivated by humanitarian concerns, but it also reflected a hesitation about taking measures to protect the revolution to their logical conclusion.

The Commune and the Issue of "Terror"

During the Commune and for long afterward Versailles entertained a shocked bourgeois world with horrific tales of its unbridled, ferocious and terrorist police regime. The bogeyman in this drama was Raoul Rigault, a 25-year-old Blanquist. He had carefully studied the Empire's law enforcement system, and was installed at the Prefecture of Police, now renamed the "ex-Prefecture."

The very existence of police (or "ex-police") was anathema to Proudhonists who, as libertarians, saw Rigault and his men as "having fallen victim to the always baleful error of believing that the enemies of the Commune should be made afraid."[153] Proudhonists believed the police "must be abolished" and an alternative force "must be created by the citizens of each area, in each arrondissement and community."[154] Laudable though this aim was in the longer term, Rigault argued that strict measures against opponents were needed straight away in order to win the civil war. A revealing exchange of views is presented in his biography:

> "We always said that we would abolish the Prefecture of Police," insisted [the Proudhonists].
>
> "Do you think that this is the right time?" said Rigault, drawing himself up, his gaze smoldering behind his glasses. "Thiers has a thousand spies in Paris. Should we let them get on with their work in peace?"
>
> "What about the sacred principles of democracy?"
>
> "I don't care a damn about them,' said Rigault, cutting them short. 'If you abolish the police service you might as well open the gates to the Versailles army."[155]

Indeed there were many covert supporters of Versailles in the capital. While many plots failed, one spy—Ducatel, gave the signal that enabled the army to enter Paris on May 21.

Although Rigault declared, "I do not do justice, I do the revolution,"[156] he was not the bloodthirsty demon depicted by Versailles. In fact repressive actions were limited, because, as he told the Communal Council, "I would prefer to let guilty people go than to persecute an innocent person."[157] The first trial of hostages for "complicity with Versailles" began on May 19. Rigault's biography tells us:

> The accused consisted of four junior officers from the gendarmerie. Yes, you read it correctly: four, just four. This was communard terror at a time when Versailles executed all the Federals that fell into its hands without any form of trial... The jury deliberated and brought in its verdict: three of those charged were considered hostages and kept under detention, the fourth was declared innocent and liberated on the spot. This was the revolutionary terror in 1871![158]

Reversion to the Terror of the Great Revolution was advocated by many ordinary Parisians in the clubs to keep down opponents of the Commune,[159] and if Rigault is criticized, it should not be so much for repression employed, but rather for the Blanquist and elitist manner by which it was carried out. A classic example of how this could backfire was when he ordered guards to seize the Bank of France on May 12, 1871, the background to which is worth studying.

The Bank of France was privately owned by the great financiers, and was a key institution of capitalism, as well as the foundation of the state's monetary system.[160] Although the Commune began boldly in the financial field, by sequestering the assets of five major insurance companies,[161] until Rigault's action it had stopped short of seizing the bank itself. Beslay had asked that the bank: "should be respected as private property belonging to the shareholders, and as the state establishment with the right to issue bank notes as currency... My mission was, above all, to safeguard public confidence so any thought of violence or pressure was removed."[162]

Perhaps such language could be expected from a moderate Proudhonist like Beslay. However, his approach was not challenged by Jourde, the left Proudhonist Delegate for Finances, or Varlin, his assistant. Jourde summed up his approach like this: "I have come to the Commune to say, 'Don't touch public credit, it is a delicate thing.'"[163] At the Communal Council Jourde was accused of "speaking like a model cashier, not like the Minister of Finance of the Commune."[164] However, when he offered to resign it was refused.

Failure to seize the bank's assets was a lost opportunity. When the Commune's accounts were presented on May 2, 1871, it emerged that 25 million francs had been spent, of which fully 21 million went to the war drive. By contrast just 1,000 francs could be spared for education![165] During its lifespan the Commune withdrew only the 9 million francs Paris had already deposited at the Bank,[166] plus an extra 700,000 francs for National Guard salaries.[167] Yet the Bank of France was awash with cash: 3,000 million francs in assets were there for the taking.[168] Lissagaray would wryly point out that the Proudhonists were "forgetting that their master put the suppression of the bank at the head of his revolutionary program."[169]

As in the case of the Bank of France, the Commune held back from exercising its authority over the stock exchange or Bourse. After March 18 businessmen feared the worst and share values plunged by 10 percent immediately.[170] An eyewitness reported this scene: "They said with sighs:

'You remember the premiums? In former times...huge pocket-books were so well filled that they nearly burst; but now we wander amidst the ruins of our defunct splendour.'" However, when the Commune left the stock exchange unmolested while Versailles mounted a vigorous assault, the stockbrokers' confidence returned. They welcomed the "bombardment, followed by a successful attack, seven or eight houses set on fire by the Versailles shells, seven or eight hundred Federals shot, a few women blown to pieces, and a few children killed..."[171] Shares bounced back and reached their former levels.[172]

The French government's attitude to finance was entirely different from the Commune's. It did not flinch from indelicate treatment of public credit. As soon as Thiers arrived at Versailles, he summoned the governor of the Bank of France and declared, "I have you, and I am keeping you... Give me money, more money. Without that all is lost." While the Commune collected little more than its own 9 million francs, the bank disbursed nearly 250 million to Thiers.[173]

This situation, therefore, was what motivated Rigault's decision to take over the Bank of France. However, he acted "without consulting anyone, neither the Commune, nor the Committee of Public Safety. It was a secret commando operation."[174] His move therefore lacked any political legitimacy, and Beslay was able to overturn it easily.[175]

The Commune's much-vaunted terror paled against Thiers's measures. In addition to the mass shooting of captured Federals, Versailles' spies fanned out across the country. All newspapers coming out of the capital were seized and burnt. All letters and correspondence were blocked, and anyone leaving Paris was interrogated. A secret decree ordered that:

> Hotels are to be kept under constant watch, their owners checked, their guests' names inscribed in the police register, and the town hall register is to be forwarded to the police commissariat or gendarmerie. Strangers to an area who are given accommodation in hostels are to be brought to the immediate attention of the town hall. All guesthouses, coffee houses and inns are to be watched. Care must be taken that no Parisian newspapers are read there.[176]

The Committee of Public Safety

The leading bodies of the Commune were in constant flux. It was restructured no less than four times in 72 days, with the National Guard Central Committee replaced by the Communal Council, and then by two Committees of Public Safety in succession. The establishment of the first Committee of Public Safety, a body whose name harked back to 1792, opened the third phase of the Commune and created a very serious split. A proposal for this five-strong leadership committee was put to the Communal Council on April 28, 1871, and reflected widespread frustration with the existing arrangements. The mover wanted to see the new entity take "the widest powers," and be able to enact "the most radical and energetic measures." The Committee of Public Safety would assume all the functions previously performed by the various Commune commissions.[177]

Forty-five Communal Assembly members voted in favor of the committee, and 23 against.[178] Their varying attitudes were set out in signed statements. Here are a few examples. Those in favor argued as follows:

> Ranvier: A month's indecision has compromised us...
> Pottier: The situation demands energy and unity of action. Despite its title I vote in favor.
> Opponents wrote:
> Vermorel: I do not believe that mere words such as "Committee of Public Safety" are effective. The people have paid too long for mere words.
> Clémence: I consider that its establishment [is] an attack on the rights that the Commune members have been given by their electors.
> Longuet: Not believing that we can be saved by words any more than talismans or amulets I vote against...[179]

Many commentators, at the time and since, have seen the issue as representing a split between the majority of "revolutionaries" (i.e., Jacobins and Blanquists), tied to the tradition of 1792–93, and a minority of "socialists" or libertarian federalists of the Proudhonist school. However, the situation was not straightforward. Members of the International were mostly Proudhonists and so might have been expected to steadfastly oppose the Committee. In fact, five abstained, 22 voted for and 13 against.[180] Equally surprising was the presence of Gustave Tridon, a longstanding and committed Blanquist, in the minority camp.

The debate over how best to fight Versailles, whether to emphasize centralized direction or local initiative, freedom or authority, suffused discussion on the Committee of Public Safety. These differences were present even though both sides had come to accept that firm action was needed. The accumulation of dissatisfaction gave the row a deep bitterness. Divisions peaked on May 15, the day the minority planned to read out a protest statement to the council. That course of action became impossible when the minority arrived to find the debating chamber empty.[181] They searched the Hôtel de Ville and found the majority in full session elsewhere.[182]

Furious, the minority publicly withdrew from the Communal Council and printed a statement to that effect:

> The Paris Commune has surrendered its authority to a dictatorship, to which it has given the name of Committee of Public Safety... Like the majority, we too want political and social renovation. However, on behalf of the voters we represent, we insist on being fully accountable for our actions to the electorate. Unlike the majority, we do not hide behind a dictatorship that the electorate have not authorized us to accept or to recognize... Therefore we will no longer appear at the council... We shall spend whatever time our respective arrondissement duties leave us among our brothers of the National Guard, and will play our part in the decisive battles being waged for the rights of the people.[183]

The majority was angered by this public denunciation in the midst of a crisis, and in intemperate terms threatened to "strike the minority down,"[184] because they "may be leading us into a civil war" within the Commune itself.[185]

In the event, the Committee of Public Safety performed no better than the Communal Council. The loss of Issy Fort led Delescluze to denounce the new institution: "The population of Paris sees the Committee of Public Safety as a weapon of war, a sharp axe. But your committee has been annihilated and crushed under the memories of the past it bears... It is just words!"[186] A second Committee of Public Safety, sitting in permanent session, was then established. By now the role of the Communal Council was considerably reduced. It met just three times a week instead of daily[187] and its members wondered aloud whether they had any further role. "We might as well not meet at all," said one.[188]

While the majority stressed the need for centralized decision making at the expense of grassroots democracy, the minority, by visibly walking away from the Communal Council, underestimated the need for unity at a time of crisis. Leading members of the latter faction subsequently recognized this to be an error. One of them confessed that they "did not fully realize the imminence of the danger. [Even if] essential principles were at stake...our appeal came too late to be heard by the people who were then fighting and who judged that before a conquering enemy this was not the moment for division."[189]

Another minority supporter was even more damning in his self-criticism:

> No matter how justified the important step taken by the minority, it was clearly flawed because it came so terribly late... By the time it was finally decided upon, the situation was too critical for our views to be expressed profitably. Without doubt the minority proved their devotion to principles that they wanted to preserve intact for the future. Yet our action had no hope of saving the Commune from the abyss toward which it was inevitably being led. Instead it meant the minority shared part responsibility for the failures which history can rightly accuse the Commune of in 1871.[190]

Toward the end of May it seemed that the row might be patched up. Most of the minority returned to the council chamber, and some of them were elected to chair the Communal Council sessions. These conciliatory moves occurred on May 21, the very day the Versailles forces invaded Paris.[191]

The Paris Commune was a tremendously ambitious movement, which held out the prospect of human liberation from tyranny and poverty. However, its difficulties also demonstrated the need to overcome the old system while building the new. Alas, the Commune never solved the conundrum of how to achieve both at the same time.

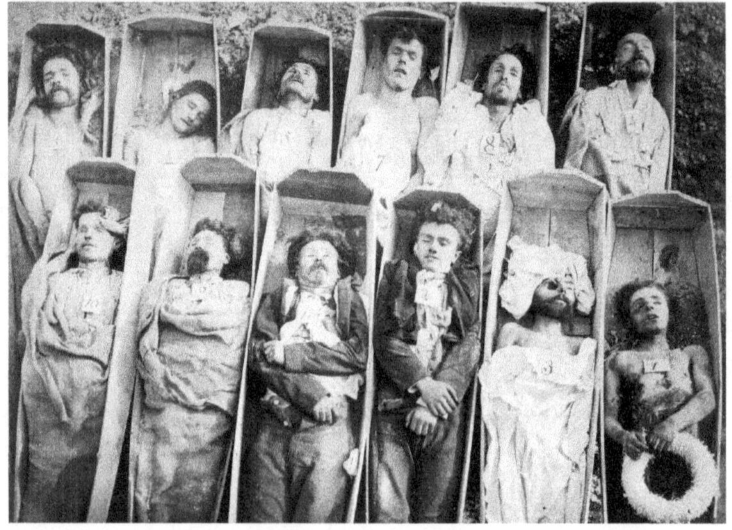

Barricade at Rue des Abbesses before the battle (above);
Twelve communards shot by Versailles (below)

Five

Bloody Week

The Communard Resistance

Then comrades come rally, and the last fight let us face

On Sunday, May 21, 1871, 8,000 Parisians attended a charity concert in the Tuileries gardens for victims of Versailles's aggression. During the performance Thiers's soldiers passed through the unguarded St. Cloud gate and poured into Paris. The city was paying the price of the Federals' disorganization. As soon as the seriousness of this incursion was realized, the atmosphere changed. There were now up to 200,000 hostile troops bearing down on one tenth of that number of Federals.[1] The breach in the hitherto impregnable fortifications completely transformed the strategic balance, giving an immense advantage to Versailles. It meant, as one insurgent put it, that communard resistance was "all the more courageous and sublime, because no person with any sense could hope for our victory. One only fought with the certainty, and I can even say the hope, of dying."[2]

Federal strategy was set by the Commune's War Delegate, Delescluze. He issued a proclamation full of magnificent and inspiring rhetoric, but which, given the poor state of military organization, made a virtue of necessity. It brilliantly encapsulated the mood of the moment:

> Citizens, enough of militarism, no more staff-officers, with their gold embroidered uniforms! Make way for the people, the combatants, the bare arms! The hour of the revolutionary war has struck. The people know nothing of planned maneuvers, but when they have a rifle in their hand, cobblestones under their feet, they do not fear all the strategists of the monarchist school. To arms! Citizens, to arms! It is a choice now, as you know, between conquering or falling into the merciless hands of the reactionaries and clericals of Versailles, of those scoundrels who deliberately delivered up France to the Prussians and are making us pay the ransom of their treachery! If you wish that the generous blood which has flowed like water these last six weeks be not infertile, if you wish to live in a free and egalitarian France, if you wish to spare your children your sufferings and your miseries, you will rise as one man and, before your fearsome resistance, the enemy, who flatters himself he will again submit you to his yoke, will win no more than the shame of the useless crimes with which he has befouled himself for the past two months. Citizens, your mandatories will fight beside you and will die beside you if need be. But in the name of this glorious France, mother of all popular revolutions, eternal home of those ideas of justice and solidarity which must and will be the laws of the world, march against the enemy; and let your revolutionary energy show them that Paris may be sold but cannot yield nor be conquered. The Commune counts on you. Count on the Commune.[3]

In response to Delescluze's appeal, Federal attack columns marched on the center of town with military bands and drums, red flags flying, and cannons bringing up the rear. An officer in the Versailles army bore witness to the fierceness of the opposition that the insurgents offered them: "Once again these people of the Commune, deprived of all solid firepower, gave proof of a tenacity comparable to our enemies, the Prussians."[4] That the true source of their bravery eluded him was shown by this passage: "If you study the organization of these dark bandits you will be struck with admiration, or rather by terror for our savage enemies who were inspired by evil and a paroxysm of hatred that gave them a formidable power."[5] Goncourt, who opposed the Commune, but observed it from within the city, had a more accurate understanding: "Why this stubborn resistance?... It is because in this battle the common people themselves are conducting their own war, are leading it themselves, and are not under the army's orders."[6]

However, the cohesion of organized forces of resistance disintegrated in the face of the onslaught, despite the prodigious efforts of experienced communard generals like Dombrowski and Wroblewski. Their work was not assisted by the Central Committee of the National Guard. In a desperate move, it proposed that the Versailles and communal assemblies both agree to dissolve themselves, to be replaced by a provisional government chosen by the larger towns.[7] This compromise was not only a distraction for the Federals but was inevitably ignored by Thiers. The leading body of the Commune, the Committee of Public Safety, remained powerless at the center because most forces had scattered to their different districts. Communal Council members therefore returned to their arrondissements to organize the barricades.[8] Soon even the vital communication links required for an effective defense were lost.[9] Mistrusting central leadership, each Federal group vigorously defended its own area, but watched helplessly while neighboring districts were crushed. By contrast, Versailles's unified command could concentrate firepower on successive points of resistance until they were entirely vanquished and then move on.

Communard fighters had turned instinctively to the urban insurrectionary tactic par excellence—the barricade. Parisians might not expect to match Versailles troops in the art of conventional warfare, but they had long experience of building barricades and could rally ordinary people in their construction. On the Rue Rivoli it took just 24 hours for a gang of 100 to construct a mighty earthwork several meters deep and six meters high, complete with trenches and embrasures for shooting through.[10] During Bloody Week up to 20,000[11] toiled furiously to assemble these structures of paving stones, sandbags, mud, mattresses and furniture.[12] Lissagaray describes how they were recruited: "We go back up Rue Saint-Antoine. At each corner groups are building barricades. All passers-by are asked to help, but not aggressively. They say, 'Come on citizen, lend a hand for the republic.' That was all."[13]

Barricades had their place in the battle, but without coordination they increased each area's isolation. Even leading anarchists, who opposed centralization on principle, realized that dependence on barricades "was an understandable instinct, but we repeat, it was absolutely contrary to good sense. Barricades localized efforts, scattering any forces capable of mounting the sort of coordinated maneuver that involved surrounding the assailants and crushing them."[14] Furthermore, unless the barricades were themselves interlinked, they could easily be encircled and lose their protective value.[15] This happened again and again.

The dilemma was tragically borne out by the Commune's very last poster, signed by Ranvier, the only member of the Committee of Public Safety still on the field of battle. It was issued to the inhabitants of Belleville on May 25, when the Federals were being attacked in eastern Paris.

> Citizens...you should be aware of a grave danger. The National Guard is refusing to march forward under the pretext of guarding barricades in districts that are under no threat at all. Lend your assistance to the 20th arrondissement and help it repel the enemy. Therein lies your security and the prize of victory. Do not wait until Belleville is itself attacked. That may perhaps be too late.[16]

Given the appalling odds, the insurgent resistance was extraordinary. Lissagaray recounts the feats of the 120 women who held out against tremendous opposition at the Place Blanche, later retreating to continue the battle at the Place Pigalle.[17] The barricade at the Boulevard Magenta offered "legendary resistance."[18] The crossroads of the Croix-Rouge "will remain celebrated in the defense of Paris"[19] because a force outnumbered ten to one held out for two days.[20] At Belleville they fought and fought, until they ran out of bullets.[21] The Hôtel de Ville itself was "a fantastic place where the death rattle and the laugh jostled each other."[22]

The Versailles army did not engage in those "brilliant charges" ascribed to it by the capitalist-owned newspapers: "Instead there was endless trench digging, night surprises and long cannonades; and once inside the city, hours of waiting while enemy positions were outflanked and the defenders, overwhelmed with gunfire, withdrew."[23] A diarist described the situation after the left bank of the Seine had fallen:

> The Versailles army now commands the riverbank and a full half of the town. Their forces accumulate hour by hour, overpowering the Parisians whose numbers decline by the minute, and are cramped into an ever more limited space. If, after the gates fell, the final issue of the struggle could not be in doubt, it is clearly nearing the end now. And yet the National Guard still resist. They do not give up an inch of ground, but they defend it just so long as they live. Dead they occupy it still with their corpses.[24]

Alongside collective bravery there were many individual acts of courage. In the preceding weeks Dombrowski, the Commune's greatest general, had tenaciously battled for the suburb of Neuilly with a handful of men, always sharing the risks himself and miraculously escaping death until he found it during Bloody Week. His aides de camp, it was calculated, survived for an average of only three days.[25] Vermorel, a Communal Council member who himself died shortly afterward, gave Dombrowski this revealing funeral oration:

> Citizens, here we are in the midst of disaster. The cause of the people is lost, and every minute that passes is filled with terrible agony. Our enemies are fighting a pitiless war against us. Triumph for them means exterminating all the combatants of the revolution, and that is what they are doing. What a tragedy! After so much heroism here you are at the mercy of implacable hangmen. It is with tears of blood that the history of these terrible days must be written. And we, the elected representatives of this unfortunate people, have we been worthy of you? No, alas! We have made many mistakes, but this is not the time for recriminations; we must fight and die!
>
> Heroic Dombrowski, noble champion of the universal republic, you are now rewarded for your admirable devotion, for your legendary courage. You are dead, despairing of the cause for which you have sacrificed yourself. At least you do not see, you will not see, the last horrors of the defeat...Dombrowski! Standing before your corpse, despite the bloody darkness which envelopes us, I cannot resist seeing a ray of hope. Yes, justice will triumph one day! And despite everything I say—long live the universal republic! Long live the Commune! Now, citizens, we will go and do our duty![26]

Shortly afterward it would be the turn of Delescluze to die. Lissagaray describes his last moments on May 25. In a final letter to his sister he wrote, "I do not wish, and am unable to act as the victim and the toy of a victorious reaction."[27] Then he set off to combat, for the last time, barely able to walk and leaning on a stick:

> We saw Delescluze... About 80 yards from the barricade the guards who accompanied him kept back, for the projectiles obscured the entrance of the boulevard. Delescluze still walked forward.
>
> Behold the scene: we have witnessed it; let it be engraved in the annals of history. The sun was setting. The old exile, unmindful of whether he was followed, still advanced at the same pace, the only living being on the road. Arrived at the barricade, he bent off to the left and mounted upon the paving-stones. For the last time his austere face, framed in his white beard, appeared to us turned toward death. Suddenly Delescluze disappeared. He had fallen as if thunderstricken on the Place du Chateau d'Eau... Delescluze walked to the barricade as the old Montagnards

> went to the scaffold. An eventful life had exhausted his strength; he had but a breath left and he gave it… He lived only for justice… It was his recompense to die for her, his hands free, in the open daylight, at his own time, not afflicted by the sight of the executioner.[28]

Innumerable unknown figures dared to resist. An English doctor told of a patient who had been shot in the lungs: "He had only half an hour to live… Suddenly he lifted himself up. I asked him what he wanted, and after a bit of effort he said: 'Citizen, I am a soldier of the universal republic. I fought in 1848 and now, in 1871, I am dying. Tell my friends that I expired shouting "'Long live the Commune!"' He then had a few convulsions and was no more."[29]

At the Hôtel de Ville Lissagaray witnessed another scene of devotion to the cause:

> They brought in a commander who no longer had a human face. A bullet had gone in through his mouth and torn away his lips, some of his teeth, and left an enormous hole in his cheek. Being unable to articulate any words, this brave man waved a red flag like a last defiant gesture, and by this means exhorted the men lying down in the Hôtel de Ville to rise for the combat.[30]

Such commitment was exhibited in different ways all over Paris. It was not the product of wickedness, as the opponents of the Commune suggested. The insurgents believed, as a poster of May 22 said, that they were engaged in "the struggle of the future against the past, liberty against despotism, equality against monopoly, fraternity against servitude, the solidarity of the peoples against the selfishness of the oppressors."[31] And for those principles "it was easy and sweet to die."[32]

Some fighters had additional personal motives for their actions, as an English journalist discovered:

> While the cannons thundered and the muskets crackled a poor woman lay prostrate with grief in a cart, sobbing bitterly. I offered her a glass of wine and a piece of bread. She refused saying, "For the little time I have left to live, it's not worth the bother."
>
> A loud noise came from our side of the barricade and I saw the poor woman seized by four soldiers who quickly stripped her of her clothes. I heard the imperious voice of the commanding officer interrogating the woman, saying, "You killed two of my men." The woman began to laugh ironically and she replied in a rough fashion, "May God punish me for not having killed more. I had two sons at Issy who were both killed, and

two at Neuilly who suffered the same fate. My husband died at this barricade, so now you can do what you want with me."[33]

Children too played a key role. Lissagaray describes the barricade of the Faubourg du Temple where:

> the most indefatigable gunner was a child. The barricade taken, all its defenders were shot, and the child's turn also came. He asked for three minutes' respite, "so that he could take his mother, who lived opposite, his silver watch, *in order that she might at least not lose everything*.' The officer, involuntarily moved, let him go, not thinking to see him again; but three minutes after the child cried, "Here I am!" and jumped on to the pavement, and nimbly leant against the wall near the corpses of his comrades.[34]

The immensity of the Versailles onslaught disoriented the insurgents. It was a sign of utter hopelessness that they turned to killing hostages, although this action paled in comparison with the carnage wrought by Versailles. In April hostages had been seized in a fruitless attempt to deter Versailles troops from slaughtering captured Federals. The Commune began to execute hostages on May 23, only after the brutality of the invading army had become clear. The victims were a man held responsible for shooting demonstrators on January 22, 1871, followed by three gendarmes. The next day a Captain Beaufort was tried for treason and acquitted, but the crowd would not accept this verdict and shot him themselves. They went on to insist that the hostage decree be fully enacted and that Versailles's violence must be met with counter-violence.

The communal leadership responsible for the hostages gave in to this pressure and decided on exemplary action. Six hostages were selected—Archbishop Darboy, Bonjean (president of the Parisian courts), two abbots and two Jesuits.[35] In the following days more followed, reaching a peak when 50 prisoners were marched from La Roquette prison to the Rue Haxo. It seems that several council members, including Varlin and Vallès, attempted to reason with the crowd and prevent further executions, but such was the popular fury they risked their own lives in persisting with this line, and the hostages were put to death.[36] Figures for the total number of executions during the period May 23 to 28 range between 63 and 107.[37] These killings filled Versailles's propaganda sheets. After all, "important" people had died at Commune hands: "They massacred the hostages without any other motive than revenge, hate, and the love of murder, sentiments very appropriate for these barbarians."[38] The accusation was false. However ineffective as a tactic, unlike Thiers's victims, hostages were not selected at random. They were seen as direct participants in the physical and mental oppression that had kept the working class in subjugation for generations.

Another desperate tactic was the setting of fires. This followed indiscriminate use of incendiary shells by Versailles,[39] which set many buildings ablaze. Naturally, the communards were blamed for all damage.[40] From May the Federals adopted the tactic of burning houses bordering their barricades.[41] This was because Versailles troops routinely smashed through the internal walls between houses so as to work around to the rear of barricades unobserved.[42]

Eventually there was a certain amount of arson as an act of revenge, even if nothing was to be gained militarily. Examples were Thiers's house and the royal expiatory chapel. There was a dreadful reasoning behind these acts:

> So we have come to this... Burn what can be burned. We are thrown to the bottom of the abyss, plunged into the pit of disasters, where they rip apart so many living bodies, where they crush so many thinking brains, where we are drowning in a sea of blood. What are these monuments, statues, books, paintings, old documents, and tapestries to us? Burn what can be burned! When an army of 200,000 bayonets, with 500 cannons and artillery pieces runs amok in our neighborhoods, when a horde of Bonapartists, clerics, monarchists and liberals combine to assault our tragic democratic and social republic; when France commits suicide at its own hands; what are a few fewer jewels around the neck of a slaughtered Paris![43]

Forgetting their own fire-starting activities, Versailles accused virtually all working-class Parisian women of being "*petroleuses*"—arsonists. Many would die as a result. The outrage expressed over property damage showed how big business and its press treasured bricks and mortar more than living, breathing human beings.

Unholy Alliance: The Commune's Enemies

The Commune's adversary in this final confrontation was Thiers's army. It had been meticulously reconstructed after the collapse of discipline on March 18, 1871. Generals such as MacMahon, Ladmirault, Vinoy and Douay,[44] who were steeped in royalism and Bonapartism, led the assault on Paris. Such people saw the insurgents as "ferocious beasts" who had to be killed.[45] Any commanders tinged with republican sympathy were purged and replaced by career officers released from Germany. As professionals, they were not the mutinous conscripts of March 18, 1871, but "were defending their salaries...their personal future."[46] From privates upward isolation had sealed prisoners of war off from the contagion of communal ideas.[47] Alongside the army and the state was the church. Faithful to the Christian injunction "Love thy neighbor," the Vicar of Versailles congratulated the government's blood-sodden troops after their unbridled savagery in these terms: "You have achieved something beautiful, great and very instructive."[48]

One member of the unholy alliance that seemed a strange bedfellow for Versailles was the German government, until recently cursed as the hated enemy. In fact the French and German authorities collaborated closely. Favre, French foreign minister, ingratiated himself with Germany's chancellor, Bismarck, by promising to annihilate the Federals. Bismarck responded to these overtures: "Although the assembling of an army at Versailles is forbidden, as the French government needs to defeat an insurrection...we are not opposed to it."[49] In return for releasing tens of thousands of prisoners he asked for only one thing: "We ask that you act promptly."[50]

The Germans still controlled over half the perimeter of Paris through their occupation of forts on the northern and eastern sides. When Bloody Week began they sealed off escape routes, and handed fleeing communards to the Versailles army. If Germany was hesitant about backing Thiers too openly[51] this was due mainly to a fear that enthusiastic intervention by a foreign power might actually heal the divide within France and produce a united opposition.[52] All restraints disappeared when mutual interest brought Thiers to hurriedly sign a full peace treaty with Germany on May 10, so that the flow of POW releases could be accelerated.

Bismarck had good reason to fear the Commune. He noted that under its influence "a common organization of socialist elements in European countries was becoming evident, with all the dangers to order that that entails." In Germany itself "socialist activity can now be seen in the large cities..."[53] His worries were shared by the Russian prime minister, who talked of "the dangers to all monarchies [from] events in Paris." His Austrian counterpart believed "that all governments must show solidarity with each other and offer mutual assistance in the struggle against this enemy."[54]

The final element in the alliance against the Commune was the press. Establishment newspapers whipped themselves up into a frenzy of denunciation, which no doubt influenced soldiers' attitudes on their entry into Paris. *L'Independance* of May 26 declared:

> At last!!! *At last* Paris is rid of the gang of bandits, of fugitives from justice, of assassins, of pillagers, of incendiaries, of robbers, who infested it for two months under the pretext of a Commune, of a Central Committee, of Committees of Public Safety, of Federations. At last the French army has returned within our walls, this valiant and noble army... *No pity for the wretches.* There is only one punishment that can expiate such crimes. *Death!*

Le Figaro was of the same opinion: "No clemency is possible for these monsters, these ferocious beasts of republicans! They represent a social danger that can only be radically suppressed. Come on...eliminate these democratic and international vermin."[55] While left-wing papers around the world rallied to the cause of the Commune, the capitalist press universally backed Versailles. The *New York Herald* in the "land of the free" was keen to offer this advice: "Make Paris a heap of ruins if necessary, let its streets be made to run rivers of blood, let all within it perish, but let the government maintain its authority and demonstrate its power. Let it crush completely every sign of opposition, no matter what the cost, and teach a lesson that Paris and all France will remember."[56]

Defeat and Massacre

After a week of intense fighting Versailles forces eventually overwhelmed the Federals. What was that experience like to live through?

> There was a constant thunder from the artillery, the crackling noise of the firing squads, the pattering rain of machine-gun cartridges... Your nervous system was shaken, hammered, weighed down by the raucous discords, by the thousand strident noises that set you on edge. It was like being in an immense workshop, yes just that, but a workshop in which it is the machine-gun that labors, and in which the product is destruction on an immense scale. Paris is transformed into an immense quarry. Here the explosives are used to blow up houses and palaces, while picks and drills bore through human flesh. It is a horrible cacophony, an infernal merry-go-round of hatred and passion.[57]

A right-wing newspaper describes what was found when the troops smashed through the barricades:

> The avenues of trees were uprooted on both sides of the street, their trunks twisted, smashed, torn apart, so that the ground was literally covered with their debris. You walked on a carpet of branches, twigs and leaves. Broken candelabras were strewn on the ground and the huts that were constructed during the siege to protect the fighters were destroyed, burnt, broken into pieces, with light piercing the holes.
>
> In most of these shelters you find the insurgents killed in battle piled up, one on top of the other. Their faces are covered in blood and mud. Bashed in by bullets they are horrible and repugnant to see. We covered them with leaves gathered from the streets... Behind the barricade made of carved cobbles and barrels of earth the dead have been removed, but they must have been numerous because their blood runs down the gutters. Cannons, broken gun carriages, piled up rifles, stained with blood, horses stretched out and stiff with death, black pools of broken bottles, empty tins and whole loaves of bread, this is what is found behind each barricade in the La Villette district.[58]

Alas, the defeat of the Commune was but the beginning.

What took place in the days and weeks that followed was a wholesale slaughter. Estimates put the number of Federals killed in actual fighting between 3,000 and 10,000 (compared to 877 for Versailles).[59] There is no doubt that the number executed afterward, in cold blood, exceeded those figures some five times over.[60]

The scale of this could not have been the result of individual soldiers' acting out a lust for violence in defiance of their officers. The entire thrust of military policy since March 18 had been to create a disciplined force. Historians are unanimous on this: "The troops remained under the direction of their officers, though Versailles apologists implied the contrary when excesses were undeniable."[61] "Bloody week was the work of the generals...all did as they were told..."[62] Even the right-wing history of du Camp affirmed that the army was "following a precise plan, step by step, and in executing it nothing was left to chance... [They were] taking their moral revenge against their compatriots."[63]

Bloody Week was a graphic example of a capitalist state stripped to its bare essentials—"armed bodies of men"—exterminating a threat to the system of domination and exploitation. The horror was organized on a mass scale, some of the tactics used prefiguring methods employed by the Nazis at places like Babi Yar in the early stages of the Holocaust:

> At the Parc des Buttes-Chaumont and Père Lachaise they began to machine-gun the eight to ten thousand Federals held at these points. Not

> all of them could be shot, so they chose the ones they disliked most. It worked like clockwork—two volleys of machine-gun fire for 40 men. In advance they had taken care to dig deep trenches. The Federals were lined up along them. When they were killed they fell into the trenches and this saved the trouble of carrying away the corpses...[64]

Lissagaray writes of a selection procedure like that of Auschwitz:

> On the Sunday more than 5,000 prisoners taken in the neighborhood of Père Lachaise were led to the prison of La Roquette. A chief of battalion standing at the entrance surveyed the prisoners and said, "To the right," or "To the left." Those to the left were to be shot. Their pockets emptied, they were drawn up along a wall and then slaughtered... It was butchery, nothing more, nothing less.[65]

The same cold, calculating counterrevolutionary fury lay behind both French army and Nazi atrocities, even if the scale and the targets were quite different.

Individual acts of cruelty can also reveal the face of barbarism. One example was the singling out of all 43 inhabitants of the Rue des Rosiers, the street where Generals Lecomte and Clément-Thomas had been shot on March 18. Young and old, they were put against a wall and executed.[66] Varlin too was brought there to die after having been beaten and dragged across Paris.[67] The anti-communard *Le Gaulois* reported how the army behaved when it reached a hospital full of wounded Federals: "At Saint Suplice there were around 400 insurgents in nightshirts, lying down and pretending to be wounded. They were all executed along with the false surgeon."[68]

In another episode a man made a last request to say goodbye to his family. The officer agreed, but when they arrived the officer cried out, "Shoot them all!"[69] This might seem to be an act of random sadism, but at least one paper saw the children of insurgents as a serious threat. *Le Gaulois* complained that not enough communards had been killed. It reckoned 64,000 had escaped "justice" and would: "always be ready to rise up should there be a call to revolt, pillage, and assassinate. These 64,000 will have children raised in the religion of their hatred, their jealousy, and their hopes. They will prepare a new generation whose only thought will be the thought of revenge..."[70]

Therefore, as one writer characterized it, the attitude was that: "while you are killing the *females* you can *get rid of the little ones at the same time*. So all the wives of Federals who went to find their husbands, or rather their corpses, and who had the misfortune to bring their children with them, were immediately seized along with their young ones, and summarily shot as arsonists!"[71]

If one man above all embodied the viciousness of Versailles it was General Galliffet, the celebrated dandy:

> On the 26th [May], in one single convoy he chose 83 men and three women, made them draw up along the talus of the fortifications and had them shot. Then he said to their comrades, "My name is Galliffet. Your journals in Paris had sullied me enough. I take my revenge." On Sunday, the 28th, he said, "Let those who have white hairs step out from the ranks." One hundred and eleven captives advanced. "You," continued Galliffet, "you have seen June 1848; you are more culpable than the others." And he had their corpses thrown over into the fortifications.[72]

Confronted by a woman desperately pleading for her life, his cutting reply was, "Madame, I have frequented all the theaters of Paris. It is pointless to continue this comedy any longer."[73]

Singling out working-class women was a particular feature of Bloody Week. Thousands of women were accused of being petroleuses simply because they wore ragged clothes, or were carrying a milk jug, vase or bottle. Their crime was to have broken out of the "feminine" roles allotted to them by society: "In their yapping voices...they demanded their place in the sun, their civil rights, and the equality that had been refused them."[74] Standing up for yourself was an unpardonable crime in the eyes of the rich and powerful, now driven into a blind rage:

> When we remember squads of women, armed, uniformed, bedecked with sashes around their waists and red cockades, running through the streets and, like hysterics in politics, preparing for the implacable resistance of the last eight days, we can only wonder from what slime the human species is made and what animalistic instincts, hidden and ineradicable, still crouch in the dark soul of mankind! (Jules Clarétie)

> What are these extraordinary beings who give up the housewife's broom and the seamstress's needle for a rifle, who leave their children to kill beside their lovers and their husbands?... What is this rage that seizes these furies? Do they know what they are doing? Do they understand why they are dying? (Catulle Mendès)[75]

Even the right-wing contemporary historian du Camp had to recognize that the accusations of widespread arson by women was unjust:

"From the morning of May 24 Paris went mad. There were stories of women who were slipping into districts already liberated by our troops throwing blazing filaments into the vents, or emptying petrol through the shutters of shops and lighting fires everywhere. This legend...was false. Not a single house burned in the area occupied by the French army."[76]

The end of May saw the most intense carnage, but the slaughter continued right up to mid-June, long after all vestiges of resistance had ended. Eventually even the establishment press could stomach no more. The *National* was sated: "Enough executions, enough blood, enough victims."[77] There are no incontrovertible figures for the final count of victims subsequent to the "victory of law and order." Estimates range from du Camp's gross underestimate of 6,500[78] through Lissagaray's 20,000[79] to 37,000.[80] A fifth of the total were women.[81] A sense of what these figures represent can be gained by a comparison with other events: "Far more had died during the last week in May than in any of the battles during the Franco-Prussian War, than in any of the previous "massacres" in French history... The Terror of the French Revolution...accounted for 2,627 in Paris and up to 17,000 throughout France during the 18 months from March 1793 to July 1794..."[82]

Death may have been a mercy when you consider the agonies that the living had to endure. Government forces killed many, but even more were arrested, marched off to Versailles, and sometimes tortured. Once again it is worth quoting du Camp, because he cannot be suspected of exaggerating in favor of the Commune:

> When a group of prisoners appeared the crowd rushed upon them and tried to break through the cordon of soldiers that escorted and protected them. The women were, as always, the most vociferous. They burst through the army lines and struck prisoners with their umbrellas, shouting "Kill the assassins! Set fire to the arsonists!" When one of these unfortunate people fell over exhausted and the gendarmes picked him up to put them in the cart that followed the convoy, there was only one cry: "No! No! Kill him! Shoot him!"[83]

The numbers seized were huge, averaging 100 every day through June and July, and the process stretched on over the next three years; 38,568 arrests were admitted by Versailles (including over 1,000 women and 651 children), but these will have been an underestimate—50,000 is probably a more accurate number.[84] Many were eventually released after suffering appalling conditions in prisons like Satory. Those convicted (numbering 10,000 plus) remained there, ended up in prison hulks, or in transports to New Caledonia; 4,000 were sent abroad.[85] They were joined by 10,000 wives and children.[86] The entire French navy was occupied for a year carrying this sorry cargo.[87]

The trials produced a variety of testimonies. Demoralization and despair meant that many tried to save themselves from the remorseless machinery of courts-martial by personal pleas or "sad defections."[88] There were also some stirring defenses of the revolution. Trinquet was proud to admit: "I have been to the barricades, and I regret not having died there..."[89] Ferré signed his own death warrant with this speech: "A member of the Commune, I am in the hands of its victors. They want my head; they may take it. I will never save my life by cowardice. Free I have lived, so I will die."[90] However, the outstanding speech from the dock was uttered by Louise Michel: "I will not defend myself; I will not be defended... Since it seems that every heart which beats for liberty has only the right to a little lead, I too demand my part. If you let me live, I shall not cease to cry vengeance, and I shall denounce you to the vengeance of my brothers... If you are not cowards kill me."[91]

She was not accorded her wish, but was transported to New Caledonia.

To the massacre and the mass arrests must be added the flight of unknown numbers who took refuge in surrounding countries like Belgium, Switzerland and Britain. (The disgusting attitude toward asylum seekers exhibited here by Tory and Labour politicians today was not shown then.) The cumulative effect of these losses on Paris was enormous. There were 100,000 fewer voters at the next Parisian elections than in February 1871.[92] The capital lost half its house-painters, half the plumbers, tile-layers, cobblers and zinc workers,[93] and large numbers from many other trades.[94] In Belleville some streets seemed to have only old women still living there.[95] The builders of sewing machines declared that their industry faced complete ruin because the workers who bought them had disappeared, while sign painters, who were usually abundant, "had completely disappeared." "Bring us back our workers" said a manufacturer of faubourg Saint-Antoine. "We don't know how we will cope..."[96]

What can explain the enormous scale of brutality visited upon the Parisian working class? Firstly, as a survivor wrote, the army command had honed its techniques of repression in colonial campaigns. They were now accustomed to: "subjecting the beautiful Arab races to the most revolting treatment and the most odious extermination. In fact, after having spent years setting fire to Algerian villages and massacring the tribespeople, the soldiers were well trained in spilling blood in our cities..."[97]

The motives that drove imperialist adventures abroad were matched in repression at home.

Secondly, the cruelty arose from the deep threat felt by the established order, a fear expressed by du Camp: "The communards wanted simply to put the fourth estate [the working class] in charge and to destroy all the privileges which caused their suffering, because they had discovered that the existing society is founded on privilege."[98] The bloodbath was a tragic compliment to the achievements of the Commune's brief tenure as the first workers' government in history.

Bloody Week was therefore a combination of established military methods and domestic political goals: "It is clear that the French ruling class, like the slaveowners of antiquity, and slaveholders of blacks today, like the barons of the Middle Ages, seem to believe that any method is permitted if it is a matter of imposing the yoke of exploitation on those who revolt. So when the soldiers faced proletarians who demanded their place in the sun, extermination was the rule."[99]

Women's prison at Chantiers a Versailles
(a contemporary reconstruction, above);
Children's quarter at Chantiers a Versailles prison (below)

Six

Interpretations: Critics and Champions

But now farewell the spirit craven
The dawn brings a brighter day

Since 1871 there have been numerous contrasting interpretations of the Commune, a body that Karl Marx described as a "Sphinx"[1] because its exact meaning was so mysterious. Unfortunately the communards did not help clarify the issue because they left no single document summing up their aims. The nearest approximation was the official manifesto of April 19. Since an agreed statement was needed it was voted through, but all groups found it disappointing and it was the lowest common denominator. Precisely because the Commune was a genuine mass democratic movement, reflecting an abundance of different ideas, no easy definition could suffice. As one writer puts it: "The 'program' of the revolution was not neatly marked out, was not a coherent entity composed of pure concepts harmoniously interlinked, or woven into 'structured thinking.' It reflected the aspirations of the actors, anonymous or named, of the revolution."[2]

This chapter will try to sift through the varied understandings. Right-wing analyses are discounted because they show little insight, merely the familiar contempt of "upper classes" for their "inferiors." They portray the Commune as either inexplicable, a drunken orgy,[3] or a criminal conspiracy masterminded by Red Professor Marx and the First International. Rather, the focus will be on accounts that broadly endorse the Commune. The first part of the chapter deals with writers who are sympathetic to the Commune but, I would argue, nevertheless fail to appreciate just how radical and forward-looking it was. The second part discusses the treatment of the Commune by Marxist writers who stress its potential but are critical of some of its methods.

The Commune as Municipal or Community Politics

A well-known slogan enjoins anticapitalists to "think globally, act locally." However, some believe the Commune's goal was little more than to establish Parisian local government. The implication is that it wished to "think locally, act locally."[4] If this had indeed been the intention, it would hardly have been very radical. Even anti-communard liberals like Ferry were arguing, "Above all else we want administrative decentralization."[5] As proof of the Commune's limited horizon this quote from 1871 has been cited: "Commune meant simply granting Paris a freely elected municipal council. Throughout the siege people did not cease repeating that Commune and municipal council were one and the same thing."[6] However, what happened after the siege is the key issue.

The March 18 revolution radically transformed the traditional demand for local autonomy. There were some—like Charles Beslay, the moderate Proudhonist and first chair of the Communal Council—who still echoed the sentiments above: "The Commune will concern itself with local affairs; the department [region] will concern itself with regional affairs; the government will concern itself with national affairs." However, Beslay's speech did not stop there. Municipal government was to be a springboard for "social regeneration…support for the weak, protection for the workers, hope for the oppressed of the world and the foundation of the universal republic."[7] Therefore, the Commune's *Journal Officiel* explicitly denied that the ultimate aim of the Commune was limited to municipal reform: "It would be a strange and even childish illusion to

The Labor Commission put forward a "proposal for organization of producers' cooperatives for women," which explicitly ridiculed "what they call municipal franchise." It asserted that "the people are not blinded by this governmental fiction, or by so-called parliamentary representation. In establishing the Commune they have unequivocally proclaimed...the creation of a new social order, of equality, solidarity, and of freedom."[41] The Women's Union did not see the Commune as limited to a council of men sitting at the Hôtel de Ville, from which women were excluded. It was a mass movement, "whose aim is to put an end to corruption, and ultimately to regenerate society by ensuring the rule of labor and justice... [It] is of as much significance to the women as it is to the men of Paris."[42] It was in this sense that Leo's *La Sociale* described the Commune as "the widest expression of free universal suffrage, whose mission is to save and consolidate the revolution."[43] In other words, the nourishment of new social relations gave both men and women real power to shape their destiny, and this took precedence over formal electoral matters. Since active participation and progress in so many areas was achieved, the Commune should not be condemned for failure to reform voting rights.

During the final days of fighting, women played a role otherwise unknown in nineteenth-century warfare. There were many like Michel who bore arms, although the most commonly adopted roles were as nurses, or as *cantinières*—people who supplied the Federal fighters with food and drink. In this context Gullickson makes great play of what she describes as a "searing article" in Leo's *La Sociale*. It tells how a group of female nurses were turned back from the fighting at Neuilly. Gullickson cites a passage detailing how the nine women were "misled by a physician, rebuffed by a superior officer, and insulted by a young officer [who] encouraged by the curtness of his superior [officers made a] jest in bad taste."[44] Unfortunately she makes only passing reference to the article's conclusion. This distinguishes between the middle- and working-class men encountered, and is worth quoting in full:

> Throughout the whole journey we noticed the very different attitudes present. Without exception the officers and surgeons showed a lack of sympathy that varied from coldness to insults; but from the National Guards came respect and fraternity... To sum up, despite the crude insult made to our devoted volunteers, the overall impression left by the journey was profoundly encouraging. Although an authoritarian, narrow, and

> mean bourgeois spirit is shared by many of the officers, our soldier citizens are bursting with a lively, deep and splendid sense of the new life. They believe in the great forces that will save the world, and acclaim them instead of resisting them. They feel the right of all to their rights.[45]

As a consequence of this article Rossel, the Commune's war delegate, turned to Leo for advice on involving more women in the military campaign.[46]

Leo was indeed frustrated by the outlook of some male communards,[47] but she did not see the interests of women and men as separate. Her criticisms focused on the Commune not taking full advantage of all the forces available to combat the real enemy—Versailles—"that old world with its rotten institutions of monarchy, religion, political and social despotism which is coming to fight the revolution…"[48] The majority of her articles dealt with subjects not specific to women. Those that did concern gender are about unity, class unity, one being entitled "Toutes avec Tous" (all women and men together).[49] She wrote with equal feeling about male "Soldiers of the Idea":

> Look at the list of the dead and wounded, and a strong emotion seizes your heart. To the names of each is attached their profession: Nicholas Châtelain—shoemaker; Louis Daniel—stonemason with two children; Louis Hainault—carpenter with four children; Marcey—blacksmith… Each has done the greatest thing that a human being can do. He has devoted his life to his beliefs, fighting for an idea he will never live to see triumph. This poor man gives up the most precious human gift—his life for humanity.[50]

Louise Michel had the same attitude. Discussing the work of the Montmartre vigilance committees she said, "People didn't worry about which sex they were before they did their duty. That stupid question was settled."[51]

If women were so irrelevant to the Commune, it is strange that its opponents were fixated on the prominent role that they played, and so vociferous in condemning them. In such displays of hostility there was little dissimilarity between women and men. Maxime du Camp, in a passage already cited, remarked that Versailles women acted viciously toward female communards.[52] As part of a prisoner convoy Michel described the treatment dealt out by Versailles women: "These creatures, hideous with ferocity, dressed in luxury and coming from who knows where…insulted the prisoners and dug out the eyes of the dead with the ends of their umbrellas… Thirsting for blood, like ghouls they were… monstrous and irresponsible like she-wolves."[53]

Unlike those feminists who regard the distinction between women and men as more important than the class divide in society, the Commune emphasized women's emancipation as part of a single, unified movement for human liberation. In this sphere the achievements of 1871 were unparalleled.

"Twilight or Dawn"?

Jacques Rougerie is one of the finest modern writers on the Paris Commune. However, his view is that the Paris Commune of 1871 was backward looking, more a reflection of the 1789 Revolution than the precursor of modern socialism or anticapitalism. He writes that it was "the last revolution of the 19th century, an end point, the final gesture of 19th century French revolutions: twilight, and not dawn."[54] If this were correct, the experience of 1871would be of only antiquarian interest, and there would be little to learn from it.

It is axiomatic that major historical events are the product of the past, and equally that they alter the future in some way. The question here is, what was the balance between these two elements? There is merit in noting the major influence of the Great Revolution on the thinking of participants in the Commune. Frankel has already been quoted on this point, and many others could be cited. Take, for example, Lefrançais, a leading Proudhonist on the Communal Council: "A philosopher has written: 'Happy are the peoples who have no history.' We would readily agree. Happy would be the Commune if it had no revolutionary traditions! The great majority of its members were indeed preoccupied by historical memories."[55]

It is no surprise that the Great Revolution was a touchstone for communards, nor that this fact would create difficulties. 1789 was a model of a successful uprising, and in destroying feudalism it cleared a path for capitalism. So it was generally revered even though many of its lessons were not directly applicable to a movement against capitalism. However, while the Great Revolution was often the subjective point of reference for communards, objectively they were forging a new path forward. It is necessary to look beyond the language they used, to the substantive character of the communal movement itself.

Consider, for example, the class composition of the Federals. Rougerie asserts that the small workshop milieu of Parisian industry made the typical communard "an old-style insurgent who belonged to the first half of the 19th century, to the prehistory of the labor and socialist movement. In no way was he part of the modern proletariat."[56] In 1871 the stereotypical horny-handed proletarian from a giant factory was indeed barely to be encountered in Paris. However, the existence of a working class does not depend on the size of the workplace or the type of product made. It is determined by social relations—whether or not there is a class of people who have no choice but to work for wages, and in so doing assist the accumulation of capital by the bosses.[57] Surface appearances may change, but capitalism's fundamental character and its exploitative mechanism remain constant.

Rougerie himself points out that "at the base of everything in the smallest, most artisanal, enterprise was the absolutely irreducible and engrained antagonism between boss and wage earner, between exploiter and exploited."[58] Then, as now, small employers struggling to survive in competition with larger rivals often treated their employees harshly, and since it was more difficult for these latter to organize and resist, feelings of bitterness could be intense. However communards (and historians) interpreted their movement, they were not sansculottes facing feudalism, but people who were challenging a capitalist system in full process of development.

An article in the Commune's official newspaper, the *Journal Officiel*, was in no doubt about the nature of the struggle:

> The proletarians of the capital, in the midst of failure and treachery by the governing classes, have understood that the time has arrived for them to save the situation by taking the direction of public affairs into their hands... The workers, those who produce all and who gain nothing from this, those who suffer poverty in the midst of accumulated wealth, the fruit of their labor and their sweat, must they always submit to this outrage? Are they never to be permitted to work for their emancipation without a torrent of abuse being hurled at them?[59]

Equally telling, the pro-capitalist republican Jules Favre believed the Commune was an immediate and fundamental challenge to the entire social system as it was presently constituted:

> How could we hesitate? Does our conscience not force upon us the serious and absolute duty of exerting all energy to overcome such a shameful attack on civilization?... Is this not open, audacious civil war accompanied by cowardly murder and pillage in the dark? Do we not see that the requisitions have begun, that private property will be violated, and that we are

> going to see, step by step, little by little, this carefully calculated perversity that undermines the very basis of society, causing its eventual collapse?[60]

Paradoxically, Rougerie is far too good a historian not to present key evidence that undermines his own argument. He undertook a detailed analysis of more than 36,000 people arrested on the Federal side. This reveals a number of things. The notion that the middle class demand of local self-government was paramount as a motivation is undermined by the social composition of the insurgents. Only 8 percent were white-collar employees, 4 percent were small businesspeople and 4 percent came from the liberal professions. The rest—84 percent—were from manual trades.[61]

Were these manual workers in fact old-style artisans from the pre-history of the movement? Traditional craftsmen were present. Shoe workers comprised 4 percent, leather workers 1 percent, and producers of artistic goods made up 7 percent. Yet workers in metal, building, and day laboring, made up 12, 16 and 15 percent, respectively. Rougerie adds, "It must also be underlined that these three professions, that we can describe as being of a new type, also formed a much higher proportion of the insurgents of 1871 than they did in the overall population."[62] He concludes, "We are convinced that in virtually all cases the communard was a wage earner… The Commune was indeed a workers' insurrection."[63] Surely this puts a question mark over his previously quoted view of the Commune as "twilight not dawn" powered by people "in no way…part of the modern proletariat."

Nevertheless, the important place of the Great Revolution in communard thinking must be recognized. Intriguingly, a great many of the Commune's opponents also accorded 1789 prominence in their beliefs, and in attacking the Commune believed they were defending "liberty, equality, fraternity." Such people included Louis Blanc, the reformist socialist whose ideas had been very significant in the 1848 Revolution. Now, as a National Assembly member for Paris he accused his own constituents of "incendiarism, pillage and assassinations."[64] Then there were republicans who exulted in the slaughter of Bloody Week. Ferry admitted that by supporting the repressive acts of Versailles he was going along: "with all that has failed…with criminal hands that one has vainly denounced for so long. I am chained to an impossible task; given the job of repairing the irreparable, under the cloak of public salvation… [It means] purely and simply worshipping the gods of hell."

And yet he learned to live with it, writing, "My eyes, burning at the sight of the fires, were soothed by the firing squads."[65]

Literary France, which prided itself as being the forward-thinking avant-garde, generally embraced notions of liberty, equality and fraternity. But apart from a few honorable exceptions like Victor Hugo and Jules Vallès, it too opposed the Commune. Gustave Flaubert wrote, "What primitive throwbacks! What savages!"[66] Georges Sand, the female writer who scandalized France by rejecting official morality, thought communards were "driven by hate…fanaticism or natural viciousness…"[67] Emile Zola, the novelist who in the Dreyfus case would play such an important role in combating anti-Semitism,[68] was sympathetic at first. Yet even he denounced the communards for "burying humanity under the ashes of the old world, in the hope that a happy and honest world would emerge. This is a terrestrial fantasy that comes of primitive legends!"[69]

That people on both sides of the civil war claimed the same principles but fought each other is not as paradoxical as it first appears, nor are references to "liberty, equality, fraternity" necessarily anachronistic. 1789 empowered the bourgeoisie, and so today its slogan is the official motto of capitalist France. George Bush and Tony Blair also use the language of freedom and democracy. However, for them this means the freedom for imperialist states and big business to oppress and exploit. It is clear that the meaning a neoliberal gives to "liberty, equality, fraternity" is the very opposite of that given by the anticapitalist and anti-imperialist movements. We stand for liberty, equality and fraternity for human beings, not for capital. Until the Paris Commune these different connotations of 1789 had never been exposed so sharply. The civil war gouged a river of blood that separated the two.

To conclude, the Commune could not leap over its own background. It was a pioneer in uncharted territory and had to describe its experiences in a language with which it was familiar, however inadequate that might be. Yet it also transcended the Great Revolution, playing the notes of the past to create the music of the future. A poster from the 12th arrondissement demonstrates this ambiguity wonderfully:

> Today, citizens, you are in the presence of two programs. The first, that of the Versailles royalists, is…perpetual slavery. It is the abasement of anything to do with the people. It is the stifling of intelligent thought and justice. It is mercenary labor. It is the collar of poverty riveted around our

necks. It is threats on every side. They want your blood, that of your wives, that of your children. They are calling for your heads.

This program makes of the people beasts of burden, working only to build up the wealth of the exploiters and the parasites, to fatten the monarchs, the ministers, the senators, the marshals, the archbishops and the Jesuits.

The other program...is the demand for the rights of man. It is the people who are masters of their destiny. It is justice and the right to live by working. It is the scepter of tyrants broken under the hammer of the worker. It is the worker's tool made equal to capital. It is intelligence seeing through lies and stupidity. It is equality from birth to death...[70]

Champions: The Marxist Tradition and the Commune

Laws cheat us and the state oppresses

Marxists have always seen the Commune as enormously significant. It symbolized the dawn of a new age, not of dictatorship (in the style of Stalinist Eastern Europe, which falsely claimed the mantle of Marxism), but an age of true human liberation and democracy. The first major statement on the Commune came from Karl Marx himself. Based in London in 1871, he monitored and reported events across the Channel for the General Council of the First International. When Versailles seized the National Guards' cannons and compelled the workers of Paris to rise up, he immediately threw all his energy into backing them. This culminated in a brilliantly argued defense that appeared on May 30, 1871, just two days after the end of Bloody Week. It was entitled *The Civil War in France.*

Yet Marx did not prophecy the Commune, or even advocate its formation. After the fall of Napoleon III in September 1870 he wrote: "The French working class moves, therefore, under circumstances of extreme difficulty. Any attempt at upsetting the new government in the present crisis, when the enemy is almost knocking at the doors of Paris, would be a desperate folly."[71]

Unlike the distorted image of Karl Marx, whom the Stalinists canonized as infallible, this passage shows he would learn from the Parisian movement. He later corrected his initial error of judgement, writing that if the Commune had been established earlier "it would have altogether changed the character of the [Franco-Prussian] war. It would have become the war of republican France, hoisting the flag of the social revolution."[72]

In the wake of the merciless onslaught by Thiers and the French army, Marx's *Civil War in France* comprehensively demolished every justification they put forward, damning them for the butchers they were. He was not, however, a mindless sycophant. He feared, for example, that the Parisian movement might be mesmerized by the Great Revolution: "They must not allow themselves to be deluded by the national souvenirs of 1792... They have not to recapitulate the past, but to build up the future. Let them calmly and resolutely improve the opportunities of republican liberty, for the work of their own class organization."[73]

Did his apprehension perhaps confirm the Commune being "twilight, not dawn"? Introducing Marx's writings on 1871, Friedrich Engels, his close collaborator, explicitly rejected that idea:

> Thanks to the economic and political development of France since 1789, Paris has been placed for the last 50 years in such a position that no revolution could break out there without assuming a proletarian character... These demands were more or less unclear and even confused...but in the last resort they all amounted to the abolition of the class antagonism between capitalists and workers [which] contained a threat to the existing order of society.[74]

Marx's writings on the Commune deal with the issue of reform or revolution. This matter is hotly debated in the anticapitalist movement, though rarely in explicit terms, discussion tending to center on whether to concentrate on particular campaigns or to challenge the system generally. The Commune's approach to capitalist production encapsulated this issue. Chapter 1 looked at how the Labor Commission set in train a workers' takeover of workshops that were the property of Parisian local government or abandoned by their owners. This would be accomplished by bodies variously entitled workers' corporations, workers' cooperatives, or social workshops. They had a long history in France and were originally promoted in Louis Blanc's influential book *The Organization of Labour* of 1847. He had predicted workers' cooperatives would: "soon be so successful in every sphere of industry that not only workers but also capitalists would join them. After a certain time, without expropriation, without injustice or irreparable disruption, the principle of association would triumph over individualism and selfishness."[75]

Blanc's formula was classic reformism. It was attractive to people in small workshops that operated with minimal machinery and depended almost entirely on human skills and energy. Superficially it did seem plausible to hope that if workers were relieved of the burden of satiating the bosses' greed, given tools, a workplace, and an order book, they could win in competition with the capitalist system.

In the *Inaugural Address* he wrote for the founding of the First International, Marx pointed out the difficulties with this plan: "However excellent in principle, and however useful in practice, co-operative labor, if kept within the narrow circle of the casual efforts of private workmen, will never be able to arrest the growth in geometrical progression of monopoly, to free the masses, nor even to perceptibly lighten the burden of their miseries."[76]

Decades of industrial development rendered it impossible to outcompete the capitalists. This restless, dynamic system was replacing small workshops with large factories, and displacing skilled craftsmen with mass-producing self-powered machines.[77] Reforms might bring short-term benefits, but capitalism would always return to erode them and nullify their effects.

However, Marx believed that in the circumstances of workers' revolution cooperative labor acquired a new significance. In *The Civil War in France* he expressed this by means of a rhetorical question:

> If co-operative production is not to remain a sham and a snare; if it is to supersede the capitalist system; if united co-operative societies are to regulate national production upon a common plan, thus taking it under their own control, and putting an end to the constant anarchy and periodical convulsions which are the fatality of capitalist production—what else, gentleman, would it be but communism, "possible" communism?[78]

Cooperative production was "possible communism" because the Commune offered hope of "national production upon a common plan." Thus the workers' government recast the relationship between limited reforms and total revolution. Promoting workers' cooperatives as a single issue campaign would have been a partial strategy ultimately going nowhere. If the insurgents of 1871 had merely talked about an ideal society but taken no practical steps to construct it, the Commune would have been an empty abstraction that failed to involve people in actively transforming their lives. Marx characterized the communards' method in this way: "They have no ready-made utopias to introduce par décret du peuple [by popular decree]... They have no ideals to realize, but to set free the elements of the new society with which the old collapsing bourgeois society itself is pregnant."[79]

Marx criticized the Commune for not acting swiftly and decisively against its enemies by marching on Versailles immediately after March 18, 1871. It was "the fault of their too great decency. They gave Thiers time..."[80] Such decency also weakened the impact of the Commune's hostage decree. At Versailles the "shooting of prisoners was suspended for a time [but only until] Thiers and his Decembrist generals became aware that the Communal decree of reprisals was but an empty threat..."[81] For his part, Engels was puzzled by the failure to seize the assets of the Bank of France: "The hardest thing to understand is certainly the holy awe with which they remained standing respectfully outside the Bank of France. This was also a serious political mistake. The bank in the hands of the Commune—this would have been worth more than 10,000 hostages."[82]

The Commune's indulgence may have not helped their struggle with Versailles, but Marx recognized in it the "magnanimity of the armed working men—so strangely at variance with the habits of the 'Party of Order.'"[83] Moreover, until the entry of Versailles troops "the proletarian revolution remained as free from the acts of violence in which the revolutions, and still more the counter-revolutions, of the 'better classes' abound."[84]

The most important sections of Marx's writing are those dealing with the Commune as a workers' government. Today we are told that the right to vote in parliamentary elections every few years is a guarantee of democracy. Marx thought such a right was hollow until the dawn of the Commune: "Instead of deciding once in three or four years which member of the ruling class was to misrepresent the people in parliament, universal suffrage was to serve the people, constituted in Communes, as individual suffrage serves every other employer in the search for the workmen and managers in his business..."[85]

What made the Parisian democratic structure so different? Firstly, "from the members of the Commune downwards, the public service had to be done at workmen's wages. The vested interests and the representation allowances of the high dignitaries of state disappeared along with the high dignitaries themselves."[86] Secondly, they were "at all times revocable"[87] so delegates could not stray from the mandate of the electors. Under our current system individuals exercise a couple of minutes of influence over the choice of representatives once every four or five years—making perhaps 30 minutes over a lifetime. Under the Commune such influence was the fruit of collective debate and was continuous. This made it quite unlike earlier forms of state power, "which claimed to be the embodiment of [national] unity independent of, and superior to, the nation itself from which it was but a parasitic excrescence."[88] Moreover, because the source of physical power, the National Guard, was the people themselves, the Commune "was a thoroughly expansive political form, while all previous forms of government have been emphatically repressive."[89]

It was principally these features that led him to conclude that this was "a working class government...the political form at last discovered under which to work out the economical emancipation of labor."[90] Therefore, "working men's Paris, with its Commune, will be for ever celebrated as the glorious harbinger of a new society."[91]

Marx was an acute observer and, as a contemporary of the Commune, his writings are invaluable. They retain an immediacy and polemical charge that come from his direct political intervention on its behalf.[92] Leon Trotsky wrote about the Commune half a century later, but brought particular sensitivities to the discussion for two reasons. During the 1905 Russian Revolution, and again in 1917, he was president of the St. Petersburg Soviet,[93] a body that operated the sort of direct mass democracy the Commune had pioneered. Later on he led the Red Army to victory in a war against internal foes and an array of foreign powers during the years 1918–21. He therefore had an understanding of the military issues confronting the Commune.

Trotsky identified parallels between Paris in 1871 and Russia in 1917. He likened the Central Committee of the National Guard to the Russian Soviets (also called Councils of Workers' and Soldiers' Deputies). Both were organs of working-class power with systems of instant recall and direct democracy. The French National Guard operated its collective control through the battalions that assembled on a daily basis and so could keep representatives under constant scrutiny. In Russia soldiers' regiments and factories played the same role. Thus, in the Petrograd Soviet delegates were elected on the basis of one per regiment, and one per 1,000 workers. Trotsky believed that:

> The Central Committee of the National Guard was, in effect, a Council of Deputies of armed workers and of the petty bourgeoisie. Such a council, elected directly by the masses who had taken the revolutionary road,

> represented an excellent apparatus for action... The entire working class, while retaining its original character and its political nuances, could act with method and firmness, without falling behind events, and each time directing fatal blows against the weak points of its enemies because, at its head, over and above the districts, the sections and the groups, there was a centralized apparatus linked by iron discipline.[94]

The key difference between the Commune and Russia's Soviets was that the former remained confined to one city and was defeated, while the latter spread across Russia and in October 1917 seized national power. (The democratic Soviet system was eventually sapped by civil war and destroyed by internal counterrevolution. The USSR was Soviet only in name; but the history of this important subject cannot be dealt with here).[95] In Trotsky's view, if the National Guard Central Committee had acted differently, its chances of success would have been greater. He was, for example, critical of its abdication of power shortly after the March 18 revolution:

> Hardly had the government retreated to Versailles than the National Guard rushed to give up its responsibility, at the very moment when this responsibility was enormous. The Central Committee thought up "legal" elections to the Commune...hoping, in the depth of their souls, that Thiers would respectfully hold back before revolutionary Paris as soon as it covered itself with the mantle of legality.[96]

What was the source of its decision? The National Guard Central Committee was founded only a few weeks before March 18, 1871, and the revolution immediately thrust full responsibility for power onto the shoulders of people who were fully representative, but thoroughly inexperienced. As Trotsky put it: "Due to its immediate and fundamental connection with the masses [the Central Committee] reflected not only all the strong sides, but also the weak sides of the masses, and from the start reflected the weak side still more than the strong. Thus it manifested a spirit of indecision, of caution, the tendency to hold back after the first successes."[97]

In one sense, the difficulties that Trotsky mentioned were inevitable. It is only in a period of crisis, when the old state can no longer maintain its monopoly of power, that alternative mass democratic structures have the space to emerge. At such times, when people break with the old ideology, but have not yet found a new one, popular ideas will be in flux. The National Guard Federation and Russian Soviets were similar in that respect. As truly democratic organizations they were bound to reflect the masses' inexperience and lack of certainty over the next step to take. However, while the Soviets overcame their initial weakness and won a civil war, the Commune never did. What was the difference between the two?

Trotsky believed the presence of the Bolshevik Party within the Soviets was crucial to their success. Its activists had years of experience organizing and learning from struggles against Tsarism. The Soviets began 1917 very much like the National Guard Central Committee in that they were unwilling to resolutely fight and defeat their capitalist enemy. They too wished to abdicate power early on. However, the Bolsheviks brought with them "the accumulated and organized experience of the proletariat...which foresees theoretically the paths of its development, all its stages, and which extracts from it the necessary formula for action."[98] Through patient argument the Bolsheviks won over the majority in the Soviets to acting on their own behalf, and in the October 1917 Revolution to creating a national state based on workers' democracy. Thus the party helped overcome the "weak side" of an inexperienced direct mass democracy, and made operative the "strong side"—the ability to represent and move vast numbers into action, and lead them to victory.

This scenario may sound all very well in the abstract. How would it have worked in practical questions such as the detailed conduct of the French civil war?

> Had there been a directing party center at Paris, it would have incorporated into the retreating armies...a few hundred or even a few dozen devoted workers, and given them the following instructions: enhance the discontent of the soldiers against the officers, profit by the first favorable psychological moment to free the soldiers from officers and bring them back to Paris to unite with the people...[99]

Although there were many currents within the Commune, none of them advocated the sort of strategy that Trotsky envisaged. Jacobins and Blanquists were too distant from the working class, or too wedded to small group conspiracies, to think in terms of such grassroots agitation. Proudhonists were too hostile to politics as such to direct action in a centralized way. Therefore no one argued for organized political agitation among the Versailles troops: "Nor was there anybody to think of it. In the midst of great events, moreover, such decisions can be adopted only by a revolutionary party which looks forward to a revolution, prepares for it, does not lose its head, by a party which is accustomed to having a rounded view and is not afraid to act."[100]

Lenin was another Marxist for whom the events of 1871 had a special significance. Although he was interested in the history of the Commune throughout his political life,[101] his chief encounter with it was during the summer of 1917. This was a particular juncture that has parallels to the situation today. At that moment the First World War was in full swing, but internationally many on the left had failed to rise to the challenge of opposing this imperialist adventure. In Russia Tsarism had been overthrown but the masses were unsure as to what to replace it with. Lenin turned to the experience of the Paris Commune, and in particular Marx's account of it in *The Civil War in France*, to help him renew the left-wing movement both abroad and at home. The result of his labor was a pamphlet called *The State and Revolution* that restated points raised by Marx, but also gave them a specific emphasis.

First of all, Lenin stressed that the Commune was not an abstract plan but a real movement of ordinary people grappling with how to overcome capitalism: "Marx did not indulge in utopias; he expected the *experience* of the mass movement to provide the reply to the question as to the specific forms this organization of the proletariat as the ruling class would assume..."[102]

The answer was the Commune, which provided an alternative vision of democracy to the dead end of capitalist "democracy": "To decide once every few years which member of the ruling class is to repress and crush the people through parliament—this is the real essence of bourgeois parliamentarism, not only in parliamentary-constitutional monarchies, but also in the most democratic republics."

The Commune did not abolish parliament with a top-down dictatorship, but replaced it with real democracy on the widest scale:

> The way out of parliamentarism is not, of course, the abolition of representative institutions and the elective principle...but the conversion of the representative institutions from talking shops into "working" bodies [where representatives] have to work, have to execute their own laws, have themselves to test the results achieved in reality, and to account directly to their constituents... from talking shops into "working" bodies.[103]

How had this been achieved in 1871? Reiterating Marx he wrote that the Commune had "replaced the smashed state machine...by fuller democracy," substituting a citizens' militia under democratic control for the standing army, submitting all officials to election and recall and paying "*all* servants of the state the level of '*workmen's wages*.'"[104]

Lenin called attention to an important development in Marx's thought brought about by the Commune. In 1872 Marx and Engels described it themselves in a Preface to *The Communist Manifesto*, their best known work. They wrote that although the original document of 1848 remained generally valid it should be updated in just one respect: "One thing especially was proved by the Commune, viz, that the working class cannot simply lay hold of the ready-made state machinery and wield it for its own purposes."[105] This alteration had profound implications.

Firstly, it was a very important counter to reformist currents. Organizations like the Labour Party promise to improve life under capitalism, but each time they operate the "ready-made state machinery" they end up running the capitalist system and sacrifice the interests of their own supporters. The Commune showed there was a better alternative—another type of state was possible.

Furthermore, not only was it more democratic than any state under capitalism could be, but it also pointed the way toward abolishing the state in general. This assertion will come as a shock to people more accustomed to the Stalinist parody of Leninism, in which worship of the state was compulsory. Lenin carefully quoted that part of *The Civil War in France,* which advocated: "'breaking state power,' which was a 'parasitic excrescence'; its 'amputation,' its 'smashing'; 'state power, now superfluous'—these are the expressions Marx used in regard to the state when appraising and analyzing the experience of the Commune."[106]

Parisian direct democracy made the masses part of the state, and the state part of the masses. In this way the notion of power from above, acting on those below, was challenged and the very foundations of the conventional state were undermined.

Lenin's emphasis on this part of Marx's account was well founded. As early as February 24, 1871, in a passage already cited, the National Guard Federation declared, "Permanent armies...have only ever been instruments of despotism."[107] Its assertion is confirmed by archaeological studies of the very oldest states, which appeared between the 7th and 3rd millennia BC in Mesopotamia (Iraq):

> [When a rich elite emerged] people could not but help notice the uneven distribution of wealth and might have been tempted to challenge the too obvious privileges... Insofar as the need to maintain order became permanent, those who were called upon to act had to be avail-

> able at all times and therefore came to form a specialized corps... The existence of such an armed force is of capital importance.[108]

An apparatus of coercion is always fundamental to the workings of the state, whose primary role is to maintain "order," i.e., existing social relations. Thus the feudal state maintained the feudal order, and the capitalist state the capitalist order.

The National Guard Federation decided that "the national citizen militia is the only national force, to the exclusion of any other,"[109] and on March 18, 1871, the revolution made this a reality, at least for Paris. Thus was released an enormous potential for human liberation and a different society. By setting up a new type of state, which fused people and power, the Commune created a situation in which the state itself could "wither away," because a system of domination by one class over another would have no reason to endure. Lenin wrote that:

> the state was bound to disappear, and that the transitional form of its disappearance (the transition from state to non-state) would be the "proletariat organized as the ruling class." Marx, however, did not set out to *discover* the political *forms* of this future stage. He limited himself to carefully observing French history... The Commune is the first attempt by a proletarian revolution to *smash* the bourgeois *state machine*; and it is the political form "at last discovered" by which the smashed state machine can and must be *replaced*.[110]

This does not mean that either Marx or Lenin accepted the anarchist belief that in 1871 the Commune had already abolished the state, even though they believed it prepared the way to that goal. The civil war demonstrated that as long as capitalism and its armies strove to reimpose the old order, workers could not dispense with a concentrated authority of their own. Lenin, recalling Marx, called this authority a workers' state, "the dictatorship of the proletariat." Engels had noted that some people were "filled with wholesome terror at the words." He defended it by explaining it was none other than the organized will of the majority class in Paris: "Do you wish to know what this dictatorship looks like? Look at the Paris Commune. That was the Dictatorship of the Proletariat."[111]

Marx, Trotsky and Lenin celebrated the Commune's strengths and studied its weaknesses. In so doing they were able to explain why it scaled such heights and yet suffered such a tragic end. Equally, they themselves learned a great deal from the Commune. This fact tells us much about the real

Marxist tradition. In contrast to the Stalinist caricature, Marxism learns from mass struggles rather than preaching sermons, and it stands for the direct democracy and liberating qualities so abundant in the Paris Commune.

The Marxist understanding of the Commune is all the more pertinent now that key traditional reference points for the left, like the 1917 Russian Revolution, are often not seen as relevant by people in the anticapitalist and anti-imperialist movements. Some react against the horrors of capitalism by what amount to Blanquist attempts at minority actions, or against Stalinism by Proudhonist/autonomist attempts to avoid politics. In 1871 these currents represented genuine, if one-sided, attempts to solve key questions and as such were embraced by masses of Parisians. While the Blanquists and Jacobins understood the need for solid organization to overcome their capitalist opponents, the Proudhonists realized that mass popular involvement was essential for the creation of a new society. Alas, isolation in one city, the novel character of what they were doing, and the sheer brutality of the enemy, meant that the communards were unable to successfully synthesize their insights. The benefit of hindsight means that this failure does not have to be repeated.

Yet we are not encouraged to look back at the Commune. After it was crushed, the government of France and its international allies tried to expunge it from history.[112] The Montmartre heights, where the March 18 uprising began, were buried beneath the Basilica of Sacré-Coeur. Numerous buildings destroyed by fire during Bloody Week, such as the Hôtel de Ville, were faithfully reconstructed. The Vendôme Column, that "monument to barbarism," stands again.

Despite these efforts, the memory of the Commune lives on through "The Internationale," a song that is sung wherever people fight back against the system, and rightly so. Nothing can diminish the magnificence of the communards' endeavor. Notwithstanding the difficulties that arose, the solutions that the Commune began to sketch out, in relation to women's rights, education, workers' control, justice, overcoming poverty, and above all the nature of a workers' state in the transition to a truly free society, were outstanding.

For these reasons, wherever the movement for anticapitalism and anti-imperialism grows, so is the last wish of the communards fulfilled:

> Whatever may happen, whether or not we will be defeated once more and be dead tomorrow, our generation is consoled! We are paid back

after 20 years of defeats and anguish. Bugles! Blow in the wind! Drums! Strike up the rhythm! Comrade, you have gray hair like me—let's embrace! And you, young kid, playing marbles behind the barricade, come here so that I can embrace you too! The 18 [of] March has indeed saved you, young fellow! You could, like us, have grown up lost in the fog, wallowing in the mud, rolling about in blood, dying of shame and the indescribable pain of humiliation! That's over! We have bled and cried for you. You will inherit the fruits of our efforts. Child of desperation, you will be free.[113]

Notes

One: The Commune's Achievements

1. The best known insurrectionary leader, Auguste Blanqui, was under arrest for a previous unsuccessful rising, while Charles Delescluze, the leading Jacobin radical, was away from Paris.
2. Quoted in L Greenberg, *Sisters of Liberty: Marseilles, Lyon, Paris and the Reaction to a Centralized State, 1868–1871* (Harvard, 1971), p95.
3. P O Lissagaray, *History of the Paris Commune* (London, 1976), pp67, 369-371.
4. See *Journal Officiel de la Commune*, March 27, 1871; and J Rougerie (ed), *1871: Jalons pour une histoire de la Commune de Paris* (Amsterdam, 1973), p52.
5. General Vinoy, *L'armistice et la Commune* (Paris, 1872), pp212-213.
6. As above, p218.
7. R Tombs, *The War Against Paris 1871* (Cambridge, 1981), p40.
8. *Guerre des communeux, 18 mars-28 mai 1871, par un officier supérieur de l'armée de Versailles* (Paris, 1871), p76.
9. See E Reclus, *La Commune de Paris, au jour le jour* (Paris, 1908), p3.
10. J Favre, *Gouvernment de la Défense Nationale du 30 juin au 31 octobre* (Paris, 1871), p210.
11. E Reclus, p7.
12. See *Guerre des communeux*, p78.
13. Quoted in G Lefrançais, *Etude sur le mouvement communaliste à Paris, en 1871* (Neuchâtel, 1871), p137.
14. L Michel, *La Commune* (Paris, 1989), p164.
15. *Guerre des communeux*, p79.
16. As above, p80.
17. P Martine, *Souvenirs d'un insurgé* (Paris, 1971), p36.
18. See P O Lissagaray, p66.
19. See Thiers's own testimony quoted in J Rougerie, *Paris libre, 1871* (Paris, 1971), p102, where he cites his memory of February 1848 as the determining factor. See also A Arnould, *Histoire Populaire et Parlementaire de la Commune de Paris*

(Lyon, 1981), p98; and *Guerre des communeux*, p83.

20 E Reclus, p14. Arnould echoes the same point. See A Arnould, 223.

21 Felix Pyat writing in *La Commune* of March 24, 1871, quoted in M Découflé, "La spontanéité révolutionnaire dans une révolution populaire: L'exemple de la Commune de Paris," in *Cahiers de l'ISEA*, August 1965, no 164, p179.

22 *Journal Officiel* (Versailles edition), May 29, 1871.

23 J Rougerie, *Procès des communards* (Paris, 1964), p177.

24 E Schulkind, *The Paris Commune of 1871: The View from the Left* (London, 1972), p144; A Vermorel (ed), *l'Ami du Peuple*, April 24.

25 A Arnould, p130.

26 J and E de Goncourt, *Journal: Mémoires de la vie littéraire*, vol 4, 1870-1871 (Paris, no date), p189.

27 C Barral de Montaud, *Notes journaliers sur l'état de Paris durant la Commune: Travail presenté à la Assemblée National (Commission d'enquête parlementaire)* (no place or date), p18.

28 A-M Blanchecotte, *Tablette d'une femme pendant la Commune* (Tussin-Charente, 1996), p38.

29 Meeting in Brussels, mid-April quoted in E Schulkind, *The Paris Commune of 1871*, p195.

30 International meeting in Geneva on April 15, 1871, quoted in E Schulkind, *The Paris Commune of 1871*, p192.

31 H Lefebvre, *La proclamation de la Commune, 26 Mars 1871* (Paris, 1965), pp21-22.

32 Cassell's new *French-English/English-French Dictionary*, London 1962.

33 Quoted in E Andréoli, *Le Gouvernement du 4 Septembre et la Commune de Paris* (Paris, 1871), p203.

34 May 1871, Quoted in M Découflé, p179.

35 P O Lissagaray, *History of the Paris Commune*, p241.

36 V Debuchy, *La vie à Paris sous la Commune* (Paris, no date), p69.

37 J Andrieu, *Notes pour servir à l'histoire de la Commune de Paris en 1871* (Paris, no date), p69.

38 F Jellinek, *The Paris Commune of 1871* (London, 1937), p166.

39 P Martine, p142.

40 P O Lissagaray, p176.

41 As above, p177.

42 Quoted in N Maclellan (ed), *Louise Michel* (Melbourne, 2004), p55.

43 Quoted in M Dommanget, *L'enseignment, l'enfance et la culture sous la Commune* (Paris, no date), pp23-24; and R Tombs, *The Paris Commune 1871* (London/New York 1999), p76.

44 V Debuchy, p113.

45 As above, p77.

46 A Arnould, p245.

47 As above.

48 C Beslay, *La verité sur la Commune* (Brussels, 1878), p55; P L Lavrov, *Die Pariser Kommune* (Berlin, 1871), p81; P Martine, p204. During this time 3,500 arrests were made. R Tombs, p88.

49 V Debuchy, p114.

50 Though a decision on establishing municipal butchers to undercut the private ones was not finalized. This was the proposal of Viard on May 8, in G Bourgin and G Henriot, *Procès-Verbaux de la Commune de 1871*, vol 1 (Paris, 1924), p253.

51 W Serman, *La Commune de Paris, 1871* (Paris, 1986), pp354-355.

52 P Martine, p104.

53 A Arnould, p236.

54 G Bourgin and G Henriot, p81.

55 C Barral de Montaud, p60.

56 V Debuchy, p75.

57 This is the point made by E Reclus, p79.

58 G Bourgin and G Henriot, p44.

59 A Bevan, *In Place of Fear* (London,

1978), p26.
60 K Marx and F Engels, *On the Paris Commune* (Moscow, 1971), p71.
61 R Tombs, p86; C Rihs, *La Commune de Paris: Sa Structure et ses Doctrines* (Geneva, 1955), p103.
62 A Arnould, p228.
63 Quoted in M Dommanget, p23.
64 A Arnould, p156.
65 S Edwards, *The Paris Commune* (London, 1971), pp79-80.
66 A Rogeard in *Le Vengeur*, April 3, 1871.
67 W Serman, p149.
68 E Reclus, p52.
69 G Bourgin and G Henriot, p53.
70 S Marcus, "Haussmannization as Anti-Modernity," in *Journal of Urban History*, vol 27, no 6 (September 2001), p725.
71 J Leighton, *Paris under the Commune: The Seventy-Three Days of the Second Siege* (London, 1871), p81.
72 *Journal Officiel de la Commune*, 21 March 1871.
73 My emphasis, G Bourgin and G Henriot, p53.
74 As above.
75 Tombs mistakenly suggests that "the Commune did not accept suggestions to requisition all empty apartments," only those abandoned since March 18. The opposite was true. After debate, the date of March 18 was deleted, the final decree stating: "Article 1—Requisition is made of all vacant apartments." G Bourgin and G Henriot, p459.
76 As above, p83.
77 See account by Barral de Montaud of how he managed to prevent this in the district where he was active. C Barral de Montaud, p16.
78 R Tombs, p107. Tombs adds that when the Versailles forces took Paris, Dugène was transported to the prison colony of New Caledonia.
79 Record of Marx's speech from Minutes of the General Council meeting of April 25, 1871, in *Documents of the First International*, vol 1 (London, no date), p72.
80 G Bourgin and G Henriot, vol 2 (Paris, 1945), p220. See also R Dumont (ed), *Organization des monts-de-piété en France et projets de réforme* (Paris, 1905).
81 G Bourgin and G Henriot, vol 2, p224.
82 R Tombs, p96.
83 E Reclus, p277.
84 In practice the Commune managed to return some 42,000 items but had no time to achieve more. G Lefrançais, p298; and R Tombs, p96.
85 G Bourgin and G Henriot, vol 2, p116.
86 P O Lissagaray, p196.
87 Many recent historians feel the need to deny any Marxist influence in Paris. Yet it is surely significant that not only was Marx in touch with the International's emissaries—Serrailler and Dimitrieff—he corresponded with both Frankel and Varlin who were central figures in the Commune. See Marx's letter of May 13, 1871, in K Marx and F Engels, *Correspondence 1846–1895* (London, 1934), p311.
88 Quoted in J Rougerie, *Paris libre*, pp175-176.
89 G Bourgin and G Henriot, vol 1, p543.
90 See details in *La Révolution Politique et Sociale* of May 8, 1871.
91 G Bourgin and G Henriot, vol 1, p539.
92 As above, p539.
93 See, for example, G Lefrançais, p298; and A Arnould, p169.
94 G Bourgin and G Henriot, vol 1, p542.
95 My emphasis. As above, p542.
96 Report by delegates on military

uniforms, signed Lévy Lazare and Evette, in G Bourgin and G Henriot, vol 2, p349.

97 Françoise Jourde quoted in G Bourgin and G Henriot, vol 2, pp353-354.

98 Quoted in J Rougerie, *Procès des communards*, p227.

99 G Bourgin and G Henriot, pp351-352. This proposal was accepted unanimously on May 12. G Bourgin and G Henriot, p355.

100 Quoted in J Rougerie, *Procès des communards*, p210.

101 Proposal by Vesinier, in G Bourgin and G Henriot, vol 2, p149.

102 *La Révolution Politique et Sociale*, April 31, 1871.

103 G Lefrançais, pp271-272.

104 W Serman, p367.

105 J Rougerie, *Procès des communards*, p221.

106 J Rougerie, *Paris libre*, p176. Our knowledge of the workings of this system of workers' control is limited, the main source being Avrial's comments as reported by Rossel, who himself was hostile to socialist experiments. But his account of liberated workers may have an element of truth to it: "At the association of mechanics they arrive when they want, chat a lot and don't do much work" [J Rougerie, *Procès des communards* (Paris 1964), p224]. The price of liberation from bosses' oppression may have been a temporary fall in production. That this was likely in any successful revolution is the general argument made by Nikolai Bukharin in *The Politics and Economics of the Transition Period* (London, 1978).

107 J Rougerie, *Procès des communards* (Paris, 1964), p222.

108 Quoted in S Braibant, *Elisabeth Dmitrieff, aristocrate et pétroleuse* (Paris, 1992), p114.

109 A Thiers, *De la Propriété*, pp485-486, 491.

110 W Serman, p35.

111 M Choury, *La Commune au coeur de Paris* (Paris 1967), p305. See also G Bourgin and G Henriot, vol 1, pp159-161.

112 R Tombs, p104.

113 A Arnould, p165.

114 G Bourgin and G Henriot, vol 2, p404.

115 V Debuchy, p75.

116 G Bourgin and G Henriot, pp366-368.

117 E Reclus, p340.

118 G Lefrançais, p245.

119 J Rougerie, *Procès des communards*, p214.

120 S Braibant, p116.

121 R Christiansen, *Paris Babylon, The Story of the Paris Commune* (London, 1994), pp314-315.

122 Letter from Dmitrieff to Hermann Jung on April 24, in S Braibant, p132.

123 Quoted in S Braibant, p141.

124 Translation in R Christiansen, p314. It has been argued that Dmitrieff "took it for granted that the cooperatives they were organizing would cover 'the trades essentially practised by women'" as though she dared not ask for anything more [R Tombs, p104]. This ignores the union's appeal, addressed to the Commune, which asks for "the money necessary for the running of factories and workshops abandoned by the bourgeoisie, *including* the trades essentially practised by women" [Quoted in J Rougerie, *Paris libre, 1871* (Paris, 1971), p182]. So all production (which included women's labor) was targeted! Furthermore, in the midst of civil war and dire poverty the Women's Union's demands were rightly shaped by the immediate needs of working-class women.

125 See G Bourgin and G Henriot, vol

2, p228.
126 S Braibant, p149.
127 As above, p153.
128 P O Lissagaray, p239.
129 V Debuchy, p140.
130 *Journal Officiel de la Commune*, April 2, 1871.
131 Letter to the Rector of Angers from a priest, quoted in A Prost, *Histoire de l'Enseignement en France, 1800–1967* (Paris, 1968), p170.
132 A Blanqui, "Le communisme, avenir de la société," in V P volguine (ed), *Auguste Blanqui, Textes Choisis* (Paris, 1971).
133 F McCollum Feeley, *Rebels with Causes* (New York, 1981), pp13-14.
134 Thiers in 1849 quoted in A Prost, p150. My emphasis.
135 G Bourgin and G Henriot, vol 2, p82.
136 W Serman, p397.
137 G Larguier and J Quaretti (eds), *La Commune de 1871: Utopie ou Modernité* (Perpignan, 2000), p418.
138 G Bourgin and G Henriot, vol 1, p104.
139 E Reclus, p79.
140 G Lefrançais, p273.
141 See G Bourgin and G Henriot, vol 1, p154, for session of April 9, 1871; and R Christiansen, p322.
142 Quoted in W Serman, p382.
143 Quoted in M Dommanget, p25. See, for example, the poster of the 3rd arrondissement, which took over three congregational schools and introduced secular education.
144 Quoted in S Edwards, p272.
145 H Bellenger in *Le Vengeur*, April 8, 1871. The Commune thus introduced what would later be the watchword of Bolshevik educators: "the bringing up of a creative personality developed on many sides." Quoted in C Rosenberg, *Education and Revolution* (London, no date), p5.
146 *La Sociale*, April 20, 1871.
147 G Larguier and J Quaretti (eds), pp335-336.
148 As above.
149 See J Harriot in a transcript of a debate on "The Commune—Utopia or Modernity," in G Larguier and J Quaretti (eds), p420.
150 *La Révolution Politique et Sociale*, April 16, 1871.
151 Paul de Saint-Victor quoted in R Christiansen, p319.
152 *Guerre des communeux*, p347.
153 As above, p349.
154 G Bourgin and G Henriot, vol 1, p64.
155 *Journal Officiel de la Commune*, March 24, 1871. He gratefully declined the commission. His letter ran as follows: "Thank you for the honor you have conferred upon me by my nomination as Commander-in-Chief of the National Guard of Paris, which I love, and whose dangers and glory I should be proud to share," March 28, 1871. Letter quoted in J Leighton, p90.
156 *Pere Duchêne*, April 12, quoted in *La chute de la colonne Vendôme, 16 mai 1871* (Paris, 1998), p20.
157 *Guerre des communeux*, p201.
158 G Bourgin and G Henriot, vol 1, p190.
159 *Les Grands Dossiers de l'Illustration*, p149.
160 G Bourgin and G Henriot, vol 1, p23.
161 As above, p141, reported in *Journal Officiel de la Commune*, April 8, 1871.
162 As above, p167. The composition was as follows: a senior officer, two officers, two junior officers, and two rank-and-file guards.
163 "On April 13 the Council of War of the XVth 295 Legion shot a National Guard for murdering his superior officer. Another Council of War, held by Melliet at Bicêtre, shot a guard, Thibault, for suspected treachery, in the presence of Dereure and Amoureux,

officially representing the Commune, which gave its approval at the session of May 12. On May 19 Johannard, Civil Commissioner to General La Cecilia, reported the shooting of a spy. It is possible that Dombrowski shot some peasants on the northern front around April 16, for murdering his men—the evidence is not very clear." F Jellinek, p294.

164 V Debuchy, p74.
165 P Martine, p148.
166 E Andréoli, p285.
167 V Debuchy, p74.
168 L M de Marancour, *Hommes et choses du temps de la Commune* (Paris, 1871), p114.
169 Villiers de l'Isle-Adam quoted in S Edwards, p308.
170 Fédération des Artistes de Paris (14 April—signed Avrial, Vaillant, Vermorel), *Les révolutions du XIX siècle, 1852–1872: Affiches, feuilles volantes, documents divers* (Paris, 1988).
171 Speech of May 19 in G Bourgin and G Henriot, vol 2, pp426-427.
172 J Rougerie, *Paris libre*, p171.
173 As above, p171.
174 Quoted in J Rougerie, p172.
175 R Tombs, p107.
176 V Debuchy, p173.
177 As above, p167.
178 Quoted in S Edwards, p308.
179 J Rougerie, *Paris libre*, p208.
180 E Schulkind, "The Activity of Popular Organizations during the Paris Commune of 1871," in *French Historical Studies* (December 1960), p396.
181 F Wey, *Chronique du Siège de Paris* (Paris 1871), p385.
182 J Bruhat, "Pouvoir, pouvoirs, état en 1871," in *Mouvement Social*, no 77, (October-December 1971), p168.
183 Quoted in C Rihs, p112.
184 *L'Avant-Garde*, April 4, 1871.
185 *L'Affranchi*, April 2, 1871.
186 J Bruhat, p168.
187 *L'Affranchi*, April 2, 1871.
188 President of the Executive Commission on April 26, in G Bourgin and G Henriot, vol 1, p488.
189 *Journal Officiel de la Commune*, April 28, 1871.
190 There were no clubs in the 8th, 10th and 16th arrondissements and little activity in the 2nd and 4th. W Serman, p292; and M Choury, p289.
191 M Choury, p290.
192 J Rougerie, *Paris libre*, p208.
193 As above, p207.
194 E Reclus, p339.
195 P Martine, p174; E Maury, *Mes souvenirs sur les Evénements des années 1870–1871* (Paris, 1999), p62; and R Tombs, p143.
196 P O Lissagaray, pp239-240.
197 M Choury, pp290-291.
198 J Rougerie, *Paris libre*, p213.
199 E Schulkind, "The Activity of Popular Organizations," p413.
200 As above, p411.
201 M Choury, p293.
202 As above, p291; and *Le Vengeur*, May 7, 1871.
203 J Rougerie, *Paris libre*, p209.
204 E Schulkind, "The Activity of Popular Organizations," p405.
205 J Bruhat, p168.
206 J Rougerie (ed), p61.
207 E Schulkind, "The Activity of Popular Organizations," pp403-404.
208 P Boisseau, "Le République démocratique et sociale de 1871: une forme originale de gouvernement du peuple par le peuple et pour le peuple," in G Larguier, p49.
209 W Serman, p319.
210 "Was it the case that the Commune simply recognized theoretically the participation of the people in its legislative procedure? No, because the daily action of the delegates in their

municipalities, the breadth of the proposals, the presence of representatives of the clubs and the International, allow us to affirm that certain measures were the result of specific requests from particular social groups. This was, for example, the case in regard to the banning of night-work for bakery workers"—P Boisseau, p51.

211 See G Bourgin and G Henriot, vol 2, pp449-469.
212 Quoted in E Andréoli, p203.
213 P Boisseau, p49.
214 J Andrieu, p203.
215 Quoted in J Rougerie, *Paris libre*, p150.
216 A Arnould, pp125-6.
217 *Le Reveil du Peuple*, April 18, 1871.
218 Quoted in J Rougerie, *Paris libre*, p157.
219 Quoted in G Lefrançais, p176.
220 International Manifesto of March 23, 1871, reprinted in *Les révolutions du XIX siècle, 1852–1872.*
221 Central Committee of the National Guard statement of April 5, 1871, printed in *Journal Officiel de la Commune*, April 7, 1871, translation in F Jellinek, pp200-201.

Two: The Capital of the Human Race

1 Cited in A Smart, "The Darkness and Claustrophobia of the City: Victor Hugo and the Myth of Paris," in *Modern and Contemporary France*, vol 8, no 3 (2000), p316; and A Horne, *The Fall of Paris, The Siège and the Commune 1870–1* (London, 1965), p79. A century later Walter Benjamin saw it as the "capital of the 19th century." Quoted in A Benjamin (ed), *The Problems of Modernity* (London, 1989), p1.
2 *Journal Officiel de la Republique Française sous la Commune*, March 20, 1871.
3 *L' Avant-Garde*, May 19, 1871. *L'Affranchi*, Grousset's paper spoke in similar terms: "The disinherited army [of workers] rose to conquer their rights and make the revolution of '89. In reality, by affirming the three indivisible principles, Liberty, Equality and Fraternity, it only produced political emancipation... It remains to destroy the economic order." *L'Affranchi*, April 2, 1871.
4 G Bourgin and G Henriot, vol 2, p397.
5 J F Varlet, *Déclaration solonnel des droits de l'homme dans l'état social* (Paris, 1793), pp3-4.
6 *Révolution politique et sociale*, translation in E Schulkind, *The Paris Commune of 1871*, p185.
7 Calculated from table in J M Merriman, *French Cities in the Nineteenth Century* (London, 1982), p88.
8 D H Pinkney, "The Revolutionary Crowd in Paris in the 1830s," in *Journal of Social History*, vol 5 (Summer 1972), p512.
9 S Gémie, *French Revolutions, 1815–1914: An Introduction* (Edinburgh, 1999), p125.
10 K Marx, "The Class Struggles in France: 1848 to 1850," in K Marx, *Surveys from Exile* (Harmondsworth, 1973), p57.
11 As above, pp58-59.
12 J Bron, *Histoire du mouvement ouvrier français*, vol 1 (Paris 1968), p115.
13 1789 led to still more state centralization. Marx wrote, "The task of the first French revolution was to destroy all separate local, territorial, urban and provincial powers in order to create the civil unity of the nation. It had to carry further the centralization that the absolute monarchy had begun" [K Marx, "The Eighteenth Brumaire of Louis Bonaparte," in K Marx, p237]. He added, "If Paris, as a result of political centralization, rules France, in moments of

revolutionary upheaval the workers rule Paris" [as above, p42].

14 G Duveau, *Histoire du people français* (Paris, no date), p90.
15 Figures from B R Mitchell, *European Historical Statistics, 1750–1970* (London, 1978), pp12-14.
16 R Tombs, *The Paris Commune 1871*, p14.
17 Napoleon III, letter to Billaut, July 9, 1857.
18 G Haussmann, *Mémoires* (Paris, 2000), p557.
19 As above, p558.
20 Serman accepts these arguments at face value, and no doubt there was an element of "civil objectives" within the mix, but only an element. W Serman, p17.
21 Parliamentary Commission of 1859 quoted in P Lavedan, *Nouvelle Histoire de Paris; Histoire de l'Urbanisme à Paris* (Paris, 1993), p421.
22 Quoted in D P Jordan, *Transforming Paris: The Life and Labors of Baron Haussmann* (New York, 1995), p110.
23 W Serman, p19.
24 A-L Shapiro, "Housing Reform in Paris: Social Space and Social Control," in *French Historical Studies* (Autumn, 1982), p487.
25 S Marcus, p727.
26 D H Pinkney, Review of "Paris La Ville" by J Gaillard, in *Journal of Social History*, vol 12, no 2 (Winter 1978), p332.
27 E Reclus, p51.
28 S Marcus, p725.
29 W Serman, p26.
30 R Christiansen, p17.
31 R Tombs, *The War Against Paris 1871*, pp3-4.
32 Quoted in J P T Bury, *Napoleon III and the Second Empire* (London, 1975), p19.
33 Figures from J Bron, pp132-3.
34 Quoted in A Plessis, *De la fête impériale au mur des fédérés, 1852–1871* (no place, 1973), p17.
35 R Price, *Napoleon III and the Second Empire* (London, 1997), p19; J P T Bury (ed), *The New Cambridge Modern History: The Zenith of European Power, 1830–70* (Cambridge, 1964), p445; A Plessis, p176.
36 H Lefebvre, p91.
37 F Mehring, *Karl Marx: The Story of His Life* (London, 1966), p319.
38 A Plessis, p59.
39 Details from A Plessis, p209.
40 R Price, p45.
41 A Plessis, p210.
42 J P T Bury, *Napoleon III*, pp86-87.
43 This was the advice of Prince Napoleon to his cousin the emperor. Quoted in J F McMillan, *Napoleon III* (London, 1991), p121.
44 Quoted in J F McMillan, p125.
45 As above, p121.
46 M Howard, *The Franco-Prussian War* (London, 1961), p1.
47 Quoted in J P T Bury, *Napoleon III*, p21.
48 These are the words of a later government study quoted in A F Kovacs, "French Military Institutions before the Franco-Prussian War," in *The American Historical Review*, vol 51, no 2, January 1946, p218.
49 M Howard, p10.
50 Engels noted the contradiction in a system that "pretends to make every able-bodied man a soldier" while "this same army is to be the armed support, the mainstay, of a quasi-absolutist government." F Engels, "How to Fight the Prussians," *Pall Mall Gazette*, September 17, 1870, in *Collected Works*, vol 22, p105.
51 A F Kovacs, p217.
52 As above, p220.
53 Quoted in M Howard, p34.
54 L J Trochu, *L'armée française en 1867* (Paris, 1895), p62.

55 A Plessis, p223.

56 J Dombrowski, *Trochu comme organisateur et comme general en chef* (December, 1870), p2.

57 Quoted in M Howard, p188.

58 G Bibesco, *Campagne de 1870, Belfort, Reims, Sedan* (Paris, 1872), p72.

59 Notes by Emile Ollivier cited in E Zola, *La Débacle* (no place, 1984), p635.

60 E Zola, p132.

61 *Campagne de 1870. Des Causes qui ont amené la capitulation de Sedan par un Officier attaché à l'Etat-Major Général* (Brussels, no date), p28.

62 *Journal Officiel de la Republique Française sous la Commune*, March 20, 1871.

63 J Bron, pp135-136.

64 As above, p140.

65 A Plessis, p130. The picture is, in fact, rather more uneven than the preceding figures suggest, there having been an actual decline in numbers of industrial workers in the 1856-66 period. 1860 was the start of a long, gradual, slowing down of the economy. [See J-C Asselain, *Histoire économique de la France* (no place, 1984), pp152-3]. Nevertheless the overall argument obtains.

66 J Bron, p150.

67 J-C Asselain, p149.

68 A Plessis, p130.

69 Incomes were two to three times greater than elsewhere. T M McBride, "The Modernisation of Woman's Work," in *Journal for Modern History*, June 1977, p238.

70 W Serman, pp38-40.

71 As above, p34.

72 There were also 200,000 white collar workers and 160,000 domestics and porters. T M McBride, p238.

73 J Gaillard, *Paris la ville 1852–1870* (Paris, 1977), p55-56.

74 See J Gaillard, "Les usines Cail et les ouvriers métallurgistes de Grenelle," in *Mouvement Social*, no 33/34 (October 1960-March 1961). Other examples could be cited. See W Serman, p22.

75 Figures are for 1860. J Gaillard, *Paris la ville*, p43. This made the average size of workshops eight employees. The figure is for 1872. In 1860 it was six. As above, p433.

76 W Serman, p23.

77 As above, p25.

78 This is the crux of Trotsky's theory of permanent revolution. Indeed Trotsky used the Paris Commune as a key piece of evidence for this: "It is possible for the workers to come to power in an economically backward country sooner than in an advanced country. In 1871 the workers deliberately took power in their hands in petty bourgeois Paris—true for only two months, but in the great-capitalist centers of Britain and the US the workers have never held power for so much as an hour. To imagine that the dictatorship of the proletariat is in any way automatically dependent on the technical development and resources of a country is a prejudice of 'economic' materialism simplified to an absurdity." L Trotsky, *The Permanent Revolution and Results and Prospects* (London, 1962), p195.

79 *L'organization des travailleurs par les corporations nouvelles* (Paris, 1861), p7. It went on to beg Bonaparte to put industry into the hands of these new associations. This type of approach shows how Proudhon's illusions in the emperor were shared by others.

80 Quoted in J Bron, p185.

81 The fact that workshops averaged only thirty-two employees did not prevent victory or the growth of radical ideas. Figure calculated from figures in *Historique de la Grêve du*

Bronze en 1867 (Paris, 1867), pp9, 25.
82 As above, p29.
83 As above, p56.
84 J Bron, p188.
85 *Grève des mineurs. Jugement correctionnel du Tribunal de Saint-Etienne* (no place, 1869), p4. These strikes were the ostensible subject of Emile Zola's great novel *Germinal*, though he also drew on the experience of strikes in the 1880s.
86 Figures in J Bron, p189.
87 *Grève des mineurs*, p3.
88 A Dalotel, A Faure and J-C Feiermuth, *Aux origines de la Commune: Le mouvement des réunions politiques à Paris, 1868–70* (Paris, 1980), p175.
89 P J Proudhon, *Qu'est-ce la Propriété?* quoted in J Bron, p166.
90 E Hyams, *Pierre-Joseph Proudhon: His Revolutionary Life, Mind and Works* (London, 1979), p44.
91 Quoted in K Marx, "The Poverty of Philosophy," in Marx, *Collected Works*, vol 6, p128.
92 Quoted in E Hyams, p45.
93 A Callinicos, *The Revolutionary Ideas of Karl Marx* (London, 1983), p113.
94 *Troisième procès de l'Association Internationale des Travailleurs à Paris* (July 1870), p128.
95 P J Proudhon quoted in E Hyams, p246.
96 P J Proudhon in 1850 quoted in J Bron, p171.
97 Quoted in E Hyams, p102.
98 Quoted in J S Shapiro, "Pierre Joseph Proudhon, Harbinger of Fascism," in *American Historical Review*, vol 50, no 4, July 1945, p724.
99 *Le Représentant du Peuple*, May 16, 1848.
100 J S Shapiro, p727.
101 My emphasis. J Bron, p132.
102 Quoted in E Hyams, p205. Proudhon also took an extremely hostile attitude toward the emancipation of women, and toward Jews. He opposed the North in the American Civil War and favored war [see Shapiro, pp731, 734 and 729]. However, Shapiro is wrong to see Proudhon as a "harbinger of fascism" because of the way his doctrines were taken up in practice by the labor movement and transformed.
103 P J Proudhon, *De la capacité politique des classes ouvrières* (Paris, 1989), pp99-100.
104 As above, p101.
105 P J Proudhon to National Assembly in July 1848, quoted in J S Shapiro, p722.
106 Quoted in E Hyams, as above, p188.
107 One with 2,000 members ran from 1866 before collapsing in November 1868. See A Dalotel, A Faure and J-C Feiermuth, p235n.
108 P J Proudhon, *De la capacité politique des classes ouvrières*, p291.
109 As above, pp291-292. It is significant that Proudhon argued *against* municipal rights for Paris, because, as an opponent of centralism he believed that this would have given the city too much power within France. As above, pp298-299, 294.
110 A Dalotel, A Faure and J-C Feiermuth, p231.
111 C Rihs, pp67-68.
112 J Vallès, *L'Insurgé* (Paris, 1923), p199.
113 Quoted in M Paz, *Un révolutionnaire professionel: Blanqui* (no place, 1984), p43.
114 A Soboul, *The French Revolution, 1787–1799* (London 1974), pp487-492.
115 E S Mason, "Blanqui and Communism," in *Political Science Quarterly*, vol 44, no 4 (December 1929), p516.
116 Quoted in M Paz, p260.

117 See S Bernstein, *Auguste Blanqui and the Art of Insurrection* (London, 1971), p203.
118 A Blanqui, "Le communisme, avenir de la société," in V P volguine (ed), as above.
119 E S Mason, p504.
120 As above, p507.
121 As above, p509.
122 S Bernstein, pp81-82.
123 M Paz, p186.
124 S Bernstein, pp283-284.
125 Quoted in M Dommanget, *Blanqui, La Guerre de 1870–71, et la Commune* (Paris, 1947), p67.
126 Some examples of Commune council members who ran newspapers are *L'Affranchi*, editor Paschal Grousset; *L'Ami du Peuple*, Vermorel; *Le Combat* and *Le Vengeur*, Felix Pyat; and *Le Reveil du Peuple*, Delescluze. Other papers worthy of mention are *La Révolution Politique et Sociale*, the International's newspaper and *Le Tribun* of Lissagaray.
127 *La Patrie en Danger*, September 16, 1870; also in J Clarétie, *Histoire de la Révolution de 1870–71*, vol 1 (no place or date), pp160-162. This affair had similarities to an uprising Blanqui attempted in 1839. His men were summoned for Sunday afternoon arms drill and only when they turned up did they discover that this would be no training exercise but the real thing. There were posters issued proclaiming a provisional government, but its members had not even been consulted!
128 L Willette, *Raoul Rigault, 25 ans, communard, chef de police* (Paris, 1984), p80.
129 Quoted in E S Mason, p519. This was not the first time that Blanqui was absent from key events because premature action had led to his imprisonment. He made the same error in 1848 and missed the June uprising of the workers.
130 M Dommanget, *Blanqui*, p128.
131 For a full discussion of the negotiations on this issue see G Dallas, "An Exercise in Terror? The Paris Commune, 1871," in *History Today* (February, 1989), pp39-44.
132 Quoted in M Dommanget, *Blanqui*, p129.
133 C Rihs, pp84-87.
134 C Delescluze, *Aux habitants des campagnes* (Paris, 1870).
135 See C Rihs, p151.
136 P L Lavrov, p35.
137 My emphasis. M Allner, "Les Communeux Jacobins: héritage idéologique et exercice du pouvoir révolutionnaire," in *Mouvement Social*, no 117 (October-December 1981), p193.
138 M A Bakunin, *The Paris Commune and the Idea of the State* (New York, 1871).
139 G Lefrançais, p41.
140 See S Braibant, as above. Like Dmitrieff, Serrailler was sent by the General Council of the International to participate, but played a relatively minor role.
141 P J Proudhon in *Le Représentant du Peuple*, May 16, 1848.
142 S Bernstein, pp294-295.
143 J Rougerie (ed), p11.
144 *The Communist Manifesto* states that "in place of the old local and national seclusion and self-sufficiency, we have intercourse in every direction, universal inter-dependence of nations." K Marx and F Engels, *Collected Works*, vol 6, p488.
145 *Documents of the First International*, vol 1 (London, no date), p288.
146 As above, p286.
147 It might be argued that Marx was simply engaged in a diplomatic sleight of hand. The founding documents do lack the incisive clarity and sharpness of, say, *The Communist Manifesto*. However,

there was more to them than that. Marx wrote to Engels that the working class was still recovering from the defeat of the 1848 revolutions and "time is necessary before the revived movement can permit itself the old audacious language. The need of the moment is: bold in matter, but mild in manner" [quoted in F Mehring, p329]. Mehring explains the strategy well: "The aim of the International was to unite the whole of the fighting proletariat of Europe and America into one great army… Marx relied exclusively on the intellectual development of the working class which would result from its united action" [p329]. Ideas would change through class struggle and vice versa in truly dialectical fashion.

148 In Britain a similar process occurred. One example of how this worked in practice was the London tailors' strike of 1866. The International's General Council minutes warned that the employers "intended to get men from the Continent to supplant those on strike." The council contacted its supporters to ensure that these plans were thwarted [*Documents of the First International*, vol 1 (London, no date), p174]. This effort was successful and soon the tailors' executive had decided their association should join the International en bloc [Minutes of April 17, 1866, p178]. Inspired by this the 1,000 members of the Coventry Ribbon and Smallwares Weavers' Association immediately affiliated.

149 See E Varlin, *Pratique militant. Ecrits d'un ouvrier communard* (Paris, 1977), pp24-25.

150 J Rougerie, *Paris libre*, p23.

151 *Troisième procès de l'Association Internationale des Travailleurs à Paris*, p58.

152 As above, p64. P L Lavrov, p28.

153 P O Lissagaray puts the figure at 200,000. As above, p11.

154 *Troisième procès de l'Association Internationale des Travailleurs à Paris*, pp40-41.

155 See E Varlin, pp109-110.

156 *Troisième procès de l'Association Internationale des Travailleurs à Paris*, pp99, 112.

Three: War and Siege

1 Quoted in E Varlin, pp124-125.

2 *Pariser Kommune 1871 Berichte und Dokumente von Zeitgenossen* (Berlin, 1931), pp85-86.

3 J-J Becker and S Audoin-Rouzeau, *La France, La Nation, La Guerre: 1850–1920* (Paris, 1995), pp55, 65.

4 Gramont, France's foreign minister, quoted in *L'Illustration*, July 16, 1870. Therefore, Marx's initial view was that "on the German side, the war is a war of defense" [K Marx, "First Address of the General Council of the International Working Men's Association on the Franco-Prussian War," in K Marx and F Engels, *On the Paris Commune*, p37]. However, he warned the German working class not to "allow the present war to lose its strictly defensive character and to degenerate into a war against the French people…," p38.

5 In Marx's words the Prussian government was guilty "of the crime of reviving, in the second half of the 19th century, the policy of conquest!" K Marx and F Engels, p43.

6 J-J Becker and S Audoin-Rouzeau, p77.

7 W Serman, p106.

8 *L'Illustration*, September 10, 1870.

9 The revolution is often described as no more than a spontaneous action by the crowd [J-J Becker and S Audoin-Rouzeau, p81]. Unlike

March 18, 1871, conscious revolutionaries were important in shaping the movement from the start. It was the Blanquists who first shouted "Vive la République!" as they led a crowd of National Guards through a platoon of soldiers sent to stop them. It was a Blanquist who first clambered over the outer gates of the parliament [M Dommanget, *Blanqui*, p24], and another (possibly Granger) who entered the assembly and proclaimed the Republic against the wishes of the platform. Trotsky wrote an interesting discussion of spontaneity and leadership in revolutions. Writing about the Russian Revolution of February 1917, he rejected an approach where "everything that happens among masses is customarily represented as an instinctive process" because the "mystic doctrine of spontaneousness explains nothing." L Trotsky, *History of the Russian Revolution* (London 1997), pp169-170.

10 J Clarétie, p241.

11 Trochu, quoted in J Clarétie, p140.

12 J Favre, p80.

13 They were called men "of the left" at that time. "Left" had a different meaning in France in 1870–71 to its modern usage. It referred to the seating arrangements in the Convention of 1792–93 when the radical bourgeois Jacobins sat on the left, a "swamp" in the middle and Girondins on the right. In this context the "left" meant liberal republican.

14 Lefrançais summed up the situation: "The [parliamentary] left, even the most radical section, were hesitant about taking decisive steps… These deputies feared that the fall of the Empire was going to open the door to the demands of the proletariat, demands which inevitably threatened the very power that they had coveted for so long." G Lefrançais, pp58-59.

15 My emphasis. J Favre, pp81-82.

16 As above, p65.

17 As above, p76.

18 Quoted by Trochu in his account of September 4 published in J Clarétie, p242.

19 F Furet (ed), *Jules Ferry, fondateur de la République* (Paris 1985), p133.

20 Quoted in J Favre, p381.

21 As above, p384.

22 A Arnould, p18.

23 *Le Combat*, September 17, 1870.

24 Poster—*La Patrie en Danger*—issued on September 6 in *Les révolutions du XIX siècle, 1852–1872*; also reproduced in first edition of *La Patrie en Danger*, September 7, 1870.

25 S Edwards, p63.

26 E Varlin, p132.

27 *Les Grands Dossiers de l'Illustration*, p140.

28 Meeting of November 3, 1870 in M D de Molinari, *Les Clubs Rouges pendant le Siège de Paris* (Paris, 1871), p61.

29 Meeting of November 4, 1870 in M D de Molinari, p61.

30 J-J Becker and S Audoin-Rouzeau, p34.

31 P L Lavrov, p45.

32 Quoted in R Tombs, *The War against Paris 1871*, p111.

33 Quoted in E L Katzenbach, "Liberals at War: The Economic Policies of the Government of National Defense, 1870–1871" in *The American Historical Review*, vol 56 (July 1951), p805. Ferry was both the founder of universal state primary education (and champion of secularism) and the colonizer of Indochina. This is sometimes seen as a contradiction. In fact one aim of secular education was to replace allegiance to Rome with allegiance to the French state.

34 A Thiers, p22.

35 As above, p49.
36 A Arnould, p17.
37 Quoted in E L Katzenbach, p812.
38 S Audoin-Rouzeau, *1870, La France dans la Guerre* (Paris, 1989), p273.
39 W Serman, p143.
40 As above, p149.
41 See, for example, the account in E and J de Goncourt, p120.
42 M D de Molinari, p230.
43 W Serman, p146.
44 E and J de Goncourt, p109.
45 A Horne, p184.
46 M D de Molinari, p38.
47 Meat rationing began on October 15, requisitioning of food supplies was delayed until November 18 and bread rationing only arrived on January 18, 1871.
48 A Arnould, pp33-34.
49 M D de Molinari, p113.
50 As above, p238.
51 See, for example, M D de Molinari, pp36, 38, 71, 113, 156, etc.
52 As above, p241—though the number is misprinted in the text as p231.
53 F Wey, *Chronique du Siège du Paris* (Paris, 1871), p390.
54 *Les Grands Dossiers de l'Illustration*, p100.
55 E Maury, p33.
56 S Audoin-Rouzeau, p275.
57 *Les Grands Dossiers de l'Illustration*, p107.
58 *La Guerre Illustrée*, February 1, 1871.
59 W Serman, p39.
60 S Audoin-Rouzeau, p275.
61 *La Guerre Illustrée*, February 1, 1871.
62 A Arnould, p34.
63 *La Guerre Illustrée*, November 19, 1870.
64 Details from J-J Becker and S Audoin-Rouzeau, p93.
65 F Engels, "Notes on the War" in *Pall Mall Gazette* of September 7, 1870, in *Collected Works*, vol 22, p87.
66 W Serman, p131.
67 F Engels, p176.
68 Quoted in A Horne, p150.
69 As above, p160.
70 G Lefrançais, p78.
71 J Brame, *Enquête sur le 4 Septembre*, quoted in P O Lissagaray, p18.
72 J Dombrowski, p16.
73 F Jellinek, p82.
74 Quoted in E Maury, p35.
75 Quoted in A Horne, p223.
76 M du Camp, *Les convulsions de Paris* (Paris, 1881), vol 2, pp11-12.
77 W Serman, p166.
78 J Andrieu, p60.
79 E Maury, p34.
80 As above, p26.
81 L Willette, p68.
82 See J Allix, *La Commune Sociale* (Paris, 1869); and A Dalotel, A Faure and J-C Feiermuth.
83 See L Greenberg, as above.
84 Quoted in J Favre, p379.
85 *Le Combat*, October 5, 1870.
86 A Arnould, p286.
87 *Les Grands Dossiers de l'Illustration*, p84.
88 See R Tombs, *The Paris Commune 1871*, p52 and W Serman, p148-9.
89 See M D de Molinari, pp5-6.
90 As above, p3.
91 General Vinoy, p84.
92 M D de Molinari, p122.
93 As above, p52.
94 Above, p129.
95 Above, p147.
96 As above, p160.
97 *Le Combat*, 27 December 1870.
98 M D de Molinari, pp175-176.
99 Poster issued by the Paris Section of the International, November 26, 1870, in *Les révolutions du XIX siècle, 1852–1872*.
100 Poster headed "Liberty, Equality, Fraternity, French Republic. International Workmen's Association" from September 1870 in *Les révolutions du XIX siècle, 1852–1872*; and also quoted in J

Rougerie (ed), p19.
101 M D de Molinari, p43.
102 G Lefrançais, p68.
103 L Michel, *Mémoires de Louise Michel*, vol 1 (Paris, 1886), p169.
104 A document quoted by Rougerie shows that on September 11 only the 11th and 18th arrondissements had given rooms to vigilance committees. J Rougerie, "Quelques documents nouveaux pour l'histoire du Comité Central républicain des vingt arrondissements," *Mouvement Social*, no 7 (October–December 1961), p4.
105 J Vallès, p202. The first vigilance committee meeting was on September 11. See J Rougerie, "Quelques documents nouveaux pour l'histoire du Comité Central républicain des vingt arrondissements," p4.
106 See, for example, poster of September 20, 1870, in *Les révolutions du XIX siècle, 1852–1872.*
107 Quoted in E Schulkind, "The activity of popular organizations during the Paris Commune of 1871," in *French Historical Studies*, December 1960, p396.
108 M D de Molinari, p37.
109 W Serman, p116.
110 M D de Molinari, p40.
111 J Rougerie (ed), p26.
112 As above, p27. See also W Serman, p134.
113 S Edwards, pp79-80.
114 J-B Milliere, *Le 31 octobre* (Paris, 1870), p4.
115 As above, p4.
116 As above, p6.
117 As above, p7.
118 *La Guerre Illustrée*, November 9, 1870. See also S Edwards, p85.
119 Figure from G Lefrançais, p103.
120 J Leighton, p6.
121 As above, pp6-7.
122 A Horne, p238.
123 F Wey, p375.
124 This was the situation *preceding* January 22! Meeting of January 19, 1871, quoted in J Rougerie (ed), p45.
125 P L Lavrov, p53.
126 This was as late as February 15. J Rougerie (ed), pp46-47.
127 R Remond, *La vie politique en France depuis 1789*, vol 2, 1848-1879 (Paris, no date), p255.
128 Karl Marx explained the fundamental character of the peasantry in these terms: "The independent peasant...is cut up into two persons. As owner of the means of production he is capitalist; as laborer he is his own wage-laborer. As capitalist he therefore pays himself his wages and draws his profit on his capital; that is to say, he exploits himself as wage-laborer, and pays himself in the surplus value." K Marx, *Theories of Surplus Value*, Part 1 (London, 1969), p407.
129 R Remond, p255.
130 W Serman, p174.
131 See, for example, figures from *Les Grands Dossiers de l'Illustration*, p102; and *Le Vengeur*, February 15, 1871 and P O Lissagaray, p38.
132 P Martine, p45. There is an intriguing exception to this general pattern, a document issued on September 6, 1870, under the name of various socialists, including Longuet and Vaillant: "Citizens, being fundamentally in the right you will be free, because you will have power in your favor. But don't forget if you are in the right but lack power that is like having the scabbard without the sword... Do we need to remind you that [in the National Guard] you nominate your officers at all grades, from the simple corporal ... up to the commander in chief, whose powers cannot last more than one year. Are

you not therefore the origin of all power?" [*Des Districts!!!* (Paris, 1870), pp2-3]. This insight did not lead to any practical conclusions at the time.

133 *Journal du 10ème Arrondissement*, December 13, 1870; and G Lefrançais, p80.
134 M Howard, p321.
135 This is a rough calculation. Serman puts the number of guardsmen and their families at 900,000 people. W Serman, p149. See also R Tombs, *The Paris Commune*, p46.
136 W Serman, p122.
137 As above, p171.
138 General Vinoy, pp101-102.
139 C Rihs, p25.
140 W Serman, p122.
141 L Lucipia, "The Paris Commune of 1871," in *International Quarterly*, no 8 (September 1903 to March 1904), p222.
142 E Varlin, *Aux citoyens du 193e batallion de la Garde Nationale* (no place, no date).
143 J-B Millière, *Le 31 octobre: Compte rendu au 208e Bataillon de la Garde Nationale*, (Menilmontant, 2-3 novembre), p1.
144 Quoted in W Serman, p152.
145 As above, p183; and V Debuchy, p15.
146 A Arnould, p74.
147 "Assemblée Nationale. Candidats socialists révolutionnaires proposes par l'Association Internationale des Travailleurs, la Chambre Fédérale des sociétés ourvrières, la délégation des vingt arrondissements," in *Les révolutions du XIX siècle, 1852–1872.*
148 L M de Marancour, p7.
149 As above, p9.
150 W Serman, p188.
151 The structure worked as follows: "Each company was to meet once a fortnight in Company-Circles to discuss immediate concerns and also general propositions which they might desire to bring up before the Battalion-Circle of the Central Committee, and, inversely, to discuss the decisions of the Central Committee and the Battalion Circle. These Battalion-Circles were to be composed of five delegates from the Company-Circle unit, one of whom was to sit on the Central Committee to discuss the large immediate concerns of the whole battalion. The Grand Council of the Committee was to be composed of three members from each district elected by the Central Committee." F Jellinek, p90.
152 "Fédération républicaine de la Garde Nationale. Comité Centrale. Statuts Déclaration préalable," in *Les révolutions du XIX siècle, 1852–1872*, September 26, 1870.
153 F Jellinek, p92.
154 P L Lavrov, p61. See also P O Lissagaray, p52.
155 E Maury, p41.
156 Quoted in J Rougerie, *Paris libre*, p89.
157 P O Lissagaray, p51.
158 J Rougerie, *Paris libre*, p99.
159 P L Lavrov, p60.
160 Quoted in J Rougerie (ed), p49.
161 J Rougerie (ed), p51.
162 H Lefebvre, p23.
163 P O Lissagaray, pp54-55.
164 As above, p55.
165 V Debuchy, p15.
166 *Guerre des communeux*, p55.
167 A Horne, p244.
168 J Favre, p93.
169 Quoted in W Serman, p187.
170 Comité central de la Garde Nationale, Paris March 4, 1871, in *Les révolutions du XIX siècle, 1852-1872.*
171 P O Lissagaray, p60.
172 C Rihs, p22.
173 G Lefrançais, p80.
174 *Les Grands Dossiers de l'Illustration*, p85.

175 A Arnould, p60.
176 General Vinoy, p126.
177 A Arnould, p61.
178 Le Rappel on February 24, 1871, quoted in H Lefebvre, p25.
179 E Maury, p37.
180 Quoted in J Rougerie, *Paris libre*, p10. See also R Tombs, *The War Against Paris 1871*, p27.
181 P O Lissagaray, p55.
182 L M de Marancour, p2.
183 *Guerre des communeux*, p64.
184 P O Lissagaray, p55.
185 A Horne, p268.
186 *Le Gaulois*, March 13, 1871.
187 *Le Vengeur*, March 9, 1871. In fact, the choice of Versailles was a compromise wrung from the royalists in the assembly who would have preferred the even more reactionary associations of Fontainebleau. But Favre argued successfully that this choice would have "provoked an immediate uprising in Paris and several other important towns." J Favre, p187.
188 Vinoy's decree quoted in G Lefrançais, p135.
189 J Favre, p209.
190 P O Lissagaray, p59.
191 J Favre, p209.
192 Quoted in J Favre, p321.
193 Unfortunately Tombs suggests that this threat was imaginary. R Tombs, *The Paris Commune 1871*, p66.
194 P O Lissagaray, p59.
195 F Jellinek, p104.
196 Viollet-le-Duc quoted in A Horne, p259.
197 A Arnould, p92.

Four: Fighting the Civil War

1 P O Lissagaray, p134.
2 A Arnould, p177.
3 P O Lissagaray, p156.
4 J Gaillard, *Communes de province, commune de Paris 1870-71* (no place, 1971), p34.
5 P Serraf, "Gaston Crémieux et la Commune de Marseille," in G Larguier and J Quaretti (eds), p102.
6 "Lyons—Fédération révolutionnaire des Communes," September 26, 1870, in *Les révolutions du XIX siècle, 1852–1872.*
7 Marx's reaction to this event was this: "These donkeys, Bakunin and Cluseret, arrived in Lyons and ruined everything." Quoted in M Moissonier, "1869–1871—Lyon des insurrections entre tradition et novation," in G Larguier and J Quaretti (eds), p117.
8 J Gaillard, p44.
9 Marseilles, November 1, 1870, in *Les révolutions du XIX siècle, 1852-1872.*
10 See J Andrieu, p78.
11 P Grousset, *La bouche de fer*, March 11, 1871, p9.
12 A Horne, p131.
13 As above, pp128-129.
14 See M César, "L'extension souhaitée nécessaire mais problématique de la Commune de Narbonne," in G Larguier and J Quaretti (eds), p83.
15 Gaillard quotes this figure—p88. Marx quotes the figure of 690,000—K Marx and F Engels, p88.
16 See A Thiers, *Discours parlementaires*, vol 4 (Paris, 1882), p213.
17 J Rougerie (ed), p160.
18 *Journal Officiel de la Commune*, March 29, 1871.
19 P Serraf, pp97-98.
20 A Duportal, *La Commune à Toulouse* (Toulouse, 1871), p4.
21 Commune de Toulouse. "Les officiers de la Garde national constitués en Commune révolutionnaire de Toulouse," March 26, 1871, in *Les révolutions du XIX siècle, 1852–1872.* My emphasis.
22 *Proclamation de la Commune à Narbonne. Compte rendu sténographique du procès Emile Digeon*

et ses 31 coaccusés (no date or place), p4.

23 G Faure (Ex-Commissaire central de la Commune de St. Etienne), *La Commune en Province. Un condamné par la Cour d'Assise de Riom, devant l'opinion publique* (Geneva, 1872), p8.

24 Commune de Lyon, "Citoyens, l'heure est venue..." April 30, 1871, *Les révolutions du XIX siècle, 1852–1872.*

25 J Gaillard, p65-6.

26 H Rochefort, *Un coin de voile aperçu des evénements de Paris* (no place, no date), p4.

27 Quoted in J Archer on Lyons, "La Commune de Lyon," *Mouvement Social*, no 77 (October–December 1971), p24.

28 G Da Costa, *La Commune Vécue*, vol 1 (Paris, 1903), pp311-312.

29 A Arnould, p149.

30 M Dommanget, *Blanqui*, p115.

31 Quoted in G Wright, "The Anti Commune, Paris, 1871," in *French Historical Studies* 10:1 (Spring 1977), p156.

32 P Martine, p50.

33 "Citoyens, Dans Paris..." March 25, 1871, signed Schoelcher, Floquet, Lockroy, Clemenceau, Tolain and Greppo, in *Les révolutions du XIX siècle, 1852–1872.*

34 J Rougerie, *Paris libre*, p117 and P O Lissagaray, p79.

35 See poster "Au people. Citoyens, Le Peuple de Paris a secoué le joug..." March 19, 1871, in *Les révolutions du XIX siècle, 1852–1872.*

36 Tridon in 1870 quoted in J Rougerie, *Paris libre*, p49.

37 "The deputies of Paris, the mayors and other elected persons who are now reinstalled in their arrondissements, and the members of the Central Committee of the National Guard Federation, are convinced that to avoid civil war, the shedding of blood in Paris and to secure the Republic, we must immediately proceed to elections..." [quoted in G Da Costa, as above (Paris, 1905), p299]. There are actually two versions of this document. The one issued by the Central Committee begins the other way round: "The Central Committee of the National Guard Federation, to whom have rallied the deputies of Paris, the mayors and other elected persons..." etc. Quoted in G Da Costa,p298.

38 L Greenberg, p103.

39 Quoted in J Rougerie, *Paris libre*, p135.

40 Bergeret at March 31 Communal Assembly in G Bourgin and G Henriot, vol 1, p77, and Central Committee statement in *Journal Officiel de la Commune*, April 7, 1871.

41 See, for example, the analysis Serman makes on p183. Analyzing the information from 28 signatories of a Central Committee poster, he makes the following observation: "The 28 signatories on the poster were unknowns. We know nothing of 11 of them... Among the others one can see the presence of four wood or stone carvers, alongside a typographer...an architect...a filemaker...a wine merchant...a brushmaker...house painter... mother of pearl turner...gas worker...bookbinder...carver and turner."

42 Quoted in J Rougerie, *Paris libre*, p135.

43 G Wright, "The Anti Commune, Paris, 1871," in *French Historical Studies*, vol 10, no 1 (Spring 1977), p150.

44 J Rougerie, *Paris libre*, pp144-145.

45 C Rihs, p58.

46 See figures in R Tombs, *The Paris Commune*, p70.

47 C Rihs, pp67-69. Incidentally National Guard Central Committee nominees did badly, gaining only some 11 seats.
48 W Serman, pp276-277.
49 A Arnould, p137.
50 *Journal Officiel de la Commune*, March 24, 1871. Central Committee document of March 22, 1871.
51 Document signed by Lefrançais, Ranc, Vallès, in G Bourgin and G Henriot, vol 1, p198.
52 *Journal Officiel de la Commune*, March 24, 1871. Central Committee document of March 22, 1871.
53 C Beslay, p40.
54 G Bourgin and G Henriot, vol 1, p46.
55 *Le Reveil*, April 18, 1871, quoted in J Rougerie, *Paris libre*, p151.
56 G Da Costa, p317.
57 As above, pp325-326.
58 A Arnould, p168.
59 As above, p293.
60 G Da Costa, p31.
61 M du Camp, p2.
62 Letter of June 2, 1871, in J Ferry, *Lettres, 1846–1893* (Paris, 1914), p119.
63 P G Nord, "The Party of Conciliation and the Paris Commune," *French Historical Studies* 15:1 (Spring 1987), p28.
64 Quoted in P G Nord, as above, p13.
65 J Favre, p326.
66 As above, p425.
67 R Tombs, *The War Against Paris 1871*, p79.
68 As above, p79.
69 R Tombs, *The Paris Commune 1871*, p161.
70 W Serman, p194.
71 E Reclus, pp245-246.
72 R Tombs, *The Paris Commune 1871*, p162.
73 P O Lissagaray, *Les huit journées de mai derrière les barricades* (Brussels, 1871), p22. Debuchy states that the Commune never had more than 25,000 National Guards available in practice. V Debuchy, p89.
74 *Journal Officiel de la Commune*, April 1, 1871.
75 Leon Trotsky, as leader of the Red Army in the Russian Civil War, put the matter well: "We must at all costs and at any price implant discipline in the Red Army—not the previous sort, the automatic discipline of the rod, but conscious, collective discipline, based on revolutionary enthusiasm and clear understanding by the workers and peasants of their duty to their own classes. We do not want the old discipline, that discipline in which every ignorant peasant and worker was slotted into his regiment, his company and his platoon, and marched off without asking why they were leading him away, why they were making him shed blood... We want a new army, a real conscious Soviet army, bound together by a discipline that has passed through the soldiers' brain, and not just the discipline of the rod." Quoted in T Cliff, *Trotsky*, vol 2 (London, 1990), pp83-84.
76 P O Lissagaray, *History of the Paris Commune*, p61.
77 R Tombs, *The War Against Paris 1871*, p69.
78 As above, p103.
79 With justice Marx would point out: "In every revolution there intrude on the side of its true agents, men of a different stamp, some of them survivors and devotees of past revolutions, without insight into the present movement...others mere bawlers. They are an unavoidable evil: with time they are shaken off; but time was not allowed to the Commune." K Marx and F Engels, pp81-82.
80 *Journal Officiel de la Commune*, April

3, 1871.

81 P O Lissagaray, *History of the Paris Commune*, p134.

82 W Serman, p272.

83 Quoted in W Serman, p273.

84 See L Rossel, *Papiers posthumes*, (Paris, 1871), pp137-138, for an interesting discussion of this.

85 G Lefrançais, p198.

86 G Bourgin and G Henriot, vol 1, p36.

87 As above, pp76-77.

88 *Journal Officiel de la Commune*, March 31, 1871.

89 G Bourgin and G Henriot, vol 1, pp78-80.

90 As above, p152.

91 Minutes of April 26, 1871, in G Bourgin and G Henriot, vol 1, p495.

92 Quoted in G Bourgin and G Henriot, vol 2, pp190-191. See also P Lanjalley and P Corriez, *l'Histoire de la Révolution du 18 mars* (Paris, 1871), pp387-388.

93 Minutes of May 2, 1871, in G Bourgin and G Henriot, vol 2, pp65-6.

94 As above, p55. See also the Central Committee appeal to the National Guard for order in G Bourgin and G Henriot, vol 2, p448.

95 P O Lissagaray, *Les huit journées de mai derrière les barricades*, p12.

96 F Jellinek, p297.

97 P O Lissagaray, *Les huit journées de mai derrière les barricades*, p21.

98 R Tombs, *The Paris Commune 1871*, p155.

99 Trotsky's view of Cluseret's approach was as follows: "It was necessary to enter into contact with sympathizers, to strengthen the hesitators and to shatter the opposition of the adversary. Instead of this policy of offensive and aggression which was the only thing that could save the situation, the leaders of Paris attempted to seclude themselves in their communal autonomy... This idealistic chatter of the same gender as mundane anarchism covered up in reality a cowardice in the face of revolutionary action which should have been conducted incessantly up to the very end, for otherwise it should not have been begun." L Trotsky, "Lessons of the Paris Commune," in *New International*, March 1935, vol 2, no 2, republished in Leon Trotsky Internet Archive (www.marxists.org) 2002.

100 E Andréoli, p244. This was later modified to include all men ages 19 to 40 [p256].

101 A Arnould, p181. See also G Lefrançais, p231; and P L Lavrov, p87.

102 P Martine, p127, and P O Lissagaray, *History of the Paris Commune*, p158. Numerous other decrees for tightening discipline among the Federals fell on deaf ears. See, for example, *L'Affranchi*, April 8, 1871.

103 E Andréoli, p255.

104 S Edwards, p235.

105 P O Lissagaray, *Les huit journées de mai derrière les barricades*, p16.

106 S Edwards, p236.

107 Quoted in P Martine, p52.

108 L Rossel, p96.

109 As above, p110.

110 As above, p103. Rougerie defends Rossel on these grounds: "He did his best to try to serve the republican patriotic cause (if not the socialist cause) by attempting to put a little order into the popular disorder. no one else, above all not the revolutionaries of 1871, thought of doing that" [J Rougerie, *Procès des communards*, p95]. In contrast Lissagaray wrote, "No man understood Paris, the National Guard, less than Rossel" [P O Lissagaray, *History of the Paris Commune*, p197].

111 L Rossel, p141.
112 G Bourgin and G Henriot, vol 2, p145.
113 L Rossel, pp119-120.
114 E Andréoli, pp327-328; G Bourgin and G Henriot, vol 2, p309.
115 E Maury, p55-56.
116 As above, p57.
117 As above, pp62-63.
118 G Da Costa, p320.
119 *Journal Officiel de la Commune*, May 11, 1871.
120 Session of May 9, 1871 in G Bourgin and G Henriot, vol 2, p301. Michel characterized the various War Delegates' methods in these terms: "The Rossel method is the reestablishment of traditional discipline. The Delescluze method appeals to the initiative and creativity of the population." H G Haupt and K Hausen, "Comment adapter les moyens révolutionnaires aux buts de la revolution. Réflexions a partir de l'expérience de la Commune de Paris (1871)," in *Mouvement Social*, no 11, (April-June 1980), p122.
121 A Arnould, p127.
122 See, for example, A Arnould, p129; P O Lissagaray, *History of the Paris Commune*, p372; P O Lissagaray, *Les huit journées de mai derrière les barricades*, pp15, 18.
123 R Tombs, *The Paris Commune 1871*, p161.
124 P Martine, p198.
125 P O Lissagaray, *Les huit journées de mai derrière les barricades*, p22.
126 *Grande remonstrance de Jacques Bonhomme au citoyens membres de la Commune*, nos 6 and 8.
127 E Reclus, p269.
128 As above, p198.
129 *Le Vengeur*, April 11, 1871. A number of deputies argued, "Today publication would be dangerous" [Frankel, Vaillant, Grousset, etc., in G Bourgin and G Henriot, vol 1, p93]. They emphasized that, "above all we must ensure the triumph of the Republic." Grousset in G Bourgin and G Henriot, vol 2, p70.
130 A Arnould, pp144-145. Lefrançais agreed that "public morale" demanded full publication. G Lefrançais, p186.
131 G Bourgin and G Henriot, vol 1, p23.
132 See G Bourgin and G Henriot, p172.
133 A Arnould, p192.
134 A Gagnière, *Histoire de la presse sous la Commune—du 18 mars au 24 mai 1871* (Paris, 1871), p156. *Le Cri du Peuple* edited by Jules Vallès objected to the Commune banning *Le Figaro* and *Le Gaulois*, as it was for absolute press freedom.
135 G Lefrançais, p269.
136 *Le Reveil du Peuple*, April 23, 1871.
137 P O Lissagaray, *History of the Paris Commune*, p96.
138 *Les Grands Dossiers de l'Illustration*, p126.
139 See proclamation in E Andreoli, pp204-205; E Reclus, p26; and J Leighton, pp67-69.
140 P O Lissagaray, *History of the Paris Commune*, p92.
141 G Wright, p154.
142 P O Lissagaray, *History of the Paris Commune*, p93, and G Wright, p154.
143 E Reclus, p72.
144 P G Nord, "The Party of Conciliation and the Paris Commune," in *French Historical Studies* 15:1 (1987, Spring), p14.
145 Quoted in E Reclus, p196. See also E Belfort Bax, *The Paris Commune* (1894) ch 9, www.marxists.org/archive/bax/1894/commune/index.htm.
146 E Reclus, p108.
147 P O Lissagaray, *History of the Paris Commune*, p68.
148 *L'Affranchi*, April 2, 1871.
149 For a powerful exposition of this point see V Serge, *What Everyone*

Should Know about State Repression (London, 1979).

150 P O Lissagaray, *History of the Paris Commune*, p138.

151 See, for example, testimony of Vuillaume in G Bourgin and G Henriot, vol 1, p122; Amouroux on May 20, in above, vol 2, p457; and P Martine, p76.

152 C Beslay, p137.

153 G Lefrançais, p268.

154 A Arnould, p189.

155 Quoted in L Willette, pp103-104.

156 As above, p128.

157 G Bourgin and G Henriot, pp382-3.

158 L Willette, p149.

159 See, for example, J Rougerie, *Procès des communards* (Paris, 1964), p192.

160 *Pariser Kommune 1871*, p341.

161 G Bourgin and G Henriot, vol 1, p73.

162 C Beslay, p76. It seems probable that Beslay was rewarded for his good offices at the bank, because its deputy governor intervened on his behalf after the Commune was crushed. Unlike many other communards who suffered death, prison or transportation, Beslay escaped punishment. See *Pariser Kommune 1871*, p342.

163 G Bourgin and G Henriot, vol 1, p77.

164 As above, p76.

165 As above, pp71-75.

166 *Pariser Kommune 1871*, p354.

167 R Tombs, *The Paris Commune 1871*, p91.

168 Lissagaray gives precise details on this score: "The bank, which Versailles believed almost empty, contained: coin, 77 millions; banknotes, 166 millions; bills discounted, 899 millions; securities for advances made, 120 m; bullion, 11 million; jewels in deposit, 7 m; public effects and other titles in deposit 900 m; that is 2 milliard 180 million francs; 800 millions in banknotes only required the signature of the cashier, a signature easily made. The Commune then had three milliards in its hands..." P O Lissagaray, *History of the Paris Commune*, p153. See also *Pariser Kommune 1871*, p346.

169 P O Lissagaray, *History of the Paris Commune*, p154.

170 L Lucipia, "The Paris Commune of 1871" in *International Quarterly*, no 8, September 1903–1904, p228.

171 J Leighton, p189.

172 L Lucipia, p228, and V Debuchy, p80.

173 M Choury, p278.

174 L Willette, p132.

175 This approach hampered other steps, such as the demand that all carry identity cards or be arrested. The system was supposed to operate from May 13 [V Debuchy, p108]. However, the bureaucratic machinery for such an immense task did not exist, and the net effect was to annoy the population rather than catch any of the "secret agents whose mission is to sow treason" that it was supposed to be aimed at. See document in E Andréoli, p342.

176 Quoted in *Pariser Kommune 1871*, p257.

177 Meeting of April 28, 1871, in G Bourgin and G Henriot, vol 1, p556.

178 May 1, 1871, in G Bourgin and G Henriot, vol 2, pp21, and 34.

179 As above, pp34-35.

180 J Rougerie (ed), p68.

181 G Bourgin and G Henriot, vol 2, p369.

182 As above, p305.

183 As above, p373. Most of the translation taken from E Schulkind, *The Paris Commune of 1871*, p187.

184 Grousset on May 17, 1871, in G Bourgin and G Henriot, vol 2, p390.

185 G Bourgin and G Henriot, vol 2, p417.

186 Meeting of May 9, 1871, in G Bourgin and G Henriot, vol 2, p303.
187 G Bourgin and G Henriot, p304.
188 Arnold on May 12, 1871, quoted in G Bourgin and G Henriot, vol 2, p365.
189 A Arnould, p222.
190 G Lefrançais, pp306-307.
191 *Le Vengeur*, May 22, 1871.

Five: Bloody Week

1 P O Lissagaray, *Les huit journées de mai derrière les barricades*, pp23, 47. Malon estimated 20,000 active Federal combatants. R Tombs, *The Paris Commune 1871*, p171.
2 P Martine, p222.
3 S Edwards, pp311-312. Original in P O Lissagaray, *Les huit journées de mai derrière les barricades*, p29; C Delescluze, "Au peuple de Paris, a la garde nationale," in *Les révolutions du XIX siècle, 1852–1872*; *L'Avant Garde*, May 23, 1871.
4 *Guerre des communeux*, pp155-6.
5 As above, p236.
6 E and J de Goncourt, p204.
7 E Andréoli, p359.
8 P O Lissagaray, *Les huit journées de mai derrière les barricades*, p36; and G Lefrançais, p319.
9 P O Lissagaray, p33.
10 As above, p38.
11 R Tombs, *The Paris Commune 1871*, p165.
12 B Malon, *La troisième défaite du prolétariat français* (Neuchâtel, 1871), p402; R Tombs, p171.
13 P O Lissagaray, *Les huit journées de mai derrière les barricades*, p49.
14 G Lefrançais, p315.
15 R Tombs, *The Paris Commune 1871*, p169.
16 The last Commune poster, dated May 25, 1871. *Les révolutions du XIX siècle, 1852–1872.*
17 P O Lissagaray, *Les huit journées de mai derrière les barricades*, p61.
18 As above, p62.
19 P O Lissagaray, *History of the Paris Commune*, p262.
20 B Malon, p417.
21 P O Lissagaray, *Les huit journées de mai derrière les barricades*, p147.
22 As above, p76.
23 R Tombs, *The War Against Paris 1871*, p197.
24 E Reclus, p373.
25 P O Lissagaray, *Les huit journées de mai derrière les barricades*, p77.
26 B Malon, pp476-477.
27 Quoted in A Horne, p401.
28 P O Lissagaray, *History of the Paris Commune*, pp287-8.
29 P O Lissagaray, *Les huit journées de mai derrière les barricades*, p64.
30 As above, p75.
31 Committee of Public Safety to Paris, May 22, 1871. *Les révolutions du XIX siècle, 1852–1872.*
32 P O Lissagaray, *Les huit journées de mai derrière les barricades*, p150.
33 As above, pp145-6.
34 P O Lissagaray, *History of the Paris Commune*, p287.
35 W Serman, p515.
36 G Gullickson, *Unruly Women of Paris* (Ithaca, 1996), p163; A Horne, p409; and W Serman, p515.
37 W Serman, p516.
38 *Guerre des communeux*, p309.
39 B Malon, p405.
40 P O Lissagaray, *Les huit journées de mai derrière les barricades*, p46.
41 W Serman, p502.
42 B Malon, p409.
43 E Reclus, p372.
44 R Tombs, *The War Against Paris 1871*, pp92-93. Tombs mentions only one important figure who supported the republic—Clinchant.
45 *Guerre des communeux, 18 mars–28 mai 1871*, p278.
46 R Tombs, *The War Against Paris 1871*, p98.
47 As above, p96.
48 Quoted in *Guerre des communeux, 18 mars–28 mai 1871*, p276.
49 *Le Gaulois*, April 29, 1871.

50 Quoted in J Favre, p427.
51 R Tombs, *The War Against Paris 1871*, p99.
52 C Witzig, "Bismarck et la Commune," in J Rougerie (ed), p197.
53 As above, p195.
54 As above, p196.
55 *Le Figaro* May 22/23, 1871, quoted in W Serman, p498.
56 *New York Herald* April 21, 1871, quoted in E Gargan, "The American Conservative Response," in J Rougerie (ed), p245.
57 E Reclus, p377.
58 *Le Français* quoted in B Malon, pp468-469.
59 B Malon, p474, gives the lower figure and G Da Costa the higher one.
60 P O Lissagaray, *Les huit journées de mai derrière les barricades*, p198.
61 R Tombs, *The War Against Paris 1871*, p165.
62 As above, p186.
63 M du Camp, p277.
64 B Malon, pp472-473.
65 P O Lissagaray, *History of the Paris Commune*, p306.
66 P Martine, p231.
67 B Malon, p481.
68 *Le Gaulois*, May 28, 1871.
69 P Martine, p282.
70 *Le Gaulois*, May 30, 1871.
71 G Lefrançais, p355.
72 P O Lissagaray, *History of the Paris Commune*, p315.
73 V Debuchy, p239.
74 Quoted in G Gullickson, p116.
75 As above, pp104-5.
76 M du Camp, p286.
77 Quoted in S Edwards, p346.
78 M du Camp, p504.
79 P O Lissagaray, *Les huit journées de mai derrière les barricades*, Brussels 1871, p197.
80 The latter estimate is from Malon. These figures are summarized by M du Camp, p501.
81 P Martine, p283.
82 S Edwards, p346.
83 M du Camp, p299.
84 See P O Lissagaray, *History of the Paris Commune*, p320.
85 R Tombs, *The Paris Commune 1871*, p181.
86 W Serman, p538.
87 H Rochefort, p21.
88 P O Lissagaray, *History of the Paris Commune*, p328.
89 Quoted in Lissagary, *History of the Paris Commune*, p328, and J Rougerie, *Procès des communards*, p85.
90 P O Lissagaray, *History of the Paris Commune*, p330; J Rougerie, *Procès des communards*, p85.
91 P O Lissagaray, *History of the Paris Commune*, p343; J Rougerie, *Procès des communards*, p88.
92 P O Lissagaray, *History of the Paris Commune*, p320.
93 A Horne, p424.
94 G Lefrançais, p386.
95 A Horne, p424.
96 G Lefrançais, p386, quoting an official municipal report of October 1871.
97 B Malon, p486.
98 M du Camp, p322.
99 B Malon, p486.

Six: Interpretations: Critics and Champions

1 K Marx and F Engels, p68.
2 M Découflé, p185.
3 This charge was not meant metaphorically. It was argued that due to siege conditions there was little food in Paris, but wine, not being perishable, was available throughout, and this combined with the loosened morals of the communards. See E A Vizetelly, *My Days of Adventure, or the Fall of France*, 1870-71 (London, no date). The accusation was, of course, absolute nonsense.
4 See, for example, L Greenberg, *Sisters of Liberty* (Harvard, 1971).

5 Quoted in C Rihs, p29. Following the September 4, revolution municipal government for Paris was actually promised, though it never materialized. J Favre, p379.
6 The quote is from Damé, who was not a prominent communard. Quoted in L Greenberg, p82.
7 G Bourgin and G Henriot, vol 1, p46.
8 Quoted in E Andréoli, p190; and *Journal Officiel de la Commune*, April 1, 1871.
9 R V Gould, "Trade Cohesion, Class Unity, and Urban Insurrection: Artisanal Activism in the Paris Commune," in *American Journal of Sociology* (January 1993), p723.
10 As above, p723. See also his book *Insurgent Identities: Class, Community and Protest in Paris from 1848 to the Commune* (Chicago, 1995).
11 J Rougerie (ed), p56.
12 A Arnould, p182. There were minor exceptions to this pattern. One was a battalion recruited from railway personnel, although it is significant that guardsmen in the latter requested that they be released to join neighborhood battalions. [*L'Affranchi*, April 2, 1871]. Jeanne Gaillard in "Les usines Cail et les ouvriers metallurgists de Grenelle," *Mouvement Social* 33/34 (October 1960-March 1961), p47, describes how the 82nd, 165th and 131st battalions had significant concentrations of workers from the 3,000-strong engineering factory of Cail.
13 J Rougerie, *Procès des communards*, p125.
14 Quoted in N Maclellan (ed), p73.
15 P Kropotkin, "La Commune de Paris," in *Paroles d'un révolté* (Paris, 1978), pp110-111.
16 A Arnould, p286.
17 *Journal Officiel*, March 27, 1871. This translation from E Schulkind, *The Paris Commune of 1871*, p111.
18 *Journal Officiel de la Commune*, April 25, 1871.
19 P Kropotkin, p111.
20 E Thomas, *Louise Michel* (Paris, no date), p89.
21 R Tombs, *The Paris Commune 1871*, p105.
22 G Gullickson, p61. There is clearly a problem citing Simon in evidence as he was one of the "three Jules" at Versailles whose forces massacred the communards.
23 Quoted in A Dalotel, A Faure and J-C Feiermuth, p172. Another example was Tolain (who would later be expelled from the International for siding with Versailles against the Commune): "'Prostitution grows in industrial countries where women go into the workshops. The health of women deteriorates because workshops produce hysteria.' When, in response, Paule Minck therefore asked, 'Is raising children all there is to life for women?' 'Yes! Yes!' was the reply to her from all sides." p173.
24 As above, p175.
25 As above, p177.
26 E Schulkind, *The Paris Commune of 1871*, p172.
27 *La Sociale*, April 12, 1871.
28 An example cited earlier was the way the Commune undermined the conventional family, by paying the same pension to "legitimate" and "illegitimate" children of dead National Guards. Tombs disagrees: "Significantly insistence on making no distinction between the married and unmarried came from a Jacobin, Grousset, whereas several socialists were reluctant to recognize equal rights for common-law wives" [R Tombs, *The Paris Commune 1871*, p104]. It is hard to see why he draws this

conclusion when the only debate on the measure was about the level of pensions to be paid, not the principle. And the decision was unanimous in its favor! G Bourgin and G Henriot, vol 1, p161.

29 J Leighton, pp282-283.
30 E Thomas, p95.
31 E Reclus, p306.
32 E Andréoli, p266.
33 E Reclus, p305.
34 It is worthwhile to compare the Commune's approach to that of the Bolsheviks, who assisted prostitutes so that they could escape having to sell their bodies. After the Russian Revolution of 1917 workshops were opened to train prostitutes in a trade, so fulfilling Lenin's dictum: "Return the prostitute to productive work; find her a place in the social economy." Quoted in R Stites, *The Women's Liberation Movement in Russia* (Princeton, 1978), p373.
35 R Christiansen, p290.
36 E Thomas, p95.
37 G Gullickson, pp134-135. Tombs makes a similar point: "Why was there no demand for the vote [for women]? There seems to have been no grassroots pressure: did most women accept the prevailing view of full citizenship as a masculine activity? Among the avant-garde elite, did they agree with the view of their male counterparts?... This unassertiveness over political equality must surely influence our overall interpretation of communarde attitudes and activities." R Tombs, *The Paris Commune 1871*, p137.
38 R Tombs, p104.
39 See E Schulkind, "The Activity of Popular Organizations during the Paris Commune of 1871," p412.
40 Quoted in N Maclellan (ed), p60.
41 This translation from E Schulkind, *The Paris Commune of 1871*, p179.
42 Quoted in E Schulkind, p171.
43 *La Sociale*, April 14, 1871.
44 G Gullickson, p95.
45 *La Sociale*, May 6, 1871. Sheila Rowbotham referring to the same article writes, "André Leo, a revolutionary feminist who was a journalist, described how obstacles were put in [the] way by the officers and surgeons who were hostile even though the troops were in favor of them. She believed that this division was because the officers still retained the narrow consciousness of military men while the soldiers were equally revolutionary." Quoted in N Maclellan (ed), p85.
46 Although Gullickson is unmoved: "However ready Rossel may have been to accept the women's help, the insolence with which they were treated suggests that the military commanders [were not], despite the need for the women's services." G Gullickson, p96.
47 See, for example, *La Sociale,* April 12, April 28, May 6 and May 8.
48 *La Sociale*, May 1, 1871.
49 *La Sociale*, April 12, 1871.
50 *La Sociale*, April 28, 1871.
51 Quoted in N Maclellan (ed), pp51-52.
52 M du Camp, p299.
53 L Michel, *La Commune* (Paris, 1898), p208.
54 J Rougerie, *Procès des communards*, p241. In a later work, *Paris libre,* he rather withdraws from this conclusion. See J Rougerie, *Paris libre,* p245.
55 G Lefrançais, p278.
56 J Rougerie, *Procès des communards*, p134.
57 This is why those in the late 20th century who predicted the demise of the working class because heavy industry declined cannot explain its reemergence in new forms such as call centers or hypermarkets. See A

Gorz, *Farewell to the Working Class* (London, 1982), and M Jacques and F Mulhern (eds), *The Forward March of Labour Halted?* (London, 1981).

58 J Rougerie, *Paris libre*, p215. Inexplicably, after this very clear exposition Rougerie adds, "This is not class hatred." What else is "the most irreducible and engrained antagonism between boss and wage earner"?

59 *Journal Officiel de la Commune*, March 21, 1871.

60 Favre on March 21 quoted in J Rougerie, *Paris libre*, p123.

61 J Rougerie, *Procès des communards*, p126.

62 As above, p128.

63 As above, p126.

64 Quoted in P O Lissagaray, *Les huit journées de mai derrière les barricades*, p235.

65 Letter of June 2, 1871, in J Ferry, p119.

66 G Flaubert, *Correspondance 1869–1872* (no date or place), p224. Letter of April 24, 1871.

67 Quoted in G Strickland, "Maupassant, Zola, Jules Vallès and the Paris Commune of 1871," in *Journal of European Studies*, (December 1983), p289.

68 In 1894 a Jewish French army officer was accused of spying for Germany. In a famous political tract called *J'accuse!* Zola came to his defense and was forced to flee the country. Dreyfus was eventually exonerated.

69 E Zola, *La Débacle* (Gallimard, 1981), p571.

70 J Rougerie, *Paris libre*, p206.

71 K Marx and F Engels, p46.

72 As above, p146.

73 As above, pp46-47.

74 As above, p23.

75 L Blanc, *L'Organization de Travail* (Paris, 1847), p90.

76 *Documents of the First International*, vol 1 (London, no date), p285.

77 See, for example, the account by H Braverman, *Labor and Monopoly Capital* (New York, 1974).

78 K Marx and F Engels, p76.

79 As above, p76.

80 Letter of April 6, K Marx and F Engels, *Correspondence 1846–1895* (London, 1934), p283.

81 K Marx and F Engels, *On the Paris Commune*, p66. "Decembrist generals" is a reference to Louis Bonaparte's coup against the Second Republic that occurred in December 1851.

82 As above, p.30.

83 As above, p63.

84 As above, p61.

85 As above, p73.

86 As above, pp71-72. Marx's assertion has been questioned on the grounds that the figure set was higher than the average worker's wage [W Serman, p322]. In fact it amounted to that of a skilled worker [A Arnould, p168]. There was also an exception to the 15 francs daily limit. First class generals earned 16.65 francs. Debuchy is therefore mistaken in suggesting that generals earned twice as much as the limit. See V Debuchy, p75.

87 K Marx and F Engels, *On the Paris Commune*, p71. Marx wrote, in *The Civil War in France*, that all public servants, with the police, were "turned into the responsible and at all times revocable agent of the Commune" [K Marx and F Engels, p71]. It seems that Marx was describing an intention rather than an accomplished fact. This was certainly the aim when the March 18 revolution triumphed, but in practice the pressure of events meant administrators were hastily co-opted to serve the cause. W Serman, p322.

88 K Marx and F Engels, *On the Paris*

Commune, p73.
89 As above, p75.
90 As above.
91 As above, p97.
92 Since Marx's *Civil War in France* was presented to the International on May 30, just two days after the fall of the Commune, it is inevitably thin on some details, in particular the initiatives dealing with workers' rights. The pamphlet stresses the Commune "aimed at the expropriation of the expropriators" [K Marx and F Engels, p75], but perhaps due to a lack of reliable information its only concrete examples are the abolition of fines, and of night work for journeyman bakers [K Marx and F Engels, p80]. R Thomas ("Enigmatic writings: Karl Marx's The Civil War in France and the Paris commune of 1871" in *History of Political Thought*, 1997, vol 18, no 3, pp483-511) meticulously details what sources of information were available to Marx for writing *The Civil War in France*.
93 In 1917 the city's name was changed to Petrograd.
94 Quoted in D Tartakowski, "1919–1939: que faut-il faire de la Commune," in G Larguier and J Quaretti (eds), p280.
95 See C Harman, *How the Revolution Was Lost* (London, 1967).
96 Quoted in J Rougerie, *Paris libre*, p109.
97 As above.
98 L Trotsky, "Lessons of the Paris Commune," in *New International*, vol 2, no 2 (March 1935), republished in Leon Trotsky Internet Archive (www.marxists.org) 2002.
99 As above.
100 As above.
101 One example was that he adopted "The Internationale" as the new Soviet national anthem. He celebrated the fact that the Bolshevik government managed to survive longer than the 72 days of the Commune, and when he died his body was wrapped in a communard banner.
102 V I Lenin, *The State and Revolution* (Moscow, 1977), p41.
103 As above, pp46-47.
104 As above, pp42-43.
105 K Marx and F Engels, "Preface to the English Edition (of the *Communist Manifesto*) of 1888"; in L S Feuer (ed) *Marx & Engels: Basic Writings on Politics and Philosophy* (New York, 1959), p43.
106 V I Lenin, p54.
107 Quoted in J Rougerie, *Paris libre*, p89.
108 J-D Forest, *Mésopotamie, l'apparition de l état VIIe-IIIe Millénaires* (Paris, 1996), p148.
109 Quoted in J Rougerie, *Paris libre*, p89.
110 V I Lenin, p55.
111 K Marx and F Engels, *On the Paris Commune*, p34.
112 On a recent visit to the Museum of the History of Paris it was interesting to note that, despite an abundance of museum staff nearby, the room dealing with the Commune could not be visited due to "lack of personnel." By contrast gallery upon gallery of fixtures and fittings from Louis XIV, XV and so on were on show. The website of Sacré-Coeur states that it "was built by the national will following the defeat in the Franco-Prussian war of 1870." There is no reference to the events in Montmartre in 1871.
113 J Vallès, p274.

Appendix 1

Chronology

1789

May 5: Opening of Estates General at Versailles.

June 20: Tennis Court Oath. Third Estate makes itself into the National Assembly in defiance of king.

July 14: Storming of the Bastille in Paris.

August 4–11: National Assembly abolishes feudal privileges.

1791

July 17: Massacre of the Champ-de-Mars. National Guard fires on a crowd of Parisians celebrating the revolution. Fifty die.

1792

April 20: France declares war on Austria.

August 9: Formation of the Revolutionary Commune in Paris.

August 10: March of sansculottes demanding a republic leads to invasion of the royal palace at the Tuileries.

September 21: Republic established.

December: Enragés led by Roux and Varlet make increasingly radical demands.

1793

January 21: Louis XVI guillotined.

March 9: Enragé demonstration is dispersed and movement dissolved.

March 18: Convention decrees capital punishment for attacks on principle of private property.

April: Rising Jacobin influence.

April 6: Formation of the Committee of Public Safety to defend Republic in time of crisis and war.

May 18–24: Arrest of Hébertists.

August 23: Levée en masse introduced to defend country.

November 10: Robespierre's "Festival of Reason."

1794

March 24: Trial leading to execution of Hébertists.

July: Thermidorian reaction leads to overthrow of Jacobins.

1796: Communist uprising by Babeuf's "Conspiracy of the Equals" in Paris.

1799: Napoleon stages coup to establish the Consulate (18th Brumaire).

1804: Napoleon declares himself emperor.

1815: Final defeat of Napoleon at Waterloo. Louis XVIII restored.

1830: Three-day June revolution in Paris overthrows Bourbon monarchy and installs Orleanist constitutional monarchy of Louis Philippe.

1831: Uprising of Lyons canuts (silk workers).

1834: Uprisings in Lyons and Paris. Thiers responsible for massacre on Rue Transnonain.

1839: Blanqui attempts first of many uprisings.

1840: Thiers is PM. Fortification of Paris developed.

1848

February: Revolution begins the Second Republic.
June: Workers' uprising follows the closure of Blanc's National Workshops. Massive repression follows, involving Clément-Thomas.
December: Louis Bonaparte elected president.

1851: Bonaparte's December coup. Second Empire begins.
1850s/60s: Haussmannization of Paris.

1864: International Workingmen's Association (First International) founded.

1868/9: Beginning of the "Liberal Empire." Striking miners killed at Ricamarie and Aubin.

1870

January: Victor Noir, republican journalist, assassinated by relative of Napoleon. His funeral seen as missed opportunity for revolution.
May: Napoleon III wins staged plebiscite.
July 19: Outbreak of Franco-Prussian War.
August 14: Failed Blanquist uprising at La Villette.
September 4: Overthrow of the Empire following capture of Napoleon at Sedan. Installation of the Government of National Defense.
September 19: Prussians begin siege of Paris.
September 28: Bakunin's coup in Lyons.
October 31: Uprising in Paris leads to seizure of the Hôtel de Ville with many government ministers inside. Uprising ultimately fails.
December 1: "Break-out" from Paris is defeated.

1871

January 5: Prussians begin shelling Paris.
January 22: Another uprising/mass demonstration at the Hôtel de Ville attempted. Crowd fired upon and many die.
January 23: Red Clubs closed and papers banned.
February 8: General elections held across France. Revolutionary left receives very poor vote.
February 12: National Assembly meets. At first this is in Bordeaux.
February 15: Formation of the National Guard Federation.
February 24: Formal structure adopted leading to National Guard Central Committee. Dual power exists in Paris.
February 28: Peace treaty with Germany ratified by National Assembly.

March 1: Germans parade through a section of Paris. Central Committee organizes passive protests.

March 10: Assembly "decapitalizes" Paris by deciding to move to Versailles (by March 20).

March 11: Blanqui and Flourens condemned to death. Papers banned.

March 13: Moratorium on overdue rents and bills is ended.

March 18: Attempt to seize National Guard cannons in Montmartre leads to the communal revolution. Central Committee controls Paris. First phase of Commune.

March 22: Right-wing demonstration in Paris is stopped. Commune declared in Lyons.

March 23: Commune declared in Marseilles.

March 26: Elections to a Communal Council that replaces rule by the Central Committee of the National Guard.

March 28: Proclamation of the Commune at the Hôtel de Ville.

March 29: Second phase of Commune begins with meeting of Communal Council. Decree on rents passed.

March 30: First clashes between National Guards and Versailles troops.

April 3: "Break-out" from Paris in direction of Versailles badly defeated.

April 10: Communal Council decides to treat legitimate and illegitimate children equally for National Guard pensions.

April 11: Foundation of the Women's Union, led by Dmitrieff.

April 16: Decree on abandoned workshops.

April 18: Final decree on overdue bills passed.

April 19: Commune "program" agreed.

April 24: Invitation issued to unions to meet to organize production in abandoned workshops.

April 28: First discussions of Committee of Public Safety. Decree passed banning night work for bakery workers.

May 1: Rossel replaces Cluseret as Delegate for War. Third phase of Commune begins with establishment of first Committee of Public Safety.

May 7: Pawnshop decree passed.

May 9: Rossel resigns.

May 10: Delescluze made Delegate for War.

May 15: Split regarding the Committee of Public Safety becomes open with publication of the minority declaration. First meeting of unions to organize production in abandoned workshops.

May 16: Demolition of the Vendôme Column.

May 21: Last full session of the Communal Council.

May 22-28: Bloody Week.

May 23: Death of Dombrowski.

May 24: Execution of hostages begins, including Archbishop Darboy.

May 25: Death of Delescluze.

May 26: Further executions of hostages.

May 27: Firing squad operating in Père Lachaise cemetery.

May 28: Final barricades fall.

1880: General amnesty granted to Communards.

Blanqui, Cluseret, Courbet, Delescluze,
Dmitrieff, Dombrowski, Ferré, Flourens,
Frankel, Grousset, Jourde, Leo,
Lissagaray, Longuet, Michel, Pyat,
Rigault, Rossel, Vallès, Vermorel

Appendix 2

Principal Figures

Andrieu, Jules, 1820–1884: Member of the Communal Council. Local government official before Commune. Head of communal administrative services. Voted against Committee of Public Safety. Condemned to death in his absence.

Arnold, Georges, 1839–1912: Member of the Communal Council and War Commission. Sentenced to deportation.

Arnould, Arthur, 1833–1895: Member of the Communal Council. Writer and leading left Proudhonist. Condemned to death in his absence. Writer of an important history of the Commune—*Histoire Populaire et Parlementaire de la Commune.*

Assi, Adolphe-Alphonse, 1841–1886: Member of the Communal Council. Previously an engineer and strike leader at Creusot. Member of the Commission for General Security. Sentenced to deportation to a fortress, he died in exile.

Avrial, Augustin, 1840–1904: Member of the Communal Council. Previously an engineer. Member of the Labor Commission and in charge of munitions production. Voted against formation of the Committee of Public Safety. Condemned to death in his absence.

Bakunin, Mikhail, 1814–1876: Leading Russian anarchist thinker and activist. In France, though not in Paris, during the Commune period. Created a short-lived Commune in Lyons in 1871. Later competed with Marx for influence over the International, which contributed to its demise.

Beslay, Charles, 1795–1878: Member of the Communal Council and as the oldest member the key figure in its inauguration. Right Proudhonist. Formerly parliamentary deputy under Orleanist rule. Member of the Communal Council's finance commission and instrumental in preventing Commune interference in the Banque de France's affairs. Author of *La Verité sur la Commune.* Died in exile in Switzerland.

Billioray, Alfred, 1840–1876: Member of the Communal Council. Previously a painter. Supported formation of the Committee of Public Safety. Sentenced to deportation.

Bismarck, Otto von, 1815–1898: Prussian chancellor and architect of German unification, Bismarck helped engineer the outbreak of the Franco-Prussian War to encourage the south German states to join the new unified state, and in January 1871 had the Prussian King crowned Kaiser at Versailles. Bismarck was a determined supporter of absolutist rule and detested republicanism and socialism. He therefore collaborated with the Versailles government in its efforts to crush the Commune.

Blanc, Louis, 1811–1882: Historian and reformist socialist theorist. His book *The Organization of Labour* had a major impact on workers during the 1848 Revolution. Elected a representative of Paris during the siege, he backed the Versailles government throughout.

Blanqui, Auguste, 1805–1881: Elected member of the Communal Council but unable to take his seat as in jail, having been arrested the day before the March 18, 1871, revolution. Veteran conspiratorial political agitator, organizer of numerous uprisings and leader of the Blanquist organization, the nearest thing to a revolutionary party operating in the Commune. Sentenced to permanent exile, but died in Paris after the 1880 pardon.

Camélinat, Zéphyrin, 1840–1932: Formerly a bronze mounter. A founder of the International in France. Put in charge of the Mint.

Chalain, Louis, 1845–1902: Member of the Communal Council. Previously a bronze worker and International member. Member of Security Commission and Labor Commission. Condemned to death in his absence.

Clémence, Adolphe, 1838–1889: Member of the Communal Council. Previously a bookbinder. International member. Member of the Justice Commission. Voted against formation of the Committee of Public Safety. Condemned to death in his absence.

Clemenceau, Georges, 1841–1929: Parisian mayor during the Commune period he was a republican liberal who rejected the Commune when it refused to compromise with Versailles. President who led France to victory during the 1914–1918 war.

Cluseret, Gustave. 1823–1900: Member of the Communal Council and Delegate for War April 3 to 21. Previously an army officer with experience in the US civil war. Attempted to form a Commune in Lyons with Bakunin. Adopted a defensive strategy. Replaced by Rossel. Member of the Executive Commission. Tried and acquitted by the Commune for treason. Condemned to death in his absence.

Courbet, Gustave, 1819–1877: Member of the Communal Council and leading member of Artists' Federation. Internationally renowned fine artist. Voted against the formation of the Committee of Public Safety. Sentenced to six months in prison and to pay for the reconstruction of the Vendôme Column.

Cournet, Frédéric, 1839–1885: Member of the Communal Council. Previously a journalist and a parliamentary deputy. Member of the Security Commission and key figure with Rigault in running the Commune's political police. Voted for the Committee of Public Safety.

Delescluze, Charles, 1809–1871: Member of the Communal Council. Leading

Jacobin politician, exiled under Napoleon III, then a parliamentary deputy (resigned). Editor of *Le Reveil du Peuple*. Last Delegate for War who adopted a strategy of mass popular initiative. Died on the barricades during Bloody Week.

Dmitrieff, Elisabeth, 1851–1910: A Russian and friend of the Marx family. Sent to Paris by the General Council of the International. Established the Women's Union and played a key role within it. Returned to Russia after Bloody Week.

Dombrowski, Jaroslav, 1836–1871: Chief communard general of Polish extraction. He fought for Polish independence against Tsarism, was exiled to Siberia but managed to escape to France. Killed on the barricades during Bloody Week.

Ducrot, Auguste-Alexandre, 1817–1882: General during the Siege of Paris and leader of the attempted "break-outs" under Trochu. Monarchist and parliamentary deputy, he was involved in the Versailles actions of Bloody Week.

Duval, Emile, 1840–April 4, 1871: Member of the Communal Council. Previously a foundry worker. Blanquist. Member of the military commission and Executive Commission. Killed at the beginning of the civil war.

Engels, Friedrich, 1820–1895: Major revolutionary socialist theorist and activist. Lifelong collaborator of Marx, including on works such as *The Communist Manifesto*. An expert in military affairs, Engels wrote extensively on the Franco-Prussian War in the *Pall Mall Gazette*.

Eudes, Emile, 1843–1888: Member of the Communal Council. Blanquist and important in the military affairs of the Commune. Very briefly Delegate for War. Member of the Committee of Public Safety. Condemned to death in his absence.

Favre, Jules, 1809–1880: French liberal politician. Member of the Provisional Government after the 1848 Revolution and leader of the constitutional opposition to Napoleon III. Foreign minister in the Government of National Defense, he was the chief negotiator in the peace deal with the Germans but then withdrew from government due to the rigorous conditions imposed.

Ferré, Théophile, 1844–November 28, 1871: Member of the Communal Council. Previously an accountant. Blanquist and second in command to Rigault as Procurator for the Commune. Close friend of Louise Michel. Voted for formation of the Committee of Public Safety. Organizer of the execution of hostages. Executed by Versailles after court judgement.

Ferry, Jules, 1832–1893: Lawyer, journalist and later liberal politician. Made prefect of the Seine by the Government of National Defense and served in this capacity during the siege and the Commune.

Flourens, Gustave, 1838–April 3, 1871: Member of the Communal Council. Teacher and Jacobin military leader. Previously fought for his beliefs in Crete. Closely involved in 31 October 1870 coup.

Frankel, Leo, 1844–1896: Member of the Communal Council. Born in Hungary and previously a jewelry worker. Leading member of the First International (German section). Corresponded with Marx. Delegate of the Labor Commission and the Executive Commission. Voted for formation of the Committee of Public Safety. Condemned to death in his absence.

Galliffet, Gaston Alexandre Auguste, marquis de, 1830–1909: French general who fought in the Crimean War, and was the most vicious Versailles commander during Bloody Week.

Gambetta, Léon, 1838–1882: Liberal republican and Minister of the Interior under the Government of National Defense. Escaped from Paris in a balloon during the siege to organize resistance to Germany elsewhere. Resigned from the government due to the peace deal.

Garibaldi, Guiseppe, 1807–1882: Radical republican military leader, he contributed to Italian unification by conquering southern Italy with his army of redshirts. Garibaldi was invited to become commander of the Paris National Guard after the March 18, 1871, revolution but declined. His son, Menotti, was a member of the Communal Council.

Gérardin, Charles, 1843–1921: Member of the Communal Council. Previously a traveling salesman. Jacobin. Member of the Security and External Relations Commissions and member of the Committee of Public Safety. Strong supporter of Rossel and left Commune with him. Condemned to death in his absence.

Grousset, Paschal, 1844–1909: Member of the Communal Council. Jacobin journalist. Editor of *La Bouche de Fer* and *L'Affranchi*. Delegate for External Relations Commission and member of Executive Commission. Voted for the Committee of Public Safety. Sentenced to deportation to island prison but escaped in 1874.

Haussmann, Georges, Baron, 1809–1891: Prefect of the Seine under Napoleon III and responsible for demolishing and rebuilding Paris in the 1850s and 1860s in a (vain) attempt to render it resistant to revolutionary takeovers. Dismissed for financial irregularities after the cost of the rebuilding became too great.

Jourde, François, 1843–1893: Member of the Communal Council. Accountant. Member of the International. Proudhonist, and Delegate for Finance. Member of the Executive Commission. Voted against formation of the Committee of Public Safety. Sentenced to deportation but escaped in 1874.

Lecomte, General, 1817–1871: Active service in Italy, Africa and Asia. Shot on March 18 after ordering his troops to fire on the population of Montmartre during the failed attempt to seize National Guard cannons.

Lefrançais, Gustave, 1826–1901: Member of the Communal Council. Accountant. Leading left Proudhonist and libertarian. Author of an important history—*Etude sur le Mouvement Communaliste à Paris, en 1871*. Briefly member of the Executive Commission and then the Labor Commission. Voted against formation of the Committee of Public Safety. Condemned to death in his absence.

Leo, André, 1832–1900: Literary name of Léodile Champseix. Exiled under Second Empire. Foremost female journalist during the Commune and editor of *La Sociale*. Influential in terms of women's involvement in Commune activities.

Lissagaray, Hyppolite Prosper, 1838–1901: Journalist, editor of *Le Tribun du Peuple*. Later he wrote the best-known contemporary history of the event—*The History of the Paris Commune*—in exile in London. He knew Marx and his book was translated into English by Marx's daughter Eleanor.

Longuet, Charles, 1839–1903: Member of the Communal Council. Previously a teacher. In 1871 journalist, and

International member. Editor of the Commune's *Journal Officiel*. Voted against the Committee of Public Safety. Later married Marx's daughter Jenny. Condemned to death in his absence.

Lullier, Charles: Naval officer and first Delegate for War under the Central Committee. Proved incompetent and was quickly replaced. Sentenced to deportation.

Malon, Benoit, 1841–1891: Member of the Communal Council. Dyer and leading International member. Husband of André Leo. Author of important history of the Commune—*La Troisième Défaite du Prolétariat Français*. Voted against formation of the Committee of Public Safety. Condemned to death in his absence.

Marx, Karl, 1818–1883: Revolutionary socialist thinker and activist. Wrote extensively on French history, including *The Eighteenth Brumaire of Louis Bonaparte* dealing with the formation of the Second Empire. In 1864 Marx was instrumental in establishing the International Working Men's Association (First International) and setting out its *Provisional Rules* and writing the *Inaugural Address*. During the Franco-Prussian War and Commune Marx wrote three separate pamphlets on the situation. The last address, delivered on May 30, was the influential *The Civil War in France*.

Michel, Louise, 1830–1905: Leading female figure in the Commune and organizer of the Montmartre Vigilance Committee located where the Commune began. An anarchist who bore arms during the civil war, she made an inspiring speech at her trial and was sentenced to deportation. Wrote important memoirs on the Commune.

Millière, Jean-Baptiste: Cooper, lawyer and socialist writer. Involved in the October 31 uprising. Elected as parliamentary deputy for Paris. Although sympathetic to the Commune he refused to join it and favored conciliation with Versailles. Shot for his socialist sympathies nonetheless during Bloody Week.

Miot, Jules, 1809–1883: Member of the Communal Council. Jacobin. Chemist and former parliamentary deputy during Second Republic. Proposed formation of the Committee of Public Safety. Condemned to death in his absence.

Parisel, François-Louis, 1841–: Member of the Communal Council. Doctor and Delegate for Science. Voted for the formation of the Committee of Public Safety. Condemned to death in his absence.

Pottier, Eugène, 1816–1887: Member of the Communal Council. Draughtsman and lyricist. Writer of the words of "The Internationale." Voted for the formation of the Committee of Public Safety. Condemned to death in his absence.

Protot, Eugène, 1839–1921: Member of the Communal Council. Lawyer. Member of the Executive Commission with responsibilities for justice. Condemned to death in his absence.

Proudhon, Pierre-Joseph, 1809–1865: Writer. Responsible for the famous phrase, "Property is theft." Proudhon's works generated an important current in the French labor movement of an anarchist-libertarian kind. In particular he stressed the idea of communes as the basis for a federal society without a central political authority. In the Commune many of his followers were more radical than he himself was.

Pyat, Félix, 1810–1889: Member of the Communal Council. Writer and journalist. Editor of *Le Combat*

(1870) and *Le Vengeur* (1871) newspapers. Veteran Jacobin and parliamentary deputy under Second Republic, before being exiled. Member of the Executive Commission and Committee of Public Safety. Voted for the formation of the Committee of Public Safety. Pyat's behavior was inconsistent and regarded by many as damaging. Malon, a key figure in the International, denounced Pyat at the Communal Coucil as "the evil genius of the revolution. Silence! Stop spreading your venomous suspicions and stirring up discord. It is your influence that is ruining the Commune, and it must be expunged" (May 9, 1871). After Bloody Week he was condemned by Versailles to death in his absence.

Ranvier, Gabriel, 1828–1879: Member of the Communal Council. Previously painter and decorator. Member of the War Commission and Committee of Public Safety. Voted for formation of the Committee of Public Safety. Last active member of the Commune during Bloody Week. Condemned to death in his absence.

Rigault, Raoul, 1846–May 24, 1871: Member of the Communal Council. Student. Blanquist who took a special interest in police matters. Head of the ex-Prefecture of Police, member of the Security Commission, Chief Prosecutor of the Commune. Killed in the fighting during Bloody Week.

Rochefort, Henri, 1830–1913: Journalist and politician. Editor of popular and criticial newspapers under Napoleon III (*La Lanterne*, *La Marseillaise*). Led the Victor Noir funeral demonstration in 1870 when one of his journalists was assassinated by a member of the Bonaparte family. Arrested for this but freed by September 4 revolution. Briefly a member of the Government of National Defense, he was too left wing to be accepted for long, although he refused to fully back the Commune, favoring compromise instead. Deported to New Caledonia as a result.

Rossel, Louis, 1844–1871: Army officer in Franco-Prussian War who escaped from captivity to join the Commune for patriotic reasons. Made Delegate for War after the dismissal of Cluseret but resigned after 8 days after his plans for an offensive failed. Suspected of plotting a coup against the Commune and arrested, but he escaped. Executed by Versailles.

Saisset, Vice-admiral: Nominated by the French government to lead the National Guard after the communal revolution. He attempted to rouse right wing forces in Paris to overthrow the Commune, but failed.

Serraillier, Auguste, 1840–: Member of the Communal Council. Molder. Member of the International and sent to Paris during the Commune period to represent it. Member of the Labor Commission. Voted against the formation of the Committee of Public Safety. Condemned to death in his absence.

Simon, Jules, 1814–1896: Philosophy lecturer and liberal politician and author of *On Liberty*. Minister of Education at Versailles.

Theisz, Albert, 1839–1881: Member of the Communal Council. Sculptor. Member of the International and Labor Commission. Delegate in charge of postal services. Voted against the formation of the Committee of Public Safety. Condemned to death in his absence.

Thiers, Adolphe, 1797–1877: Long-standing

politician of Orleanist sympathies. Author of *On Property*. Responsible for the massacre on the Rue Transnonain in 1834, and for the construction of the system of forts and walls around Paris. Head of the Versailles government in 1871 and chief political organizer of the repression of the Commune. Eventually came to accept that the monarchy could not be restored.

Thomas, Clément: Remembered in Paris for his role in crushing the workers' rising of June 1848. Made head of the National Guard during the winter of 1870/1871. Shot on March 18, 1871, during the communal revolution.

Tridon, Gustave, 1841–1871: Member of the Communal Council. Lawyer and writer. Member of the Executive Commission and War Commission. Voted against the formation of the Committee of Public Safety. Died in August 1871 in exile.

Trinquet, Alexis-Louis, 1835–1882: Member of the Communal Council. Previously a shoemaker. Made one of the outstanding speeches during the trial of Communards. Sentenced to forced labor (in perpetuity) until the pardon of 1880.

Trochu, Louis, 1815–1896: Military governor of Paris, in 1870 he switched allegiance from the emperor to the Government of National Defense and became its president. Despite hopes of a "Trochu plan" that would deliver Paris from the Germans none materialized and in 1871 he was replaced when the new government of Versailles was elected.

Vaillant, Edouard, 1840–1915: Member of the Communal Council. Previously civil engineer. Member of the International. Member of the Executive Commission and Delegate for Education. Voted for the Committee of Public Safety. Condemned to death in his absence. Later a leading figure in the French socialist movement.

Vallès, Jules, 1832–1885: Member of the Communal Council. Journalist and writer. Editor of *Le Cri du Peuple*. Author of an important semi-autobiographical account of the Commune—*L'Insurgé*. Condemned to death in his absence.

Varlin, Eugène, 1839–May 28, 1871: Member of the Communal Council. Previously bookbinder. A leader of the International in France. Finance Delegate with Jourde. Holder of several other important posts under the Commune. Voted against the formation of the Committee of Public Safety. The last significant communard figure to die in Bloody Week.

Vermorel, Auguste, 1841–June 20, 1871: Member of the Communal Council. Editor of *l'Ami du Peuple*. Member of the Executive Commission and Security Commission. Voted against the Committee of Public Safety. Died in captivity as a result of injuries sustained during Bloody Week.

Vésinier, Pierre, 1826–1902: Member of the Communal Council. Voted for the formation of the Committee of Public Safety. Condemned to death in his absence.

Vinoy, General: Replaced Trochu as commander of Paris in January 1871. Organizer of the attempt to seize the Montmartre cannons on March 18. Involved in the Bloody Week action.

Appendix 3

"The Internationale"

Lyrics by Eugene Pottier, music by Pierre Degeyter

Arise ye starvelings from your slumbers
Arise ye prisoners of want
For reason in revolt now thunders
And at last ends the age of cant.
So away with all your superstitions
Servile masses arise, arise
We'll change forthwith the old condition
And spurn the dust to win the prize.

Chorus

Then comrades, come rally
And the last fight let us face
The Internationale unites the
human race.
So comrades, come rally
And the last fight let us face
The Internationale unites the
human race.

No more deluded by reaction
On tyrants only we'll make war
The soldiers too will take strike action
They'll break ranks and fight no more
And if those cannibals keep trying
To sacrifice us to their pride
They soon shall hear the bullets flying.
We'll shoot the generals on our own side.

No saviour from on high delivers
No faith have we in prince or peer
Our own right hand the chains
must sever
Chains of hatred, greed and fear
E'er the thieves will out with their booty
And give to all a happier lot.
Each at the forge must do their duty
And we'll strike while the iron is hot.

Laws cheat us and the state oppresses;
Their taxes drain the people more
The rich themselves escape such stresses
So what rights have the poor?
We've enough of languishing in slavery
Equality is why we fight
No right without any duty
And no duty without our right.

Those mining bosses and the rail kings,
It's them, the real monsters,

Throughout their lives they do nothing
But rob the poor workers?
While in their bank vaults they hoard
All our labor does produce
By demanding that it's restored
We ask only for our dues.

We peasants, artisans and others
Enrol'd as daughters, sons of toil
Let's claim henceforth the earth
for workers
Drive the indolent from the soil
On our flesh long has fed the raven
We've been too long vultures' prey
But now farewell the spirit craven
The dawn brings a brighter day

"L'Internationale"

Debout, les damnés de la terre
Debout, les forçats de la faim
La raison tonne en son cratère,
C'est l'éruption de la fin.
Du passé faisons table rase,
Foule esclave, debout, debout
Le monde va changer de base,
Nous ne sommes rien, soyons tout.

Chorus

C'est la lutte finale;
Groupons-nous et demain
L'Internationale
Sera le genre humain.

Il n'est pas de sauveurs suprêmes
Ni Dieu, ni César, ni tribun,
Producteurs, sauvons-nous nous-mêmes
Décrétons le salut commun.
Pour que le voleur rende gorge,
Pour tirer l'esprit du cachot,
Soufflons nous-même notre forge,
Battons le fer quand est chaud.

L'Etat comprime et la Loi triche,
L'impôt saigne le malheureux;
Nul devoir ne s'impose au riche;
Le droit du pauvre est un mot creux
C'est assez languir en tutelle,
L'Egalité veut d'autres lois;
Pas de droits sans devoirs, dit-elle
Egaux, pas de devoirs sans droits.

Hideux dans leur apothéose,
Les rois de la mine et du rail
Ont-ils jamais fait autre chose
Que dévaliser le travail?
Dans les coffres-forts de la banque
Ce qu'il a créé s'est fondu,
En décrétant qu'on le lui rende,
Le peuple ne veut que son dû.

Les rois nous soulaient de fumée,
Paix entre nous, guerre aux Tyrans
Appliquons la grève aux armées,
Crosse en l'air et rompons les rangs!
S'ils s'obstinent, ces cannibales
A faire de nous des héros,
Ils sauront bientôt que nos balles
Sont pour nos propres généraux.

Ouvriers, paysans, nous sommes
Le grand parti des travailleurs,
La terre n'appartient qu'aux hommes,
L'oisif ira loger aileur.
Combien de nos chairs se repaissent!
Mais si les corbeaux, les vautours,
Un de ces matins disparaissent,
Le soleil brillera toujours.

Appendix 5

MAP OF PARIS, 1871

1 Notre Dame
2 Palais de Justice
3 Arc de Triomphe
4 Avenue des Champs Elysees
5 Place de la Concorde
6 Tuileries
7 Louvre
8 Place Royale
9 Hotel de Ville
10 Place de la Bastille
11 Place Vendome
12 General Staff
13 Bourse
14 Place du Chateau d'Eau
15 Cimetiere Pere Lachaise
16 Place de Clichy
17 Cimetiere Montmartre
18 Place des Abbesses
19 Butte Montmartre
20 Place Pigalle
21 Invalides
22 Cimetiere Montparnasse
23 Jardin du Luxembourg
1 - 20 Arrondisements
St Denis
Ft de l'Est
Canal de St Denis
Ft d'Aubervilliers
Canal de l'Ourcq
Pantin
La Villette
Ft de Noisy
Ft de Romainville
Belleville
Menilmontant
Montreuil
Ft de Rosny
Charonne
Vincennes
Ft de Nogent
Reuilly
Ft de Vincennes
Bercy
Bois de Vincennes
Charenton
Marne
Ft d'Ivry
Ft de Charenton
Ft de Bicetre
Villejuif
Vitry
Seine
Marne

Index

© Penny Gower

About the author

Donny Gluckstein's previous books include *The Nazis, Capitalism and the Working Class* (Bookmarks, 1999), *The Tragedy of Bukharin* (Pluto, 1994), and *The Western Soviets: Workers' Councils Versus Parliament 1915–1920* (Bookmarks, 1985). He is the coauthor with Tony Cliff of *The Labour Party: A Marxist History* (Bookmarks, 1988) and *Marxism and Trade Union Struggle: The General Strike of 1926* (Bookmarks, 1986). Gluckstein is a lecturer in history in Edinburgh and is a member of the Socialist Workers Party.

About Haymarket Books

Haymarket Books is a nonprofit, progressive book distributor and publisher, a project of the Center for Economic Research and Social Change. We believe that activists need to take ideas, history, and politics into the many struggles for social justice today. Learning the lessons of past victories, as well as defeats, can arm a new generation of fighters for a better world. As Karl Marx said, "The philosophers have merely interpreted the world; the point, however, is to change it."

We take inspiration and courage from our namesakes, the Haymarket Martyrs, who gave their lives fighting for a better world. Their 1886 struggle for the eight-hour day reminds workers around the world that ordinary people can organize and struggle for their own liberation.

For more information and to shop our complete catalog of titles, visit us online at www.haymarketbooks.org.

Also from Haymarket Books

The Women Incendiaries: The Inspiring Story of the Women of the Paris Commune Who Took up Arms in the Fight for Liberty and Equality
Edith Thomas

Witness to the German Revolution
Victor Serge

Vive la Revolution: A Stand-Up History of the French Revolution
Mark Steel

Subterranean Fire: A History of Working-Class Radicalism in the United States
Sharon Smith

Sin Patrón: Stories from Argentina's Worker-Run Factories
edited by the lavaca collective

Revolution in Seattle: A Memoir
Harvey O'Connor

Ours to Master and to Own: Workers' Control from the Commune to the Present
edited by Immanuel Ness and Dario Azzellini

Live Working or Die Fighting: How the Working Class Went Global
Paul Mason

www.ingramcontent.com/pod-product-compliance
Lightning Source LLC
Jackson TN
JSHW080157141224
75386JS00029B/880

* 9 7 8 1 6 0 8 4 6 1 1 8 9 *